PORTUGAL IN EUR

PORTUGAL

IN EUROPEAN AND
WORLD HISTORY

Malyn Newitt

REAKTION BOOKS

Published by
Reaktion Books Ltd
33 Great Sutton Street
London EC1V 0DX, UK
www.reaktionbooks.co.uk

First published 2009, reprinted 2010
Transferred to digital printing 2013

Copyright © Malyn Newitt 2009

Printed and bound in Great Britain
by CPI Group (UK) Ltd, Croydon CRO 4YY

British Library Cataloguing in Publication Data
Newitt, M. D. D.
Portugal in European and world history.
1. Portugal – History.
2. Portugal – Foreign relations.
I. Title
946.9-DC22

ISBN 978 1 86189 519 6

Contents

List of Maps

Glossary and Abbreviations

Águas livres	The aqueduct built in Lisbon in the eighteenth century
Auto da fé	Literally 'Act of faith'. The ceremony at which those condemned by the Inquisition were punished
Banda Oriental	The East bank. This refers to the region on the left bank of the Río de la Plata, which later became Uruguay
Câmara	Municipal council
Carreira da Índia	The passage of Portuguese Indiamen between Lisbon and Goa
Cartaz	A pass or safe conduct sold to Asian ships by the Portuguese
Comissários dos Armazéns	Commissioners for the arsenals
Comissários volantes	Itinerant traders
Comité de Salut Public	Committee of Public Safety
Concelho	Council. Self-governing communes in medieval Portugal
Conto	A thousand escudos
Converso	A Jew who had converted to Christianity or who was descended from one who had converted
CPLP	Comunidades dos Países de Língua Portuguesa
Cruzado	A silver coin valued at 400 reis
Dobra	Gold coin minted in Morocco and Castile. Monetary reform in Portugal led to the minting of escudos in 1435–6 with a parity with the dobra

Dom	From the latin *dominus*. Courtesy title used by all Portuguese kings and by noblemen
Encoberto	The hidden one. Refers to the prophecies of Bandarra, which were the origin of the cult of Dom Sebastião
Estado da Índia	The State of India. Portugal's empire in the East centred on Goa
Estrangeirado	A Portuguese who has become influenced by foreign culture through living abroad
Felicissima armada	The most fortunate Armada. The name given by Philip II to the most unfortunate Great Armada of 1588
Fidalgo	A knight or gentleman
Flota	Fleet. Used for the convoys bringing silver from the Indies to Seville
Golpe	*Coup d'état*
Governadores	Name given to regents appointed to govern the kingdom in the absence of the king
Inconfidência mineira	The Minas conspiracy
Infante	The title of a Portuguese prince
Junta	Board or council
Landsknecht	German pikeman of the sixteenth century
Lei das Sesmarias	The law of the wastelands
Longue durée	The long term. Used for long term trends in historical development
Mapa Côr de Rosa	Rose Coloured Map
Mare Clausum	Closed sea. The doctrine that the sea is not open to all
Mare Liberum	Freedom of the sea
Moidore	From the Portuguese *moeda de ouro*. A gold coin minted in Portugal after the Restoration. The double moidore was worth slightly more than the guinea and had a value equivalent to 27 shillings
Moradia	Pension
Morgado	Entailed estate
MFA	Movimento das Forças Armadas (Armed Forces Movement)

MPLA	Movimento Popular de Libertação de Angola
Nau	Carrack or ocean-going ship
Nu-pieds	Bare feet. The name given to rebels in Normandy in 1639
Ordenações Filipinas	Laws promulgated in Portugal by Philip III
Ordenança	Village militia
Padroado Real	Portuguese royal patronage over the church
PAIGC	Partido Africano para a Independência da Guiné e Cabo Verde
Pancada	Blow with a stick or the flat of a sword
Pays d'état	French province with its own elected estates
Philosophe	Thinker of the Enlightenment
Portolan maps	Sea charts produced in Italy and Majorca in the Middle Ages
Povo	The (ordinary) people
Praça	A garrison town or fortress
Prazo	Grants of land in Zambesia
Procunciamiento	Military uprising
Real	The basic unit of currency in Spain and Portugal
Reconquista	Reconquest. Used especially for the reconquest of Portugal and Spain from the Moors
Regimento	Instructions given to captains of ships or fortresses
Rei natural	Native king
Requerimento	The summons to surrender which the Spanish conquistadors were obliged to make before attacking Indians
Retornados	Settlers who returned to Portugal after the independence of the African colonies
Roça	A cocoa estate in São Tomé
Roteiro	English rutter. Sailing directions, usually including coastal maps
Salinas	Salt pans
Segunda Linha	Militia
Senhor(es)	Lord or seigneur

Sertão	Backlands
Soltura de lingua	Loose language, swearing
Tercio	Regiment
Ultramar	Overseas territories
Vellon	Debased copper coinage issued in Spain
Voortrekkers	Boers who went on the Great Trek out of Cape Colony in the 1830s
Zavra	Also Zabra. A small boat used in the Biscay region

Introduction

The history of metropolitan Portugal has been little studied outside Portugal itself and even among Portuguese is often little understood. 'What happened between the discoveries and the present?' asked Maria Isabel Barreno, one of the 'Three Marias' whose book *Novas Cartas Portuguesas* led to their prosecution by the dying Salazarist regime in 1972.[1] 'This question will encounter silence, loss of memory and *meae culpae*.' Portugal may indeed be a small country but at various periods it has played a leading role in European and world affairs, and there are aspects of its history which illuminate themes more usually explored in the history of other countries. The purpose of this book is to explore the importance of Portugal for the rest of Europe through eleven episodes in its history, ranging from the twelfth to the twentieth centuries. Four of the chapters deal with Portugal's overseas expansion, as the self-evident importance of Portugal in initiating what today is called 'globalization' can hardly be ignored. Three of the chapters focus on the strategic importance of Lisbon and the struggle to control this great port-city. Three chapters deal with Portugal's important role in major European Wars – the Hundred Years War, the Thirty Years War and the Napoleonic Wars – and two of the chapters provide a commentary on episodes of Europe's cultural and social history, the Inquisition and the Enlightenment.

In a longer book there would be other chapters – on Portugal's role in the liberal revolutions of the nineteenth century, in the creation of Brazil and in the slave trade. Or there might be one on Salazarism, which would provide a commentary on European fascism. There might also be a chapter on Portugal's contribution to European literary culture which would highlight the importance of its great writers from the incomparable medieval chronicler Fernão Lopes to João de Barros and the Renaissance poets, through to the realist and post-romantic writers like Eça de Queiroz and Fernando Pessoa.[2] There might also be room for a chapter on Portugal's greatest contribution to the visual arts, the marvellous tradition of ceramic tile painting which illuminates the history, society and cultural life of a nation in a way that is not easy to find paralleled elsewhere in Europe. Moreover, in spite of its own cultural conservatism, Portugal has been the doorway through which in the sixteenth and seventeenth centuries Europe received the ideas, cultures and tastes of the rest of the world. It was the purveyor to the rest of Europe of American and Asian foodstuffs, medicines and drugs, cotton textiles, Chinoiserie, exotic cultural artefacts and new fashions in everything from cooking to hairstyles, the use of hammocks and the wearing of pyjamas, not to speak of the representations of non-European societies that were so influential in forming the ideas of the Enlightenment.

Portugal's importance in international affairs has always depended first and foremost on its strategic location. In Nuno Severiano Teixeira's felicitous phrase it is 'caught between the devil of continental pressure and – literally – the deep blue sea'.[3] In 1949, when Portugal entered NATO, this was clearly and explicitly understood.

> Portugal's entry into the Defence Pact of the Atlantic Alliance is of great importance; not only does her coast line of 520 miles cover the largest part of the Iberian Peninsula, of greater importance still is her possession of the Azores, Madeira and the Cape Verde Islands as well as her bases in Africa.[4]

NATO turned a blind eye to the dubious democratic credentials of Salazar because of the vital strategic importance of Portugal and its islands. Its geographical location made Portugal a significant participant in countless European conflicts from the twelfth to the twentieth centuries. Lisbon, situated near the mouth of the River Tagus, is the greatest natural harbour on the Atlantic coast of Europe. Protected by a narrow, easily defended mouth, the Tagus broadens out into a great protected deep water basin where ships can be built or repaired and whole fleets can lie safely at anchor. It was here that the Genoese based their Atlantic operations in the Middle Ages, where the Great Armada assembled in 1588, where British fleets were stationed in the wars of the eighteenth century, where Admiral Senyavin sheltered his Black Sea fleet on its way back to the Baltic in 1807 and where in 1937 the Companhia União Fabril built the great Lisnave shipyards capable of servicing

Lisbon at the beginning of the 16th century, from *Cronica de D. Afonso Henriques* by Duarte Galvão.

international oil tankers. From the conquest of the city by the crusaders in 1147, Lisbon has been vital to the development of Atlantic Europe and has been the port used by armies invading the Iberian peninsula in the Hundred Years War, the War of the Spanish Succession and the Napoleonic Wars. Moreover, as the port gradually developed as a major entrepôt for European trade, it meant that Portugal's 'commerce did not suffer the fate of the shifting and temporary fairs'[5] of medieval Europe but became a secure base for commercial and maritime expansion.

The fact that Lisbon was situated in Portuguese territory would have been reason enough for European nations to court Portugal's alliance but Portugal also came to possess Madeira, the Azores and the Cape Verde Islands. The Azores were crucial to the control of the North Atlantic from the time of Philip II to the two World Wars and were most recently used as a base for US bombers operating in Iraq. The Cape Verde Islands lay across the shipping lanes linking Europe to South America and Asia. They were the favoured rendezvous for fleets of all nations and a crucial link in the perilously slender lines of communication that connected Europe with the Indian Ocean. In the nineteenth century they became the point where submarine cables came ashore before being redirected to Africa and South America and where steamships could supply themselves with coal. In the twentieth century they formed a vital link in the development of long-distance aviation. As V. de Bragança Cunha wrote in 1936,

> England knew she could always rely on Lisbon, Horta and St Vincent 'situated at the corner of that important triangle of naval strategic importance'.[6] She could not disregard the Azores, and particularly the harbour of Horta, which is approximately equidistant from Europe, Africa and America, as a naval base or a place for sheltering her squadrons. 'It has been the opinion,' said Lord Palmerston, in the House of Commons, 'of the ablest Englishmen that it is important to the security of England that the Tagus should be in the hands of a friendly power. It has been thought by the most competent judges that with Gibraltar our own and with an ally at Lisbon we might face the combined hostility of any powers.'[7]

And Portugal occupied yet another port of great strategic importance. In the nineteenth and twentieth centuries Delagoa Bay (now Maputo Bay) in southern Mozambique became vital for the development of South Africa and the security of the British empire.

The second reason why Portugal has continually featured strongly in the strategic thinking of the great powers in Europe is precisely the fact that it is not Spain. The idea of the unity of the Iberian peninsula, a reality under the Romans, seems to be dictated by the logic of geography. This great peninsula, surrounded by the sea and cut off from France by the Pyrenees, was surely destined to be a single state if not a single nation. Moreover this geographical logic has often seemed to make economic sense to the merchants, nobility, clergy and royal families of Castile and Portugal whose self-interest continually drew them to contemplate unity. If the elites of Portugal looked to Spain for marriages, careers and patronage, the kings of Portugal themselves, notably the kings of the house of Avis who ruled between 1385 and 1580, constantly sought to unite their kingdom with Castile through dynastic marriages. This was nearly achieved in 1501 when both kingdoms recognized a common heir to the throne, and was finally realized in 1580. Yet the lower orders of Portugal have shown a distinct anti-Castilian sentiment that constantly came to the surface, being harnessed by one faction among the ruling elite to assert Portugal's independence in 1383–5 and again in 1640 and 1807. Similar anti-Castilian sentiment has been very much alive also in Spain's Catalan and Basque provinces, but only Portugal among the kingdoms of the peninsula has been able to preserve its political independence. How is this to be explained?

Portugal is separated from Spain by high mountains in the north and by the Guadiana river in the south. This has given some geographical underpinning to the idea of independence but is hardly a sufficient explanation in itself. There are two reasons over the *longue durée* why Portugal has remained independent of Spain. Those states of Europe which feared the power of Spain, and in particular the possibility of France and Spain in combination, have always had a vested interest in Portugal's independence. During the Hundred Years War it was the English who sought an ally to counter the alliance between France and Castile; in the sixteenth and early seventeenth centuries it was France, during the long duel with the Habsburgs, that intermittently supported Portuguese independence; in the late seventeenth century to the end of the Napoleonic Wars it was Britain again that had most to fear from the Family Pact that linked France and Spain in an alliance that threatened Britain's imperial supremacy. While Portugal remained independent neither Spain nor France could ever mobilize enough resources to secure European domination. An independent Portugal left an open door into the Iberian peninsula for commerce, arms, intelligence, ideas, exiles and invading armies.

Portugal also owed its continued independence to its overseas empire. The empire provided the Portuguese Crown with financial resources, and more importantly resources of patronage with which to wean churchmen and nobles away from dreams of union with Castile. The empire later gave Portugal significant leverage in international affairs, so that in the nineteenth century it could negotiate with the great powers almost on terms of equality, while under Salazar it enabled Portugal to make itself indispensable to the Allies during the Second World War and to seek security, not least from Spain, under the umbrella of NATO.

There has been nothing inevitable about this history, however, and in 1580 Portugal was not protected from absorption by Spain either by

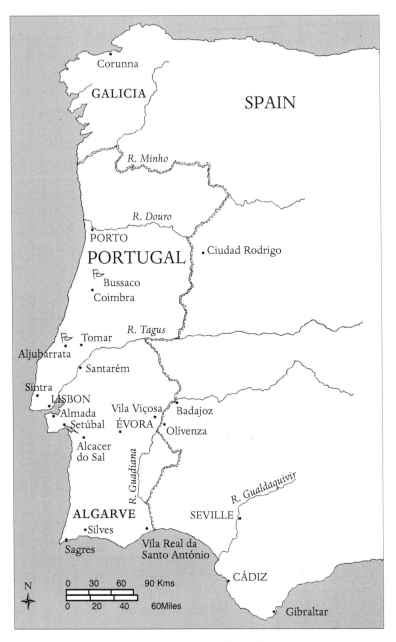

PORTUGAL AND WESTERN SPAIN

English interest, or its geography or by popular sentiment. More recently Portugal's Nobel laureate, José Saramago, in an interview with the newspaper *Diário das Notícias* declared that 'it is inevitable that we will end up joining with Spain'.[8] It was the realization that this was a very real possibility that led Portugal's leaders, notable among them Mário Soares, to seek a future within the European Union once the empire had been given up. Within the framework of Europe Portugal, like other small nationalities, would be safe from the predatory nationalism that might otherwise threaten its survival.

If Portugal is a country that is small and lacking resources, this has not always been perceived as a source of weakness. Portugal's overseas expansion had begun in the fifteenth century largely because of the poverty of the land and its scanty resources, and learning to 'live within your means' was an art that the Portuguese were forced to learn. 'The very modesty of our resources has been the source of precious learning . . . for people to acquire the sentiment of living in an advanced human community.' It was something that Salazar was to make into a virtue.[9] Meanwhile the fact that Portuguese is the language not only of five African countries but of the rising superpower of Brazil continues to give Portugal an importance on the world stage which its size alone would never have warranted.

I

The Second Crusade
and the
Capture of Lisbon

The Crusades

In 1099 an army raised in the feudal territories of western Europe invaded the Middle East and, taking advantage of divisions which existed within the Islamic world, captured Jerusalem and established four Frankish states stretching along the whole coast from Edessa in modern Turkey to the borders of Egypt. The crusades were an assertion of the power and influence of the Papacy and the term itself, originally used to describe wars to win control of the holy places of Christendom, came to be used for any war specifically sanctioned by the Papacy as a holy war, whether aimed exclusively at the recapture of the holy places, or more generally against Islam in the Iberian peninsula, the pagans on the eastern frontier of Germany or Christian heretics in the south of France. A crusade was often preached by Popes against their political enemies in the convoluted politics of the Italian city states and in 1135 was employed as a way of dealing with the problem of an anti-Pope. The Christian ideology of holy war fills contemporary accounts of these crusades, whether they are direct narratives of the expeditions and wars or indirect documentation to be found in wills and charters. In the same way a later generation of chroniclers was to invoke the ideology of the crusades to justify the actions of those who carried their conquests to the Americas and the Indian Ocean at the end of the fifteenth century. This ideology served to sanctify almost any action undertaken in the name of a crusade and became deeply embedded in the psychology of the Christian west which, over the centuries, always represented its insatiable appetite for expansion as the march of religion and progress.

The crusades have to be seen, over the *longue durée,* as part of the process by which the societies of western Europe constantly sought to expand their wealth and their control of territory through conquest. This was not a story of unbroken success. The spectacular early conquests of

Sicily (between 1060 and 1091) and the fall of Toledo to Christian forces in 1085 were followed by the conquests in the Middle East at the end of the century. However, the settlement of the Holy Land proved unsustainable and the last Frankish outposts there were eliminated in 1291. The thirteenth century also saw Poland, Germany and Russia thrown onto the defensive by the invasions of the Mongols. In the fourteenth century the Black Death severely curtailed western Europe's expansionist drive, while in the fifteenth century Christendom actually contracted as the Balkans and the eastern Mediterranean fell under the control of the Ottoman Turks. During these centuries it sometimes seemed as if western Europe itself would be absorbed by one or other of the powerful military empires of Asia.

Nevertheless the territorial expansion of western Christendom continued even in the most unpropitious circumstances. In the thirteenth century Frankish kingdoms were established in Greece at the expense of the Byzantines and permanent conquests were made on the eastern frontiers of Germany. The expansion of Christian territory in the Iberian peninsula continued, although at an uneven pace, and acquired the character of a crusade in the reflected glory of Christian triumphs in the Middle East. In fact it was only after the First Crusade that fighting the Moors in the Iberian peninsula came to be considered a form of crusading.[1] The Norman military aristocracy also engaged in almost continuous warfare on its Celtic frontier, conquering first southern Wales and then crossing to begin the conquest of Ireland and launching a series of attempts to conquer Scotland and northern Wales as well. While these wars were not crusades sanctioned by the Pope, they nevertheless shared many of the characteristics of the expeditions undertaken against the declared enemies of Christendom and such enterprises continued to appeal to men whose status was derived from their military prowess and whose fortunes were made from the spoils of war. A vow to 'take the cross' continued to earn public approval well into the fifteenth century and was frequently the way in which the most outrageous criminal behaviour could be expiated. Throughout these centuries, however, the fundamental motivation remained constant, the establishment of lordships which allowed the levying of feudal rent on subject populations, or simply plunder.

During the period from the eleventh to the thirteenth century the expeditions to the Middle East were among the most high profile and prestigious of these expansionist enterprises, and France provided the greatest number of the crusaders. However, the organization of large military expeditions presented formidable problems and the secular lords of western Europe seldom had the capacity for war on this scale. So the military aristocracy organized itself. Orders of knights were created, combining the ideals of the military class with the prevailing values of monasticism. The Templars and the Hospitallers were originally formed between 1113 and 1118 to defend the Latin states in the East, but the idea of independent corporations of knights, forming a standing army, caught on and similar orders were formed to fight on the eastern frontiers of Germany (the Teutonic Knights) and against the Muslims in the Iberian Peninsula (the orders of Calatrava founded in 1158 and Santiago in 1170). These military corporations did not owe exclusive allegiance to any single feudal overlord. The knights were organized on an international basis and the loyalty of their members was first and foremost to their Order, whose headquarters, in the case of the Templars and Hospitallers, was in Jerusalem. However, once they were established, no feudal ruler could do without their services. The Latin states in the Middle East depended almost entirely on their arms and on the castles they built and garrisoned; the German and Iberian princes also employed the knights to defend their frontiers, rewarding them with grants of land where they built their castles and extracted revenues and services from their vassals and subject populations. The orders of knights became powerful 'multinational corporations' with the capacity to act independently of the secular state.

Once the kingdom of Jerusalem and the other Latin kingdoms had been established, a wide variety of people travelled eastwards to take advantage of the Christian control of the holy places. Many of these were traditional pilgrims but there were also common soldiers, settlers, merchants and ship owners. Pirates and lawless adventurers, coming from the maritime coasts of northern Europe as far away as Norway and Scotland, were also attracted to this frontier zone. They made little secret of the fact that their interests lay in plunder, slaving and ransoms, sanctified of course by the notion that they were going on a crusade. What was true of the crusades was to be repeated, in an almost seamless fashion, when western Europeans began their expansion into Africa, the Americas and the Indian Ocean – the desire of all classes of society to plunder the wealth of the non-European world in the name of the Church, blessed and sanctioned by the Papacy, proved irresistible. It has been maintained that material gain did not feature prominently in the motivation of crusaders. In 2001 Jean Flori wrote of the First Crusade, 'as the majority of crusaders could hope to win little or nothing, this could not have constituted a motivation for setting out'.[2] Such a comment could have been written about the majority of those who enlisted with the Spanish and Portuguese expeditions in the sixteenth century or who went to Australia or California in the nineteenth-century gold rushes but it is a logic that again and again has been proved false when men have been faced by the lure of instant riches. Rather more in tune with the mentality of military adventurers, Matthew Bennet countered by writing of the Second Crusade, 'the crusaders were motivated, not only by religious zeal, but by greed for booty',[3] while Jonathan Riley-Smith, after quoting a number of passages detailing the plundering exploits of the first Crusaders, concluded that 'all leaders, from the great to the small, had to live with the reality that their followers expected from them at the very least a subsistence level of provisioning: this alone would account for an obsession with loot.'[4]

The Second Crusade

The first major setback for the crusading enterprise in the Middle East was the reconquest in 1144 of most of the County of Edessa by the Seljuk ruler of Aleppo and Mosul, Imad al-Din Zangi. This prompted the preaching of what became known as the Second Crusade. Bernard of Clairvaux led the campaign, touring the lower Rhineland and famously preaching to assembled crusaders at Vézelay. Expeditions set off from various parts of Europe, among them armies led by Conrad of Germany and Louis, king of France, accompanied by his young queen Eleanor of Aquitaine. Having marched across Hungary and the Byzantine-controlled Balkans the crusaders were defeated by the Turks in Anatolia before reaching the Holy Land, where they mustered at Jerusalem. A combined assault on the city of Damascus proved a humiliating failure, after which the crusading army broke up and its survivors, including Louis and Conrad, left for home.

However, although the Second Crusade may have failed in the Holy Land it achieved one resounding and lasting success against the forces of Islam – a success which was to have incalculable consequences for the development of western Europe long after the crusader states of the Middle East had disintegrated and Jerusalem had been lost.

While the crusaders from France and Germany, inspired by the teachings of St Bernard, made their way through the heat of summer across Hungary and Anatolia, a large fleet of between 160 and 200 ships (accounts differ) had assembled at Dartmouth on the southwestern coast of England. On board this fleet were contingents from the Low Countries, the Rhineland and Scotland as well as men from Normandy and the coastal English towns of Hastings, Southampton and Bristol. Although this force was led by some minor nobles and knights, it was primarily an expedition of ordinary adventurers who elected their own 'justices' to arbitrate disputes and the distribution of loot and who made little secret of the fact that they were bent on piracy and plunder.

The Second Crusade in the Iberian peninsula

The crusader fleet that gathered at Dartmouth in May 1147 was almost certainly the result of Bernard of Clairvaux's preaching tour in the Rhineland. Although its ultimate destination was the Middle East it seems likely that St Bernard had encouraged the idea that the crusaders should mount a campaign against the Muslims in the Iberian peninsula while en route to the Holy Land, even though such an enterprise had not specifically been declared a crusade by the Pope.[5] The political and military situation in the Iberian peninsula was very unstable. While Alfonso of Leon was trying to assert his supremacy throughout the peninsula by declaring himself emperor and receiving homage from Christian and Muslim lords, Afonso Henriques, described at the time as *princeps* or *dux portugalensium,* was attempting to establish undisputed control over the lands on both sides of the Minho and in the process to escape from dependence on Leon, whose vassal he was in both religious and secular matters.

South of the Douro was an open frontier where raid and counter-raid took place between Christian and Muslim forces and in 1131 Afonso Henriques had moved the centre of his operations to Coimbra, which at that time was a frontier town, and round which he began the construction of a line of fortified castles, the most important of which was Leiria built in 1135. The adoption of Coimbra as the capital of his state has been described by José Mattoso as 'the most transcendant of all his decisions for the survival of Portugal as an independent nation'.[6] Key to Afonso Henriques's strategy of breaking away from Leon was an alliance with the Papacy, to which in 1143 he offered to do homage.

Confusion also existed among the Muslims, where the Almoravid garrisons of southern Portugal and Spain were facing hostility from the local population as well as increasingly severe threats from Almohad nomads in their rear.

It was in this confused situation that an alliance with a powerful crusading army offered Afonso Henriques a decisive advantage against both his Christian and Muslim enemies. An alliance with the crusaders fitted into an already established pattern of military adventuring. Some contingents recruited for the First Crusade had campaigned in the Iberian peninsula and it seems that in 1140 (or 1142) a force of mercenaries from northern Europe had joined Afonso Henriques in an attack on Lisbon. This attack had failed and the Muslims had successfully driven a wedge between Afonso and the 'crusaders' by offering to pay tribute to the former. As a result the Portuguese had signed a truce which was seen by some of the crusaders as a betrayal.

It seems likely that in 1147 Afonso Henriques knew of the imminent arrival of the crusading army and intended once again to profit from its presence, while the crusaders for their part had come prepared to undertake siege operations, which suggests they had some specific objective in mind. Afono Henriques appointed the bishop of Porto to meet the crusaders and provide them with refreshment, while he himself set off on a preliminary raid against the Muslims in the Tagus valley. With the help of forces supplied by the Templars, he launched a surprise raid on Santarém that resulted in a brilliant and opportunistic seizure of the city in March 1147, sending its Muslim inhabitants fleeing downriver towards Lisbon. Lisbon could now be cut off by a combination of an advance down the river valley and an assault from the sea.

The crusader fleet set sail from Dartmouth in May, and from this time till the termination of the siege the expedition is the subject of two detailed narratives almost certainly contemporary with the events they describe.[7] After enduring the storms of the Bay of Biscay, the fleet made a landfall in northern Spain and then continued down the coast to Porto. There the leaders of the expedition coordinated the plans for an attack on Lisbon with the bishop, who offered them an alliance on behalf of Afonso Henriques, who since 1140 had been calling himself 'king' of Portugal.[8] Although Afonso Henriques was in a position to advance on Lisbon he had neither the manpower nor the military expertise to capture the city without mercenary aid[9] and the bishop was authorized to 'promise money to your forces so far as the resources of the royal treasury will permit',[10] in other words to pay the expenses of the army. The crusaders clearly did not trust the word of the bishop and it was agreed that he would come with them to Lisbon, where a meeting could be held with Afonso Henriques himself.

At the end of June the fleet entered the Tagus and effected a land-
ing west of the city. There they found Afonso Henriques waiting for
them 'for he had heard in advance of our coming'. 'As the king approached we almost all went out to meet him, rich and poor mixed up
together', and there was some difficulty in determining who could
speak for the crusaders. Afonso Henriques then addressed the assembled crusaders with an irony that comes through clearly in the account
that was sent back to England. He said he did not believe 'that our
promise to enrich you with gifts would suffice to induce men as wealthy
as you are, and as numerous as you are, to remain with us at the siege
of this city.' Nevertheless, he assured the crusaders that the promises of
reward that had been made to them would be kept. The crusaders now
became deeply divided between those who trusted the king and those
who remembered that in 1140 similar promises had been broken. The
English, in particular, wanted 'to sail quickly past the coast of Spain and
then extort much easy money from the merchant vessels of Africa and
Spain.'[11] The crusading army split up and retreated to different locations.

Eventually the dissidents gave in and agreed to stay on condition
that 'sufficient provisions were in store for them, but not a day longer
unless they should be retained as stipendiaries of the king'.[12] A charter
was drawn up which granted to the 'Franks' 'all the possessions of the
enemy, myself and all my men having absolutely no share in them'
and also the ransom money of any captives who were taken.

> If perchance they should take the city, they shall have it and hold
> it until it has been searched and despoiled, both through putting
> everyone to ransom and otherwise. And so, at last, after it has been
> ransacked to their full satisfaction, they shall hand it over to me.

Afterwards 'the city and subjugated lands shall, with me presiding, be
divided among them in accordance with their respective ranks . . . I
myself retaining in them only the overlordship.'[13] Thrown in as a bonus
was a provision to exempt the ships and goods of those who took part
in the siege 'and their heirs' from payment of tax. There was then an
exchange of hostages to guarantee the terms of the agreement. The priest
who recorded these events had few doubts about the real motives of
the crusaders.

The siege of Lisbon

The siege operations lasted three months and are described in great detail in the two contemporary accounts. There appears to have been an early parley in which the city was summoned to surrender before the siege began in earnest. Such a formality, so reminiscent of the *requerimento* by which sixteenth-century Spanish conquistadors summoned the Indians of America to submit before any attack was launched, served the purpose of clearing away any moral scruples there may have been before the killing and looting began. An early success for the besiegers was to seize control of the western suburbs outside the wall. This enabled them to confine the defenders within the city and prevent their getting food and reinforcements. A portable shelter, called a sow, was then constructed to protect those trying to mine the walls, and a siege tower ninety-five feet (29m) high was manoeuvred up to the walls until it became stuck in the sands. According to one account two towers were built and 'the English who were less careful in guarding their tower, were unable to extinguish it after it was unexpectedly set on fire'.[14] Floating bridges were also built to be manoeuvred into position from the river on seven boats. All these were destroyed or disabled by the defenders.

While the morale of the besiegers suffered from these reverses, raiding parties were sent to plunder the settlements round Sintra and across the river in Almada, while intercepted messages cast doubt on whether the defenders could expect help from the south. While a second tower was being built the Flemish and Germans successfully mined the wall. Although this succeeded in bringing down a section of the ramparts, the breach could not be stormed and the surrender of the city had to wait for the second siege tower to be moved into position on the river side of the city. Here the accounts differ. One version suggests that this second tower was built by the Normans and English, but the German 'Letter' attributes it to a Pisan engineer who was with the army and says it was paid for by the king and built 'by the labour of the whole army'.[15] Meanwhile, according to the English account, the Portuguese withdrew all their forces from the city, leaving the siege operations to the northerners, while the German account says that the Portuguese fighting in the tower 'were frightened of the Saracens' mangonels and fought less bravely',[16] the tower only escaping the fate of its predecessor by the actions of the crusaders.

Eventually, after being cut off for two nights by the rising tide in the river, the siege tower was moved into position, at which point the defenders asked for a truce. They may well have hoped for a repeat of the events of 1140 when the king and the crusaders had fallen out and, indeed, this nearly happened. The defenders offered hostages, who were taken under the protection of the king. Immediately there was an uproar in the English camp as it was assumed that the king was about to doublecross them again. At one point armed men roamed the camps threatening to seize the hostages and take the law into their own hands. Eventually terms were agreed that the goods of the citizens should be collected together in the castle prior to distribution among the conquerors. However, as the crusaders entered the city, a lawless element among the besiegers (the English account says it was the Flemings and men of Cologne)

> observed not the bond of the oath or plighted faith. They rushed about hither and thither; they pillaged; they broke open doors; they tore open the innermost parts of every house; they drove out the citizens and treated them with insults, against right and justice; they scattered utensils and clothing; they insulted maidens . . .[17]

They even murdered the bishop of the Mozarabe Christian community within the city.

As well as plundering the city, the crusaders were given the opportunity to obtain land in the neighbourhood while an English priest accompanying the expedition, Gilbert of Hastings, was made the first bishop of Lisbon. Whatever their spiritual motivation may have been, it is clear that many of the crusaders did very well out of the conquest.

The capture of Lisbon in its contemporary setting

The capture of a city of such economic and strategic importance as Lisbon was always going to be seen as an event of great significance, but to many both at the time and since it was a defining moment in the evolution of Europe. As Maria João Branco has written, 'the echoes of this conquest can be heard in almost all the annals and chronicles of Christendom'.[18] The capture of Lisbon was 'indissolubly linked to the struggle of the first Portuguese king to affirm the sovereignty of his dominion, both internally and externally and in its political, material and symbolic dimensions'[19] and the accounts of the conquest written at the time or soon after were part of a sustained propaganda campaign.

In contrast to other episodes in the long reign of the first Portuguese king, such as S. Mamede or Ourique, which only much later came to feature in the chronicles of the kingdom as founding moments, and in contrast to other conquests equally hard and troublesome such as Leiria, Santarém or even Évora, about whose success little or nothing is said in the annals and chronicles, the conquest of Lisbon was an event about which a written record was at once created as though there existed a desire or a necessity to preserve from the very first the details of that moment.[20]

Moreover, the establishment of the See of Lisbon immediately after the capture of the city, and the consecration of the new bishop by the Archbishop of Braga, to whom an oath of obedience was taken, was part of a long and frustrating campaign to 'mould the ecclesiastical geography to the political geography of the nascent kingdom'.[21]

And the detailed account of the conquest, complete with elaborate passages of reported speech, although written by a Norman priest, was intended to be a piece of royal propaganda. The author was able to transcribe documents from the royal chancery to 'reproduce sermons and discourses as if he had the text before him'. As such it ceases to be just a private letter to a friend and becomes

the mirror of a world evolving and under construction, made up of interests, political struggles and factions of every kind, but also a mental and emotional world which at the same time is unfolded in this narrative, made up of profane and pious intentions, full of the contacts between cultures and permeated with the tolerance and intolerance which characterized the vision of the world which was held by the men of the North and the men of the South, by warriors from the peninsula, crusaders, Muslims and Mozarabes.[22]

In the eyes of the Christian priests who described the siege, there was something apocalyptic about the fall of Lisbon. The English priest, Raoul, described Muslim Lisbon as an earthly paradise. The city is situated on the Tagus river, where

gold is found on its banks in the early spring after it has returned to its channel. It contains fish in such quantities that it is believed by the natives to be two parts water and one part fish; and it abounds in shellfish like the sands . . . To the south of it lies the province of Almada which abounds in vines, figs and pomegranates. So fertile is the soil that two crops are produced from a single seeding. It is celebrated for its hunting and abounds in honey . . . The surrounding country is second to none and comparable with the best, rich in products of the soil, whether you are looking for the fruit of trees or of vines. It abounds in everything, both costly articles of luxury and necessary articles of consumption. It also contains gold and silver and is never wanting iron mines. The olive flourishes . . . They do not boil their salt but dig it. Figs are so abundant that we could hardly eat a fraction of them . . . The air is healthful, and the city has hot baths . . . In its pastures the mares breed with wonderful fecundity.[23]

And so on. This earthly paradise supports a dense population which, the priest innocently observes, is the result of there being 'no prescribed form of religion among them, for everyone has a law unto himself'.

Nowhere can the link between the crusades and the Iberian conquest of the New World be more clearly seen, for this description recalls Bernal Diaz's description of Tenochtitlán when it was first seen by the Spaniards in 1519 – and before they unleashed fire, sword and massacre on the inhabitants in the name of religion. The crusades had created a mind-set which feared the exotic and which constantly sought to deny the plurality of human experience. Having recognized the benefits of religious pluralism in populating the city and creating an earthly paradise, Raoul continues in the same breath to condemn what he has seen on the grounds that 'the most depraved elements from all parts of the world had flowed together as it were in a cesspool and had formed a breeding ground of every lust and abomination'. And the fall of Lisbon, like the fall of Tenochtitlán, was followed by utter destruction.

> Then there followed such a pestilence among the Moors that throughout the desert wastes, in vineyards, in villages and squares, and among ruins of houses unnumbered thousands of corpses lay exposed to birds and beasts, and living men resembling bloodless beings went about the earth, and, grasping the symbol of the cross, they kissed it as suppliants . . .[24]

The Crusaders in Portugal

The fall of Lisbon led to the rapid occupation of Sintra, the Almada peninsula, the castle of Palmella and the Alentejo region as far south as Évora. It was not, however, the last intervention of crusading armies in Portuguese affairs. Crusader mercenaries were recruited for the attack on Alcácer do Sal in 1157, the Muslim stronghold of Silves in the Algarve in 1187 (where the crusaders plundered the city in scenes reminiscent of the capture of Lisbon) and Alcácer do Sal again in 1217. In each case the pay-off was to be the right to sack the captured cities. With Santarém and Lisbon in Christian hands, the future of the Islamic communities in central Portugal became unsustainable. In the next thirty years the Portuguese orders of knights overran the Alentejo region, the city of Évora finally becoming Portuguese in 1166. In 1179, after receiving a discreet gift of a thousand gold coins, the Pope formally recognized the independent kingdom of Portugal. However, the Muslim kingdom of the Algarve was not finally conquered until 1249.

The crusading orders of knights had apparently played little part in the siege of Lisbon but they remained important institutions in Portugal and kept alive the traditions and mentalities of crusading warfare. After the destruction of the Templars in 1310 the lands of the order were taken over and used to endow the Portuguese Order of Christ. The Order of the Hospital, which had assumed the defence of Santarém after its capture, survived and other purely Iberian orders came into existence, linked with their counterparts in Castile, the orders of Calatrava (which was later called the Order of São Bento de Avis), and the Order of Santiago. As the *reconquista* proceeded these orders obtained vast lands as well as castles and towns in central and southern Portugal. After the Portuguese military frontier with Islam was closed in 1249, the *raison d'être* of the orders changed. In 1288 Pope Nicholas IV allowed the Portuguese Order of Santiago to be separated from that in Castile since 'the king of Portugal always risked seeing the knights who were his subjects serving in the ranks of his enemies and, what was worse, delivering up to the Castilians the castles which the Portuguese monarchs had given them'.[25] They remained corporations of knights which owed military service to the Crown but became increasingly absorbed in administering their vast estates. Portuguese *fidalgos* and noblemen sought entry to the orders to supplement their incomes with commanderies and the control of lands and revenues.

By the end of the fourteenth century the Crown was casting envious eyes on the wealth and military potential of the orders. In 1385 the

Master of the Order of Avis became king of Portugal and a process began by which the Crown took control of the orders, first by placing members of the royal family at their head and then by annexing them to the patrimony of the Crown itself. In 1419 the Infante Henrique (Henry the Navigator) was made governor of the Order of Christ, which was absorbed by the Crown when Dom Manuel, the head of the Order, became king in 1495. The last of the orders to be absorbed into the patrimony of the Crown was the Order of Santiago, which passed into the hands of the king in 1550 on the death of the Infante Dom Jorge.

The orders of knights were also of fundamental importance in the story of Portugal's expansion overseas. The Infante Dom Henrique used the funds of the Order of Christ to finance his expeditions and employed its members as his captains and officials. It was a knight of the order, Gomes Eannes de Zurara, who became the chronicler and most effective propagandist for the prince and his enterprises. Moreover Henrique obtained from the Papacy the right of the Order of Christ to control the revenues and patronage of the church outside Portugal. These Bulls not only gave Portugal's overseas expansion a crusading veneer but conferred vast revenues and patronage on the kings of Portugal, who came effectively to control all the Christian communities in Africa, Asia and Brazil.

The other orders played a lesser role but the rivalry of the Order of Christ and the Order of Santiago underlay the debates and decisions over expansionist policy at the end of the fifteenth century. The reluctant financing of the expedition to India in 1497 as well as the appointment of Vasco da Gama, a relatively unknown knight of the Order of Santiago, as commander, can probably best be explained in terms of rivalry between the orders and the need to compensate Dom Jorge, the head of the Order of Santiago, for being denied the crown.

The role that the orders played in the early stages of Portuguese overseas expansion probably also accounts for the strong crusading ideology which marked Portugal's attitude to Muslims. Whereas Venetians and Genoese were able to establish peaceful and co-operative relations with Muslim commercial classes, the Portuguese military aristocracy assumed from the start an attitude which identified Islam as an irreconcilable enemy.

Throughout the sixteenth century there were various attempts made to purify the orders and rededicate their members to the crusading ideal – most notably during the reign of Dom Sebastião, whose disastrous invasion of Morocco in 1578 was certainly seen by his contemporaries as a new crusade. However, with the death of the king at Alcazar el Kebir and the subsequent absorption of Portugal by the Spanish monarchy the orders again became little more than a system of honours used to reward servants of the crown.

Conclusion

The capture of Lisbon was an event of such importance that it easily transcends the failure of the Second Crusade to take Damascus. Had Damascus been captured, the long-term viability of the crusader states in the Middle East would not have been greatly altered. They would have remained vulnerable to any Muslim revival, such as that led by Nur al Din and Saladin which resulted in the recapture of Jerusalem in 1187. In contrast the capture of Lisbon was a decisive and permanent victory. At the time of the siege Lisbon was said to be a city of sixty thousand families and was described as 'the richest in trade of all Africa and a good part of Europe'.[26] The finest seaport on the Atlantic coast of Europe was now in Christian hands and soon developed as an important way-station between the Mediterranean and northern Europe. Genoese and Venetians began to use the port as a base for their penetration of north-ern markets and in the fourteenth century English armies made use of Lisbon to invade the Iberian peninsula in pursuit of their endless wars of expansion in France and Castile. Lisbon became the base from which European expansion into the Atlantic was launched in the fifteenth century. Without the capture of Lisbon the reconquest of the Iberian peninsula would have been impossible and the subsequent shift of Europe's economy from the Mediterranean to the Atlantic seaboard unthinkable.

2

The Hundred Years War and the Crisis of Portuguese Independence

Medieval Portugal

By the time of his death in 1185 Afonso Henriques had been recognized by the Papacy, and by implication by the rest of Europe, as king of an independent Portugal. However, the exact shape of this kingdom was fought over for another century. The Portuguese kings continued to have designs on Galicia, where the population spoke a language close to Portuguese, while on the confused southern frontier Christian armies loyal to the Portuguese crown campaigned as far as Seville. In 1212 Portuguese forces took part in the Christian victory at Las Navas de Tolosa, opening up the possibility of a frontier on the Guadalquivir. Castilians for their part claimed sovereignty over the Muslim territories in the Algarve and, although the Portuguese had captured most of the Muslim towns by 1249, Castile maintained its claim to Silves until 1253.

By the mid-thirteenth century Portugal's southern frontier had become fixed along the Guadiana river, but the rest of the frontier with Leon and Castile remained undefined and, to use a modern phrase, was highly 'porous'. Conflicts of jurisdiction in the church had been largely resolved in the 1170s with the sees of Santiago and Toledo being forced to give up their claims to control the church in Portugal in return for the archbishops of Braga, whose primacy over the church in Portugal was now uncontested, abandoning any claims in Leon. However, Portugal still remained linked to Castile and Leon by many corporate, family and religious ties. The interests of the military orders of knights extended across the Iberian kingdoms and many families owned property and contracted marriages that created networks spanning the kingdoms and raising complex problems of loyalty and allegiance. Portugal's position as an independent kingdom remained fragile, particularly in the years 1245–6 when the two brothers, Sancho and Afonso, contested the crown, and the Papacy and the neighbouring Spanish kingdoms all seized the opportunity to intervene.

In the second half of the thirteenth century the Portuguese monarchy began slowly to consolidate its position. The Orders of Calatrava and Santiago were nationalized and acquired a separate Portuguese corporate identity. The Order of Santiago separated from its Castilian counterpart in 1288 and the Order of Calatrava also separated and took a new name from the town of Avis with which it had been endowed by Afonso II. With the abolition of the Order of the Templars the extensive lands owned by the knights were taken over by the Crown and used in 1319 to endow a new Portuguese Order of Christ with headquarters at Castro Marim on the southern borders with Castile.

The reign of Dom Dinis (1279–1325) has usually been seen as the golden age of medieval Portuguese kingship when the tradition of courtly poetry flourished, a university was founded in Coimbra and the commercial life of Portugal expanded. According to Bailey Diffie, 'Portugal combined the advantages of good ports, incoming foreign goods to be exported, and, most important of all, domestic products in demand in northern Europe.'[1] However, the country remained poor and all classes struggled to make a living. In the coastal regions of northern Portugal land was controlled by feudal *senhores* and, although further inland and further south society was organized in self-governing *concelhos*, there was a shortage of good agricultural land and the custom of dividing inheritances made it increasingly difficult for the population to subsist on tiny landholdings. José Mattoso describes what might be called 'a noble proletariat of small knights, even from the most powerful and respected families, who lived miserably' and a society which had to 'develop strategies of inheritance which rejected a section of the members of the community and of the noble families and obliged them to find success and subsistence away from the land'.[2] The struggle for the control of southern Portugal, which had continued until the 1250s, had discouraged intensive settlement of the region beyond the Tagus. As a result the military orders continued to dominate a thinly populated countryside and a subjugated Muslim peasantry from their castles.

In this hostile economic environment the Portuguese increasingly looked to the sea for their living and the maritime economy became of particular significance for the development of an independent Portuguese monarchy. Salt production flourished in the *salinas* of Aveiro and Setúbal; seaweed was collected as fertilizer and ship-building, fishing and overseas trade absorbed the energies of a significant part of the population. The rivers of Portugal led from inaccessible mountains through broad and fertile valleys to a sea coast that faced the Atlantic.

Here relatively prosperous trading towns, such as Viana do Castello and Porto, grew up from which Portuguese merchants developed commercial networks in places such as Bruges and London. Lisbon in particular was becoming a port of European significance. Italian trading houses established themselves there towards the end of the thirteenth century and the port became a way-station for Venetian and Genoese ships trading to northern Europe. The Portuguese crown subsidized shipbuilding and a galley fleet. The Genoese even contracted to provide Portugal with captains for the royal galleys and a Genoese was appointed hereditary admiral of Portugal in 1325. The reward for this activity was the growth of royal revenues from customs dues. This contrasted with the stagnant and meagre returns from landed estates, which kept the nobility of Portugal poor and dependent on the patronage of the orders of knights and of the crown to maintain its status.

The long and relatively prosperous reign of Dom Dinis contrasts with the fifty years which followed, years which saw the Black Death devastate the country and the kingdom drawn into the ever widening European conflict of the Hundred Years War. As with other medieval monarchies, political instability frequently arose from disputed successions which split society along the social fissures of class interest and noble faction. Portugal had experienced civil wars in the thirteenth century and in the fourteenth century the irregular sexual partnerships of its kings were to exacerbate class tensions and in the end endanger the very survival of the country's independence. It was the threat to this independence and the struggle to control this small kingdom during the 1380s that made Portugal the arena where the outcome of the wider conflict north of the Pyrenees would be decided. For a few years the ambitions of the European military elite, and the attentions of the chroniclers who recorded their activities, became focused on events in Portugal.

The Hundred Years War

The Hundred Years War, which began with the disputed succession following the death of Charles IV of France in 1328, was not at first a new phenomenon. In the twelfth century dynastic marriages had resulted in the creation of the great Angevin kingdom which stretched from the borders of Scotland to the Pyrenees. Although its rulers, Henry II, Richard and John, found great difficulty in controlling this vast domain, and still more in mobilizing its resources, it nevertheless overshadowed the kingdom of France to which its Norman and Aquitainian lands were nominally subject. The kingdoms of England and France had few effective institutions and depended on feudal loyalty to control the military elites, who constantly sought to boost their fortunes through the spoils of war. The conquest of Normandy by the French early in the thirteenth century had hugely increased the power of the French monarchy and had removed Angevin influence from the area of the Low Countries but the kings of England, who were expanding their political power into Ireland, Wales and Scotland, still ruled extensive lands in the south of France bordering the Pyrenees.

When Edward III of England claimed the French crown there was no reason to suppose that the war which resulted would spread so far, and become so damaging and so difficult to bring to a resolution. The early stages of the conflict can be understood as an attempt by Edward to reverse the loss of Normandy with the help of allies in the Netherlands who had close commercial ties with England and feared constant French interference. Although the dramatic English victory at Crécy in 1342 did not lead to the reconquest of Normandy, it did enable the English to establish a bridgehead in northern France and seriously weakened the prestige and hence authority of the French Crown. Moreover Crécy made the war popular in England and persuaded generations of English knights and soldiers to look to campaigning in France as a way to make their fortunes.

Although the war was temporarily interrupted by the Black Death, the 1350s saw devastating English raids mounted from Aquitaine against southern France. There was little pretence that these raids served any purpose other than to obtain plunder. Abbeys, towns and castles were ransacked and, to protect themselves, communities throughout southern France threw up the defensive walls which characterize their layout to this day. Attempts by the French king, Jean, to defend the southern part of his kingdom met with disaster at the battle of Poitiers in 1356 where the French army suffered not only defeat but humiliation and where the king was captured.

Mediation by the Papacy and the prolonged negotiations over the ransoming of the king temporarily halted the war but the fact that the English now controlled great swathes of France did nothing to resolve the basic problems of a weak state and divided loyalties, while the so-called Free Companies, mostly English freebooters, continued to range across France plundering and devastating the countryside. France was without government and in the power vacuum social breakdown and chaos reigned. Meanwhile Europe was becoming increasingly sucked into the conflict as English and French sought allies in order to acquire a decisive advantage. Brittany on the borders of English and French territory was bitterly fought over until the decisive victory of the pro-English party in 1364, while Navarre, whose territories bordered Gascony in the south, sought the protection of an English alliance, allowing its king to meddle constantly in French affairs from the lands he possessed in Normandy. The activities of the king of Navarre brought the war perilously close to the Iberian peninsula.

The war comes south of the Pyrenees

What caused the war to spill over south of the Pyrenees was the issue of sea power. English ability to campaign in France was dependent on the control of the sea and the French appreciated that this, together with the turbulent Scottish border, was the weakness of the English position. Raids launched against southern England from the sea or by Scots across the Tweed would keep England preoccupied with its own defence. It was here that the galley fleets maintained by Castile and, to a lesser extent by Portugal, became of great strategic importance. Nor was it lost on the French that control of Castile or Aragon would enable a second front to be opened and force the English in Gascony onto the defensive. Even so, it took the fratricidal struggle within the royal house of Castile to move the main focus of the war south of the Pyrenees.

After his victory at the battle of Poitiers the Black Prince, who was his father Edward III's regent in Gascony, sought to seal an alliance with Castile, which had been involved in almost constant warfare with Aragon since 1346. The Aragonese for their part found an ally in Pedro of Castile's illegitimate half-brother Enrique de Trastámara who lived as an exile in France and was determined to gain the crown. During the truce which followed the battle of Poitiers, Enrique was able to recruit unemployed mercenaries from the so-called Free Companies to campaign against Pedro. This increased the pressure on Pedro to conclude an alliance with the English in Bordeaux.

In 1364 the war in Brittany came to an end following the English victory at Auray, and a peace treaty was signed. The same year Charles V became king of France and began to put together a system of alliances designed to undermine English dominance in the south of France. His allies were to be the king of Aragon and the Castilian pretender Enrique, and Navarre was to be the immediate object of attack. At the end of 1365 the French knight Bertrand Du Guesclin led a mixed force from Montpellier across the Pyrenees. This army was made up partly of mercenaries (some of them English and Gascon) but mainly of French knights who had enlisted in this campaign as a way of pursuing the war against the English. In 1366 this army invaded northern Castile through Navarre and enabled Enrique to declare himself king of Castile on Castilian soil. King Pedro meanwhile retreated south to Toledo and then Seville which brought him close to the Portuguese frontier. It was to Portugal that he now turned for help against Enrique. The king of Portugal, also called Pedro (r. 1357–67), refused to offer his namesake sanctuary but allowed him to pass through the country en route for the loyal province of Galicia where he still had support. From Galicia Pedro of Castile went in person to Bordeaux to seek the help of the Black Prince.[3]

There was now a real danger that both Navarre and Castile would fall into the hands of allies of France, creating a situation which would pose a huge danger to the English lands in Gascony. Although slow to react to the collapse of Pedro's position, the Black Prince and his brother, John of Gaunt, Duke of Lancaster, eventually crossed the Pyrenees in the summer of 1367. The result was the battle of Nájera, which utterly destroyed the allied forces ranged against Pedro and left the Black Prince temporarily the arbiter of events in the peninsula. Although this great military victory had the effect of establishing a fear of English military intervention which lasted for a generation, in the short term its effects were squandered as the Black Prince fell out with his ally and, with his soldiers unpaid, returned to Gascony. Enrique and his French allies were soon back in the ascendancy.

None of these events directly affected Portugal, which had so far survived on the extreme edge of the European War, but, as the struggle for the Castilian throne became a second front in the European conflict, the Portuguese found that neutrality was an increasingly difficult option – particularly as the English and French parties in Castile each saw great advantages in a Portuguese alliance. The bitter civil war in Castile had already made Portugal a place of refuge for exiled noblemen of both parties. During the period of Pedro of Castile's ascendancy it had been Castilians aligned with his half-brother, Enrique, including some with lands and titles in Portugal, who formed the most important exile faction. Principal among these were Álvaro Peres de Castro and the children of Martim Afonso Teles. These Castilian exiles were soon to wield enormous influence within the Portuguese ruling establishment, not least through the sexual attractions of female members of their families. Dom Pedro, when still heir to the Portuguese throne, had formed a passionate liaison with Álvaro de Castro's sister Inês, by whom he had four illegitimate children, while Leonor Teles (daughter of Martim Afonso Teles) was later to marry Pedro's legitimate son and become queen of Portugal. The Infante Pedro's liaison with the exiled Castros had been an extreme embarrassment for his father, Dom Afonso (r. 1325–57), who had wanted to maintain good relations with the king of Castile, and in 1355 the king had taken the drastic step of having Inês murdered. Afonso feared that, if his son were successful in getting a Papal dispensation to marry Inês, thereby legitimizing her children, the way would be open for a disputed succession between her sons and Pedro's son by an earlier wife.

Dom Afonso of Portugal died in 1357 and was duly succeeded by Dom Pedro whose ten-year reign (1357–67) was the first in the history of Portugal in which there was no war – no mean achievement with neighbouring Castile and Aragon, not mention the rest of Europe, torn apart by conflict. Pedro tried to maintain Portugal's neutrality by judiciously shifting his support between Pedro of Castile and Enrique de Trastámara. He also left a full treasury – in short, a country ripe to be plundered.

The murder of Pedro of Castile at Montiel in 1369 secured the complete triumph of Enrique of Trastámara but did not bring immediate peace. Instead it sucked Portugal and Castile deeper into the wider international struggle. Pedro of Castile's supporters, who were particularly strong in Galicia, refused to accept Enrique as king and large numbers took refuge in Portugal where they tried to recognize the new Portuguese king, Dom Fernando, as legitimate king of Castile. Fernando renounced any claims he might have in 1371 with the result that the factions hostile to Enrique de Trastámara then recognized Constanza, Pedro of Castile's daughter, instead.

Meanwhile relations between the English and French were drifting towards a renewal of the war and both sides were beginning to realize that victory would be won not on the battlefields of France but in the Iberian peninsula. So in 1371 the English re-entered Castilian politics by arranging a marriage between the Black Prince's brother, the Duke of Lancaster, and Constanza, a marriage which enabled Lancaster to claim the Crown of Castile for himself and to become the leader of the Castilian 'legitimists'. As the English involvement in Castilian politics deepened, King Edward III and his advisers formally recognized that 'the *chemin d'Espaigne* was the royal road to victory over France'.[4]

As Lancaster struggled to put together an alliance that would at the same time win him his crown and destroy French influence in Castile, Dom Fernando of Portugal, without waiting for English aid, foolishly embarked on a war with Castile which rapidly turned into a disaster, Castilian forces taking Coimbra and threatening Lisbon. Fernando hastened to make peace in 1373 and to align himself publicly with Castile and France. This was a dangerous situation for Portugal. The Franco-Castilian alliance now posed a real threat to the survival of Portuguese independence and, not for the last time, Portugal was forced to submit to its powerful neighbour as the only viable alternative to annexation. Portuguese galleys were sent to strengthen the Castilian fleet while Fernando agreed to expel Enrique's enemies among the Castilian exiles. However, just as the prince regent, Dom João, was to do when faced by a similar dilemma in 1807, Fernando sent emissaries to England to explain that he was acting out of *force majeure* and actually to conclude a semi-secret agreement with the English – the informal beginning of the famous Anglo-Portuguese alliance.

The Franco-Castilian alliance, which the French had built up with such care since 1365, now began to pay handsome dividends. Between 1372 and 1380 the Castilian galley fleet raided the southern coasts of England with relative impunity, turning the tide in the Hundred Years War decisively in France's favour. As a result it became a priority of English policy to find some way of rekindling the war in the Iberian peninsula to put a stop to the depredations of the French and Castilians. The opportunity arose with the unexpected death of Enrique of Trastámara in 1379, followed by that of the king of France and his chief military commander, Du Guesclin, in 1380.

The drift towards civil war in Portugal

The divisions within Portuguese society now became more exposed as the rival factions edged towards civil war. On the death of Dom Pedro of Portugal in 1367 the succession had passed to his legitimate son, Fernando, who was unmarried. In 1372 Fernando had secretly married Leonor Teles, installing this daughter of a Castilian exile (who incidentally was already married) as queen, with the result that the influence of the Castilians at the Portuguese court greatly increased. Fernando's marriage aroused bitter opposition among those who feared and resented the rise of the Teles de Meneses family, and from this moment the hostility of the native Portuguese nobility and the population of

Lisbon towards the Castilian noble families entrenched at court came out into the open, preparing the ground for English and French intervention on a grand scale. While Dom Fernando lived, the cracks in the social structure were papered over and Leonor Teles was able to strengthen the position of her family and friends among the exiled Castilian nobles at Court. However, she did not bear the king a male heir and it was not difficult to foresee that his death would precipitate a succession crisis.

The great historian-chronicler Fernão Lopes was to represent Portugal's slide into civil war as the consequence of the disastrous marriage which Fernando made with Leonor Teles, a marriage which had resulted not from wise dynastic considerations but from sexual obsession. The moral weakness of the king had brought disaster on his country – history still being seen in terms of the power of the (divine) ruler to bring happiness or disaster to his country through his own physical well-being and moral conduct. However, Fernão Lopes was also to draw a vivid picture of the popular protest that arose during Fernando's reign and which became focused on the king's unwise marriage. This popular protest gave the civil war which followed the king's death something of the appearance of a social revolution. Yet the discontent that erupted in Portugal, and which was largely concentrated in the capital, was not dissimilar to the popular revolts which had occurred in Paris after the battle of Poitiers and in London in 1381, when the young King Richard II had come close to losing his throne. In Portugal popular discontent had lain just beneath the surface ever since the death of Dom Dinis in 1325. Severe social dislocation followed the outbreaks of plague in the 1340s and the 1360s when the countryside was depopulated, food production fell and the economic and social order was threatened with collapse. The depopulation of the countryside had the effect of undermining the incomes of the nobility and forcing them to look for other ways of maintaining themselves – not least through the patronage at the disposal of the Crown and the military orders and through the spoils of war in general. It also led the king in 1375 to pass the important *Lei das Sesmarias* which created a framework for bringing unused land back into cultivation and which was to prove so important when the Portuguese began their overseas expansion. However, such 'laws and ordinances were powerless to forestall the move of a large part of the rural population from the countryside to the city'.[5]

Meanwhile, following the death of Enrique de Trastámara in 1379, John of Gaunt prepared to renew his bid for the Castilian throne, which had stalled during the disastrous decade of the 1370s when England had lost the military initiative in France and had suffered the humiliations resulting from the control of the seas by France and Castile. In 1380, after the failure of lengthy peace negotiations with France and with the two countries more divided than ever, this time over which Pope to recognize following the Schism of 1377, the English parliament was at last persuaded to vote a large subsidy to send an army to Portugal and to mount an invasion of Castile. In the short term, it was hoped that such a threat would keep the Castilian galley fleet in home waters while the longer-term result of a successful war might be the break-up of the Franco-Castilian alliance. The invasion route through Portugal was chosen partly because, now that Enrique was dead, Dom Fernando was willing to take the field to recover some of Portugal's lost prestige and partly because Enrique's final war against Navarre had resulted in the closure of the Pyrenean passes through which the Black Prince had invaded Castile in 1367.

In 1381 Edmund, Earl of Cambridge, brought an army of 3,000 men to Portugal to mount an invasion of Castile. According to Fernão Lopes, the Castilian commander heard that 'Dom Fernando has been pregnant with the English for more than nine months, and has at last given birth to them in Lisbon.'[6] The expedition was poorly led and the English soldiers aroused deep resentment among the population as they requisitioned horses and lodgings for themselves and plundered the countryside around Lisbon. Two forays were made into Castile itself, during which the English were accompanied by the Master of the Order of Avis, who used Cambridge's presence in Portugal to establish close ties with the English leaders.[7] Meanwhile no English reinforcements arrived and Fernando and his advisers decided to use the presence of the English army, which apparently still bore some of the (by now rather tarnished) reputation of Nájera, to negotiate a favourable peace with Castile by which Portugal obtained the restitution of the galleys and their crews captured early in the war by the Castilians. The Earl of Cambridge, apparently, was not consulted and returned humiliated to England with his mutinous army. The historian Peter Russell pointed out that, ineffective as Edmund of Cambridge had been, the presence of the English army had led to the modernization of military organization in Portugal in ways that were copied by the Castilians. 'These changes by both sides gave formal recognition to the fact that, from a military point of view, both Castile and Portugal had now been completely drawn by events into the orbit of the general struggle in Europe.'[8]

The futility of the English intervention, in such marked contrast to the Black Prince's campaign in 1367, led Fernando and his advisers, supported by the queen, to undertake a major rethink of Portugal's peninsula policy. Whereas the Anglo-Portuguese alliance had brought little advantage to either party, the alliance between Castile and France remained strong and effective. Not only had it secured the throne of Castile for the Trastámara dynasty but it had turned the tide of the Hundred Years War decisively in France's favour. Up to this point the Castilian exiles had believed that their return depended on an English alliance and a successful invasion of Castile with English help. The failure of Cambridge's expedition now convinced them to seek a guarantee for their future by managing the succession of the Castilian king to the throne of Portugal after the death of the ailing Fernando. Early in 1383 hurried negotiations were conducted by queen Leonor's lover, João Fernandes Andeiro, Count of Ourém, and on 14 May Juan of Castile was married to the heiress to the Portuguese throne – a move which would have led, and was intended to lead, to the union of the Castilian and Portuguese Crowns. Five months later Dom Fernando died and Leonor Teles was duly declared regent for her daughter.

The Duke of Lancaster now saw another opportunity to make good the failures of his brother's campaign and to renew his bid for the Castilian throne. The Castilians for their part sought aid from France. Once again, as in 1365–7, a disputed succession attracted the main protagonists of the Hundred Years War, each seeking a decisive advantage in the peninsula which would swing the political balance north of the Pyrenees. If Portugal passed under the control of Juan, the French, through their clients in Castile, would control the fleets of Castile and Portugal and be able to deploy decisive military power against Gascony. For England it was vital that no such union of Crowns should take place. Political calculations were made in fourteenth-century London which were not dissimilar to those that would subsequently be made in European wars in the seventeenth, eighteenth and nineteenth centuries. Whether or not John of Gaunt would be able to make good his claims to Castile, French influence in the peninsula had, at all costs, to be curtailed.

Although the truce still held in France itself a decisive moment had now been reached in the European power struggle and all attention was focused on the outcome of the disputed succession to the Portuguese Crown.

The war of 1383–5 and the battle of Aljubarrota

In the year immediately following Dom Fernando's death the Castilian king pursued his objective of taking the Portuguese Crown, with a ruthlessness worthy of his father. The bastard sons of Dom Pedro and Inês de Castro, who were possible rivals, were imprisoned and Queen Leonor herself was forced to surrender the regency and was sent to a convent. Juan quartered the arms of Portugal with his own, and demanded homage from Portuguese nobles and the surrender of Dom Fernando's seals. He was strongly backed by the Castilian exiles in Portugal and by much of the Portuguese nobility, and in 1384 advanced with a large army with the intention of taking possession of Lisbon.

The long pent-up forces of civil conflict now erupted in Portugal. Opposition was strong not only among the citizens of Lisbon and the other coastal cities but among the minor nobility, who felt themselves excluded from the inner circles of court patronage. Elsewhere Juan received the submission of towns and castles. However, as he advanced into the country opposition grew and found leaders among the knights of the military orders: João, the young Master of Avis who was a bastard of the former king Dom Pedro, and Nun'Alvares Pereira, whose father had been Prior of the Hospitallers. João of Avis had become something of a hero after his murder of the queen's Castilian lover but he was only twenty-six years old and had few military supporters. He was reluctant to take up arms and claim the throne without a powerful ally and turned to the English, not surprisingly considering his early association with Edmund of Cambridge who had intervened to save his life when he had been imprisoned on the orders of the queen in 1381.

The English response was lukewarm as England was engaged in another round of peace negotiations with France. However, Portuguese agents were allowed to raise troops in England, while João of Avis offered Portuguese galleys to help defend the English coasts and, like Afonso Henriques in 1147, agreed to pay the expenses of any English army. Peter Russell has painted a sad picture of the picaresque group of villains and charlatans who enlisted under João's banner – if taken at face value, one of the most useless bodies of mercenaries ever to have been raised in any cause. Moreover Russell believed that possibly only 200 men actually sailed to Portugal, or at best only 800. Meanwhile Juan laid siege to Lisbon and seemed poised to crush the inexperienced levies that had been raised to defend the city. In the event it was the plague, not João's forces, that defeated Juan's attack, forcing him to abandon the siege and

causing the death of many of his best troops and commanders, including the admiral of his galleys, the formidable Sancho de Tovar, who had
brought terror to the towns of southern England. Before any serious
aid could reach him from France, Juan was compelled to withdraw to
the frontier, there to prepare a wholly new army to enforce his claims
the following season.

This breathing space allowed João of Avis to build up his support
and gave time for the forces recruited in England to arrive. It is clear
that during the winter of 1384–5 his position was strengthened to such
an extent that he was encouraged to summon a Cortes to Coimbra to
consider the question of the succession to the throne. Up to that time
the only serious rival to Juan had been the Infante Dom João, the son of
Inês de Castro – but he had the great disadvantage of being a prisoner
in Juan's hands. The Cortes was not accustomed to be asked to declare
on the legitimacy of the succession but eventually the Master of Avis's
case won over the delegates. He was duly declared king and hastened to
send emissaries to England to announce the adoption of his new title.

Meanwhile the succession struggle in Portugal had begun to
arouse widespread interest in the rest of Europe. A union of Castile and
Portugal would clearly tip the military balance in France's favour and
by combining the fleets of Castile and Portugal would open the way for
a French invasion of England. Moreover the increasingly bitter struggle for recognition between the Roman and Avignon popes might be resolved definitively if Portugal was attached irrevocably to the Avignon
cause supported by France and Castile. On the campaign that was begun
in the summer of 1385 therefore hung not only the future of Portugal but
also the outcome of the Hundred Years War, the future of the English
provinces in France and the resolution of the Papal schism. Meanwhile
Jean Froissart, reporter in chief of the Hundred Years War and the
greatest journalist of his age, also turned his attention to what was
going on in central Portugal.

By late summer 1385 English and Gascon forces had begun to arrive
in significant numbers and João's army, which had won some morale-
boosting victories in minor engagements with Castilian forces, had
begun to concentrate for the defence of Lisbon. Juan's newly raised
army was also joined by a strong force of French knights led by Geoffroi
de Parthenay, described ominously by Russell as a 'veteran of Crécy
and Poitiers'.

João's army barred the advance of the Franco-Castilian army
from Coimbra just as the Portuguese levies were to bar the advance

of Marshal Masséna's French at Bussaco four hundred years later.
Around the hermitage of São Jorge, near the village of Aljubarrota,
7,000 English, Gascons and Portuguese faced an invading army that may
have numbered 20,000 men. Apparently there were few veterans of
Nájera in the Castilian army, though the king's adviser Pedro Ayalla was
certainly aware of the lessons of that battle. Full-scale battles were relatively rare in medieval warfare, where sieges of towns and castles and
the harrying of the countryside were the preferred methods for gaining
military advantage. The battle which now took place was comparable
in scale to Crécy, Poitiers, Nájera and Agincourt but was to prove far
more decisive than any of these. It was chosen by Froissart as one of his
set pieces of chivalrous action and led the chronicler in his excitement
to give two distinct and rather different accounts of the conflict.[9]

Attacking a strongly prepared defensive position in the late evening,
the Castilians and French were caught by the fire of the archers and,
as at Crécy, cut down as the enveloping wings of the enemy surrounded
and confined their main force in what can only be described as 'a killing ground' –

> where the Englishmen by their policy had fortified them: and
> because the entry was so narrow, there was a great press and
> great mischief to the assailants, for such English archers as
> were there shot so wholly together that their arrows pierced
> men and horse, and when the horses were full of arrows, they
> fell one upon another. Then the English men of arms, the
> Portugalois and Lisbonois came upon them crying their cries,
> 'Our Lady of Portugal!' with good spears and sharp heads,
> wherewith they strake and hurt many knights and squires.[10]

Over two thousand French and Castilian men at arms were killed while
the rest scattered and fled. The magnitude of the Castilian defeat was
fully recognized at the time though historians of medieval warfare in
general, and the Hundred Years War in particular, largely ignore its significance. In his book *Medieval Warfare,* for example, Peter Reid says
only that 'King James [sic] of Portugal defeated the Castilians at the
Battle of Aljubarrota in Portugal'[11] and gives no index entry for the
king, the country or the battle. Yet the battle tactics that won so decisive a victory were clearly those that had brought the English their
great, if ultimately unprofitable, victories at Crécy, Poitiers and Nájera,
and Russell concluded that 'in terms of results achieved, the battle of

Aljubarrota must rank among the most decisive engagements of medieval warfare'.[12]

The aftermath of the battle

Among historians of Portugal, however, there has been an extremely unusual unanimity in recognizing that this victory guaranteed the survival of Portugal as an independent nation. Dispute, of course, there has been. Did the triumph of Dom João lead to a 'bourgeois revolution' in Portugal as António Sérgio maintained and as Russell incautiously endorsed; or did it simply lead to a realignment of Portuguese noble families – the fall of the nobles who had dominated Portugal since the death of Dom Dinis and the rise of the supporters of Dom João who were duly rewarded with the lands, titles and privileges of the defeated? There is also disagreement about the role of the English. Froissart represents the battle very much in terms of another conflict between French and English chivalry – but Froissart was not present. Russell largely discounted the English contribution but the latest Portuguese research states definitively that the victorious army at Aljubarrota was an Anglo-Portuguese force.[13]

The importance of this victory to the wider European conflict became apparent in 1386. With Castile prostrated by the defeat and French prestige also seriously damaged, England and Portugal renewed their formal alliance. The treaty signed at Windsor, and confirmed in London in the Star Chamber, guaranteed the political integrity of Portugal and the commercial privileges of English and Portuguese merchants in each other's countries. For England the immediate advantage was the naval alliance which brought Portuguese galleys to help in the defence of the coast of south England. Parliament also granted subsidies for John of Gaunt to renew his ultimately futile pursuit of the Castilian throne, enabling him to land with an impressive army of 7,000 men in Galicia in August 1386. The dispatch of this army at a time when England feared a French invasion is a remarkable indication of how important the balance of power in the Iberian peninsula was to the outcome of the struggle further north. The campaign in fact opened with a satisfactory naval victory when a squadron of Castilian galleys was seized by the Portuguese while its defenders were ashore.

The English army overran much of Galicia and in anticipation of further conquests Dom João signed an agreement with Lancaster for substantial Portuguese military aid and for the marriage of himself to Lancaster's daughter Philippa. In return Portugal was to gain a considerable accession of territory including all the castles that guarded the Castilian frontier – the only time in its history that Portugal seriously envisaged expanding its frontiers at the expense of its neighbour. The marriage with Phillipa was duly solemnized on 14 February 1387. This marriage with the granddaughter of Edward III, and niece of the Black Prince, completed the process of legitimization that had raised a young bastard nobleman to a European throne.

Although the events of 1383–5 must be seen as a Portuguese civil war, the victory of the 'bastard' João of Avis was not followed by the strife which had marked the victory of the 'bastard' Enrique de Trastámara in Castile. Dom João proved highly successful in uniting the Portuguese, an important part being played by Philippa, the heroine of Fernão Lopes's and Zurara's chronicles, who gave birth to the princes who were to dominate Portuguese politics until 1460 and who were to preside over Portugal's expansion as an Atlantic power.

In other respects the battle of Aljubarrota proved less decisive. French victory in the Hundred Years War now seemed more distant than ever and the stalemate in that debilitating conflict continued. The papal schism continued its furious battle of the anathemas with Portugal now firmly allied to the Roman cause. However, unlike Nájera, the battle of Aljubarrota did not usher in another generation of civil conflict in Castile. Gaunt was now an old man and finally agreed to abandon his claims to the Castilian throne in 1387, after two unsuccessful campaigns in Galicia and Leon in conjunction with the Portuguese. Juan of Castile, for his part, unchallenged at home but unable to pursue a fruitless war against Portugal, died unexpectedly in 1390 leaving an infant son to occupy the throne. Although a formal peace between Portugal and Castile was not concluded till 1411, the Iberian peninsula had at last found a level of stability.

Dom João's long reign saw Portugal wisely withdrawing from any further involvement in the Hundred Years War and enjoying a period of internal peace which was not broken until the armed clash between the Infante Dom Pedro and the Duke of Braganza in 1449. The energies of the military nobles were turned outwards to crusades against the Moroccans while rivalry with Castile worked itself out relatively harmlessly in slaving expeditions to the Canary Islands. Not until the 1580s was Portugal to be involved again in a European-wide conflict and until then enjoyed a 'peace dividend' that few if any European states could emulate.

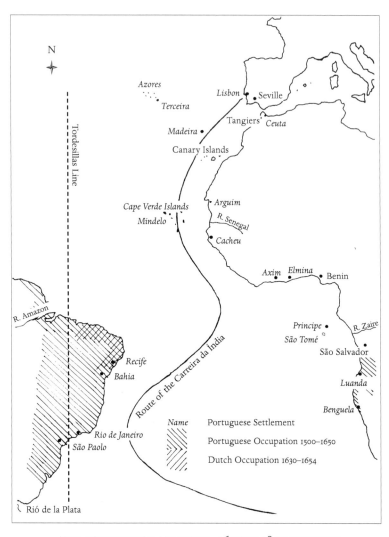

THE PORTUGUESE ATLANTIC, 16TH TO 18TH CENTURIES

3

Portugal and the Discoveries

Introduction

The activities of Portuguese seamen between 1420 and 1520 in opening the sea routes of the world are the best-known and most frequently described aspect of Portuguese history.[1] In outline the story is well known; Portuguese navigators mapped the coasts of West Africa between 1430 and 1490 and discovered the sea route round the Cape of Good Hope. Between 1490 and 1520 they sailed from Europe to India, Indonesia and China, and discovered and charted the coasts of Brazil. Moreover Columbus, a Genoese in Castilian service, must in many respects be seen as a product of the Portuguese maritime community. He and his brother had lived in Lisbon, and he had married the daughter of the governor of Porto Santo, from where he had probably made a voyage to the Mina coast. His navigational knowledge and skills were all learned from the Portuguese.

In addition to these well-known navigational achievements, Portuguese seamen explored the coasts of Newfoundland and North America, the mouth of the Río de la Plata and the coasts of Madagascar, East Africa, the Arabian peninsula and the Indian Ocean islands, scattering the world map with the names they bestowed on their discoveries – Labrador, Lagos, Cameroon, Natal, the Mascarenes, Tristan da Cunha, Formosa and many more. Meanwhile in 1502 Portuguese cartographers made the Cantino map, the first recognizably modern map of the world and in 1520 Fernão de Magalhães discovered the Magellan Strait and made the first crossing of the Pacific. It seemed there was nowhere the Portuguese could not sail and nowhere they did not attempt to explore. For a poor and remote kingdom, far from the centres of European civilization, learning and commerce, this has always seemed not only a remarkable but an almost inexplicable achievement. However, if the history of fifteenth-century Portugal is studied, a narrative unfolds that is at the same time more pedestrian and more believable.

The Moroccan crusades

The new dynasty that secured the throne of Portugal after the Anglo-Portuguese victory at Aljubarrota established its legitimacy through a combination of the arts of propaganda and a judicious use of patronage. Dom João I replaced much of the old nobility of Portugal with his own supporters and, as Queen Philippa duly did her duty and produced a succession of healthy male children, the king was able to create an upper layer of nobility closely related to himself. As his sons grew to manhood they were endowed with titles, lands and lordships, were granted economic privileges and were placed strategically as administrators of the Military Orders of Santiago and Christ.[2]

According to Zurara, who succeeded Fernão Lopes as the official royal chronicler of the Avis dynasty and who is the principal source for the early years of Portuguese expansion, it was the young princes who encouraged their father to mount an attack on the Moroccan city of Ceuta in 1415. Zurara wrote his account of the expedition thirty years after the event when he was concerned to enhance the reputation of his patron the Infante Dom Henrique. He described the expedition against Ceuta very much as Froissart would have done, as a chivalrous enterprise undertaken to enable the princes to display their knightly valour and religious devotion. Zurara asserted that the king was concerned to find active employment for the military class of knights, now that the war with Castile was finally over, but subsequent historians have speculated that he also wanted to close Ceuta to the Muslim corsairs and to obtain a share of the trade of Morocco, which passed through the port of Ceuta.[3] Whatever the real reasons for the expedition, it seems likely that the idea of making substantial conquests in Morocco had a very wide appeal not only to the nobility and the church but also to merchants and ship-owners.

The amphibious expedition that was organized over a period of three years and which eventually set sail in August 1415 consisted of over a hundred ships, escorted by twenty royal galleys and carrying 19,000 men – an extraordinarily large expedition by the standards of the day.[4] Ten days earlier João's cousin by marriage, Henry V of England, had set sail to conquer France with 12,000 men and in October fought the battle of Agincourt with at best 7,000.

The capture of Ceuta was an impressive military achievement and planted the Cross in lands that had been under Muslim control for eight hundred years, but it was more a propaganda victory than one of real

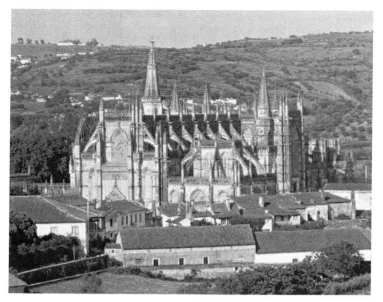

Batalha abbey, founded after the victory at Aljubarrota.

substance. Ceuta was easily blockaded from the landward side and the
Portuguese were never able to break out of the city to begin the *reconquista* of Morocco. However, so much prestige had been invested in this
conquest that it proved politically impossible to give it up and Portugal
was forced to pour resources of men and money into defending this tiny
North African outpost. In the royal council there was constant argument
about whether to abandon the conquest or invest yet more resources in
attempting to expand it. The principal advocate of further expeditions to
Morocco was the Infante Dom Henrique, the king's third son and governor of the Order of Christ, who saw crusading warfare as the way of
advancing his own interests and those of his order, and who took seriously
the vows of celibacy that the knights of the order still formally made.
While Dom João I lived, warfare in Morocco was limited to the defence
of Ceuta but when he was succeeded in 1433 by his son, Dom Duarte,
Henrique was able to persuade the new king to mount an attack on Tangiers which, if successful, would have given Portugal control of a solid
wedge of Moroccan territory. The expedition sailed in 1437 and was a disaster, the Portuguese being forced into a precipitate retreat, abandoning
the young Infante Dom Fernando as a hostage in the hands of the Moors.

Dom Duarte died in 1438, leaving his small son, Afonso, as his successor. The Regency was contested between Dom Pedro, Duarte's eldest

brother and his queen, Leonor, but Pedro triumphed and during his time in power further Moroccan adventures were firmly discouraged. However, he fell out of favour and was dismissed from the Regency in 1448, being succeeded by his great rival, his illegitimate half-brother the Duke of Braganza, who engineered a military confrontation in 1449 in which Pedro was killed.

The Duke of Braganza now became the power behind the throne and Dom Henrique hastened to align himself with the new political order, receiving confirmation of all his estates, titles and privileges. It was in the context of this new political dispensation that Zurara wrote the famous chronicles extolling the prince's life and achievements. By 1458 Henrique had won the young Afonso v over to supporting the idea of further Moroccan conquests and an expedition was sent to capture the coastal town of Alcazar. Although Dom Henrique died in 1460, Afonso retained his enthusiasm for Moroccan warfare, dispatching expeditions to raid the coast in 1464 and 1468 and in 1471 sending an army which conquered Arzila and Tangiers. Portugal now possessed four Moroccan towns and controlled a considerable section of the coastline receiving the homage of the sheikhs in the neighbourhood of the Portuguese garrisons. Early in the sixteenth century there were to be further conquests of Moroccan coastal towns extending as far down the coast as Agadir. The *reconquista*, it seemed, was at last underway.

Over a period of at least a hundred years, it was the promise of conquests in Morocco which preoccupied the Portuguese nobility and military class and which remained the focus of the ambitions of the crown and of the royal princes, who followed the example of Dom Henrique. Moroccan warfare not only established the military reputations of individual knights but could prove very lucrative. It was a warfare of raids which might result in substantial plunder or in the taking of captives for ransom. A successful plundering raid in 1511, for example, netted 1,000 head of cattle, 300 camels and horses and 567 prisoners.[5] This kind of warfare fitted well with the traditional crusading values of a conservative military elite. Morocco was also close at hand so it was relatively easy to send reinforcements and to repatriate the spoils of war.

If the commercial rewards of the Moroccan enterprises were less spectacular, they were by no means negligible and Portuguese merchants traded extensively in cloth, metalware and horses, which they exchanged for Portuguese salt. However, the permanent conquest of Morocco proved far beyond the resources of a country that simply did not have the military capacity to defeat the increasingly well-organized

Moroccan sultanates. By the early sixteenth century Portugal's control of the Moroccan ports was becoming precarious and could only be maintained by constant reinforcement and supply from the sea. It was an enterprise doomed to failure.

In 1542 Agadir was captured by Moroccan forces and in the following years the Portuguese vacated four of their Moroccan towns.[6] Even then the decision to abandon completely the conquests of Dom Henrique, already by this time something of a national icon, was not taken and during the reign of Dom Sebastião (1557–78) there was a revival of the idea that Portugal's real destiny lay in crusading in Morocco rather than in exploiting the vast potential of the Estado da Índia and the South Atlantic. In 1562 Mazagan was heroically defended against a massive Moroccan assault, three relief expeditions having to be organized at vast expense, and in 1578 Dom Sebastião invaded Morocco with an army of 20,000 men.[7] The king met his death at the battle of Alcazar el Kebir and with him died the idea of a Moroccan crusade. The Crown passed to Cardinal Henrique, the last legitimate male descendant of Dom João I, who was terminally ill and childless. On his death early in 1580 Portugal was invaded by a Castilian army and Philip II of Spain was proclaimed king.

Slaving Voyages and Island Settlements

The Moroccan wars were not only disastrous for Portugal but were of little long-term significance for Europe or even for Morocco itself.[8] Yet some historians have tried to see in them the genesis of Portugal's and ultimately Europe's overseas expansion. It has been suggested, for example, that it was in Morocco that Portugal learned about the gold trade of West Africa and was encouraged to seek out allies, perhaps Christian allies, in Africa or the East to help in the wars against the common Muslim enemy. However, far from aiding overseas maritime expansion, the Moroccan wars were seen at the time as a competing enterprise which diverted resources from other activities.

From at least the 1420s the rival interests of maritime trade and territorial conquest were defended by distinct factions in the royal council. Where Dom Henrique advocated crusade in Morocco, his brother Dom Pedro supported the mercantile interests of Lisbon, Porto and Lagos, which significantly expanded their maritime enterprise during Pedro's Regency. During the reign of Afonso V Moroccan warfare was back in fashion but his successor, João II, focused attention once more on commercial and maritime enterprise. With his premature death in

1495 the pendulum swung back yet again as Dom Manuel, who succeeded him, was a religious devotee who was easily persuaded to support the idea of a crusade against the Moors, giving the commercial exploitation of Portugal's maritime discoveries a relatively low priority. The rival claims of Morocco and overseas commercial expansion continued to be contested until the ultimate disaster of 1578. So how was it that, in spite of the distraction of the expensive wars in Morocco, Portuguese seamen, rather than those of any other country, came to pioneer the exploration of the Atlantic that was to have such momentous consequences for the history of the world?

Portugal had a long Atlantic coastline. For centuries its seamen had visited the fishing grounds of the eastern Atlantic while the coastal communities had made a living from the sea – from salt making, inshore fishing, the collecting of seaweed for use as fertilizer and from long-distance trade. During the Hundred Years War slaving and piracy had been added to these maritime pastimes. Such activities were shared with the Atlantic communities of other countries and during the fourteenth century Castilian, French, Italian as well as Portuguese corsairs had preyed on any Moroccan ships that were found sailing along the Atlantic coast and had sailed to the Canary Islands, whose inhabitants were carried off as slaves. Some noble adventurers had tried to claim seigneurial rights in the islands, while early in the fifteenth century a handful of French had even established short-lived settlements there.[9]

It was the rivalry resulting from these slave-raiding expeditions which encouraged the Portuguese Crown in 1419 to take formal possession of the Madeira archipelago, islands which had frequently been visited by fishing boats but never settled. The attempts to settle the Canary Islands had not proved successful as the indigenous inhabitants were warlike and the islands themselves presented a dry and hostile environment. Madeira, however, was not only uninhabited but had fertile volcanic soil and plentiful rainfall. Dom João I decided to grant these islands to captains with the obligation to build settlements and provide for their defence. The captains found no difficulty in recruiting settlers from among the impoverished rural communities of Portugal and were also able to attract Genoese sugar masters who were looking for fresh land to cultivate. The Madeiran settlements prospered to such an extent that Dom Henrique petitioned to be granted the seigneurial rights in the islands and for the spiritualities to be conferred on the Order of Christ.[10]

In Madeira the Portuguese and their Genoese partners were not challenged but in the Canary Islands clashes between Portuguese and

Castilians increased and even threatened the precarious peace that had been maintained between the two kingdoms since 1411. In 1425 the Portuguese sent a large expedition to the Canaries which achieved little of permanence and it was probably a desire to pre-empt further Castilian rivalry that convinced Dom João of the need to settle the more distant Azores. These remote islands were also known to seamen and had appeared on fourteenth-century maps but no permanent settlements had been attempted until the 1430s when the Portuguese king began to make grants of captaincies as he had in Madeira. The seigneurial rights over the islands were divided between Dom Henrique and Dom Pedro but their settlement proceeded more slowly and colonists had even to be recruited from the Netherlands.[11]

The Portuguese settlement of the Atlantic Islands had resulted in frequent voyages between the islands and mainland Portugal, making seamen familiar with the winds and currents of this region of the Atlantic. Moreover the settlements in Madeira and the Azores created new communities that looked outward into the Atlantic. Azoreans used their islands as bases to exploit the fishing grounds further out in the unexplored ocean, while the Madeirans began to send their own slaving expeditions to Africa. The participation of Italians was of the greatest importance but the Genoese were quite happy to work with the Portuguese and posed no threat to their possession of the islands, while they were able to bring their skills in making sea charts to Portugal and helped to improve the design of ocean-going ships. In the 1440s it appears that lateen-rigged caravels, modelled on those familiar in the Mediterranean, began to be built in Portugal for use in Atlantic navigation.

During the 1430s and '40s Portuguese and Castilians continued their desultory piracy in the Canary Islands and along the western coasts of Morocco and the Sahara and many of these expeditions were recorded in detail by the chronicler Zurara. According to his account the slaving voyages were usually sponsored by a nobleman or other person of importance while the ships would be captained by some minor figure from the noble household. Most of the expeditions consisted of only a handful of small ships and were not costly to organize. The slave raiding yielded profits to the organizers and enabled young squires to demonstrate leadership in the face of hostile conditions and an enemy who sometimes put up stiff resistance. By the 1440s these voyages were bringing back quite large numbers of slaves who were landed and sold at Lagos. The success of the voyages tempted others to take part and during the Regency of Dom Pedro (1440–48), when no expeditions to

Morocco were launched, increasing numbers of young men saw expeditions to the Atlantic coast of west Africa as the best way of securing their advancement. Here is Zurara describing a young man setting out on a slaving expedition:

> One of the signs by which a noble heart is recognised is that it is not content with small matters, but always seeks to do better in order to increase its honour and to surpass the deeds of the most noble both in its own land and abroad. This can justly be said of João Gonçalves captain of the island [of Madeira], because he was not satisfied with the voyage that his ship had made in the previous year to the land of the blacks. He wanted to send the same Álvaro Fernandes again with his well-armed caravel, and charged him to sail as far, and to try to obtain some prize which by its novelty and importance might give proof of the great desire he had to serve that lord who had brought him up.[12]

However, it would be wrong to see these slaving voyages as being conducted exclusively by Portuguese, for French and Castilian raiders were also active along the African coast during this period. What distinguished Portuguese enterprise was the degree of support it received from the royal family. The Portuguese Infantes, Henrique and Pedro, who had received grants of seigneurial rights in the islands, both invested in voyages, and Álvaro Fernandes found that because his 'caravel went further this year than all the others [he received] 200 *dobras* by way of reward, that is to say 100 which the Infante Dom Pedro, who was then Regent, ordered to be given and another 100 which they received from the Infante Dom Henrique'.[13] Meanwhile Henrique obtained the right to grant licences for voyages and to levy a tax of a fifth on all trade with the African coast. Henrique was also instrumental in establishing the Casa da Guiné, a department of state that handled all the matters concerned with West African trade and the issuing of trading licences. The rivalry of Portugal and Castile was beginning to intrude into wider European diplomacy and in 1436 the Portuguese sought a Papal grant of the Canary Islands and became involved in frantic lobbying in Rome in competition with the Castilians. However, beyond securing his commercial and fiscal interests in these areas, Henrique's role in maritime enterprise was largely passive, for in the 1450s he had turned his attention once again to Morocco and the organization of the expedition that took place in 1458.

Trading voyages to western Africa continued on a purely private commercial basis. Although Zurara detailed many of the slaving voyages that took place up to 1448, he was only able to record the experiences of the seamen at second hand. In the 1450s, however, a young Venetian, Alvise da Cadamosto, obtained a licence from Henrique to trade on the African coast and subsequently wrote about his experiences. By the time Cadamosto sailed slave-raiding had largely ceased and the Portuguese had embarked on peaceful trade with the powerful rulers of the Senegambia region, exchanging salt, cloth and especially horses for slaves and gold. Cadamosto described how Portuguese ships sailed first to Madeira or the Canary Islands and then skirted the coast of the Sahara, keeping more or less within sight of land. For trading purposes they anchored in the lower reaches of the rivers of upper Guinea. Cadamosto was able not only to go ashore but to travel extensively in the Senegal hinterland visiting the royal court and the local markets. His observations on sub-Saharan Africa ranged from the care of horses to the function of polygyny and the nature of African kingship. Although he recorded rumour and legend about the trade of the interior, including the famous silent barter of the gold traders, he tried always to describe things as he saw them with a minimum of religious or racial prejudice. For the first time an intelligent European was reflecting on a culture built around institutions and values wholly different from his own.[14]

It was inevitable that vessels sailing as far as upper Guinea would eventually encounter the Cape Verde Islands. In the 1450s these islands were visited and once again the Portuguese crown laid claim to them and began to distribute them as captaincies to Italian and Portuguese adventurers. When they were discovered the Cape Verde Islands appeared green and well-wooded like Madeira and the Azores, the vagaries of their hard climate being discovered painfully and at a later date, but the small settlements that grew up in the Islands were different from those that had taken root in the other archipelagos. The settlers found themselves far from Portugal but close to the African mainland and turned their eyes towards Africa rather than back to Europe. The import of large numbers of slaves meant that the population of the islands became predominantly African and African cultural traits merged with, and at times threatened to swamp, the culture of distant Europe. The Cape Verdians developed their own Creole language and formed commercial and family relationships with the mainland of Africa rather than with Portugal.

Castilian rivalry again

The settlement of the Cape Verde Islands took place during the reign of Afonso v when the concerns of the Portuguese ruling elites had once again become focused on Morocco and on events in neighbouring Castile. Trade with Africa was of little interest to the Court and in 1466 the Cape Verde settlers were granted the right to trade in upper Guinea while the privilege of granting commercial licences for African voyages was devolved, first on the young prince Fernando and then on a private Lisbon merchant. In 1469, with the expenses of the Moroccan wars beginning to take their toll, the African trade was leased for a lump sum to Fernão Gomes. A condition of Gomes's contract was that he should explore a hundred leagues of Africa coastline every year. Why this provision was introduced into his lease is not known, for it does not appear that Afonso's court was very much interested in sub-Saharan Africa. One can only speculate that this policy was framed in consideration of the old rivalry with Castilian seamen and adventurers that still continued in the Canary Islands and was soon to spread to the Cape Verde Islands as well.[15]

The trading ships sent out by Gomes soon made a discovery that was to transform Europe's relations with sub-Saharan Africa and ultimately with the rest of the world, and was to focus European attention for the first time on the importance of the commerce which the Portuguese had developed. In the early 1470s ships trading along the African coast discovered that they could obtain gold in large quantities in the area which later became known as the Gold Coast. Within a short time rumours of the magnitude of the gold trade began to attract other Europeans, principally Castilians, who Gomes regarded as interlopers. Fearful of losing the benefits of his monopoly Gomes pressed on with his exploration of the coast and within two years his ships had reached the equator and had discovered yet another island, which was named Fernando Po after its discoverer (the other islands in this archipelago – São Tomé, Príncipe and Ano Bom – being sighted later between 1478 and 1484).

Meanwhile a new war had broken out between Portugal and Castile. It is one of the ironies of Portuguese history that the very monarchs who were the living symbols of Portugal's independence constantly worked to bring about the union of Portugal with Castile through dynastic marriages. In 1474 Enrique IV of Castile died, leaving a daughter, Juana. Castilians were soon divided between the supporters of the young princess, whose paternity was strongly suspect, and supporters of Isabella Enrique's sister. Afonso of Portugal saw in this conflict an opportunity for himself and his dynasty and proposed to offer himself as a husband to Juana, who was his niece. As Afonso prepared to invade the country to assert the claims of himself and his betrothed, Portugal and Castile were soon at war.

The war brought out into the open the maritime rivalry between the Portuguese and Castilians. Armed Castilian fleets sailed for the Gold Coast and seized the island of Santiago in the Cape Verde archipelago, sending its captain, Antonio da Noli, and the Portuguese settlers as prisoners to Castile. While this war, the first overtly colonial war between European kingdoms, was fought thousands of miles from the European mainland, Portuguese forces joined Castilians opposed to Isabella in an invasion of Castile which ended in spectacular defeat at the battle of Toro in 1476.

Soon after the outbreak of war, Gomes surrendered his lease to the Crown as he was not able to deal with the threat posed by armed Castilian warships. The heir to the Portuguese throne, the Infante João, assumed responsibility for co-ordinating the Portuguese response and was successful in driving off the Castilians and reasserting Portuguese supremacy on the West African coast. The Portuguese victory in the maritime war showed the value of the central direction that the Portuguese were able to provide through the direct intervention of the Crown and through the Casa da Guiné that coordinated maritime and commercial affairs. The Castilian seamen, by contrast, had no central direction and suffered from the rivalry of their various noble patrons.[16]

The war was brought to an end in 1479 by the Treaty of Alcaçovas. This treaty contained the bizarre proposal that the heirs to the thrones of Castile and Portugal, both babies, should be brought up together with a view to a later marriage and a union of the kingdoms. Of much wider significance was the agreement that Portugal would finally recognize Castilian possession of the Canary Islands while the Castilians would accept Portugal's possession of the other island groups and the lands in Africa 'discovered and to be discovered'. This treaty was soon to be superseded by the much more important Treaty of Tordesillas but it set a precedent of far-reaching international importance. By this treaty European kingdoms were not only partitioning maritime space and allocating sovereignty over non-European territories but were deciding the terms of maritime trade thousands of miles from Europe. Moreover, these decisions were being taken in order to resolve conflicts that were in essence struggles for power within Europe itself.

Dom João II

In 1481 the Infante João succeeded his father on the Portuguese throne as Dom João II. João had learned the lesson of the war with Castile and, as one of his first acts as king, decided to fortify the principal gold-trading station on the Gold Coast. In 1482 he sent a fleet, equipped with soldiers, stone masons and carpenters, to construct a castle that came to be called São Jorge da Mina or Elmina. Elmina was not conceived as being a bridgehead for invasion and conquest, like the fortified towns in Morocco. It was rather a trading 'factory' whose fortifications were primarily intended to provide defence against attacks from the sea. It became the prototype for many similar trading stations which were established in the Indian Ocean in the following century. In contrast to what was to happen when the Castilians discovered gold in the New World ten years later, the Portuguese traded relatively peacefully with the African gold merchants and there was no attempt to conquer, enslave or massacre the African population.[17]

While charters were still granted to Portuguese captains to settle newly discovered islands, João was determined that the fort at Elmina should become a royal factory with all trade being carried on directly by the crown's agents. This was a daring innovation and one that had great significance for João's political aims in Portugal itself, for the king had embarked on a decisive struggle to wrest judicial and seigneur-ial authority and the control over the resources of the Crown from the principal noble factions in Portugal. The gold of Mina vastly increased the financial resources of the Crown and underpinned the system of royal absolutism to which João, like his contemporaries Henry VII of England and Louis XII of France, aspired.

The growth of the trade in gold and slaves with West Africa, the settlement of the islands, the Papal Bulls granting extra-territorial rights to the Order of Christ and the Castilian-Portuguese struggle for control of the trade of Mina had all served to attract European-wide attention. Many Italians had taken part in these enterprises providing capital and maritime skills for the Portuguese – Perestrello, the first captain of Porto Santo and the father-in-law of Columbus, Antonio da Noli, the discoverer and first captain of Santiago in the Cape Verde Islands, Cadamosto and Italian bankers like the Marchioni were all active in financing commercial voyages. Italian makers of portolan maps had begun to incorporate more information about western Africa onto their charts. Maps such as those of Benincasa and Fra Mauro showed the extent to which the maritime information coming back to Lisbon was finding its way into the cartographic bloodstream. Germans also enlisted in the Portuguese garrisons in Morocco, and a German Bohemian, Martin Behaim, may have accompanied Diogo Cão to the Congo in 1484. A Danish sea captain made a voyage under Portuguese colours and Flemish colonists were recruited for the settlement of the Azores. By the 1470s the Azoreans were not only using their islands as bases for fishing but were applying to the Portuguese Crown for licences to discover and settle new islands in the ocean to the west about whose existence rumour was circulating.

In spite of this growing European interest in Atlantic commerce Portugal still held a pre-eminent position, partly because of the accumulated knowledge and skills among its seamen and island settlers which were not widely available to others, and partly because of the Papal Bulls, the treaty with Castile and the evident ability of the Portuguese Crown to organize this growing Atlantic-based activity. By the accession of Dom João II the kingdom of Portugal had effectively expanded its territory from the narrow strip of land in the west of the Iberian peninsula to include four groups of islands, and a commercial and religious monopoly in the African lands bordering the Atlantic. However, it was the fear that Portugal's pre-eminence might soon be challenged that convinced João to divert resources from profitless warfare in Morocco to building a system of alliances with African rulers and to securing for Portugal the sea route to Asia about which geographers and entrepreneurs were now actively speculating.

Between 1482 and 1489, while regular trade with West Africa continued, João dispatched three official expeditions which differed from most previous voyages in having no immediate commercial objective and in being quite explicitly for the purposes of exploration. So little is known about these expeditions that some historians have speculated that their details were deliberately kept secret but there can be little doubt that João's objective was to chart the coast of West Africa and to discover a sea route to Asia. This became clear when in 1484 he rejected out of hand the project advocated by Christopher Columbus for reaching Asia by sailing westwards and in the same year announced to the Papacy that his seamen had indeed discovered a route to India – propaganda which departed quite far from the truth but helped to maintain Portugal's primacy in the navigation of the Atlantic.[18]

The captain of the first two expeditions was Diogo Cão, a member of the king's household. On his first voyage he explored the mouth of the Zaire and established diplomatic relations with the kingdom of Congo. His second voyage, which took him down the coast of modern Angola, ended with his death somewhere off modern Namibia. In 1487 the king sent out a third maritime expedition under the command of Bartolomeu Dias and dispatched Pero da Covilham, an Arabic-speaking spy, to travel overland along the caravan routes to Ethiopia and India. It was Dias who in 1488 rounded the end of Africa and, although he was forced to turn back by a mutiny of his crew, in effect opened the sea route to the East.

The world divided: The decade of the 1490s

The decade which followed Dias's epic voyage saw events which were to transform Europe's relations with the rest of the world and were to achieve unprecedented advances in scientific knowledge. Portugal was at the very centre of these events and the particular circumstances of Portuguese politics had a profound influence on how these developments played on the world stage. The return of Dias in 1489 did not immediately result in a follow-up voyage; instead Dom João sent a major expedition to further the relations that had been established by Diogo Cão with the kingdom of Congo. Establishing firm diplomatic relations, which included the conversion of the royal lineage to Christianity and the establishment of another royal trade monopoly, seemed to the king at the time to be a priority and a logical extension of the successful operation of the royal factory at Elmina. However, these plans were thrown into disarray by two quite unexpected events. In 1491 the heir to the Portuguese throne was killed in a riding accident. The king had no other legitimate children, though he did have a bastard son, Dom Jorge, who was Master of the Order of Santiago and the leader of an important faction at court. The other claimant was Dom Manuel, a cousin of the king and the queen's brother, who was a member of the Braganza family which had been humbled by Dom João in his reassertion of royal power at the start of his reign. The prospect of Dom Manuel rehabilitating the powerful Braganzas was not a welcome prospect for Dom João. A disputed succession loomed.

Then in 1492 came the news that Christopher Columbus, sailing with a commission from Isabella of Castile, had discovered some more islands to the west, immediately reawakening the prospect of a return of the old Luso-Castilian rivalry in the Atlantic that had been temporarily allayed by the Treaty of Alcaçovas. Dom João tried to defend the

Alcaçovas settlement and claimed the new islands for Portugal but events escalated as the Castilians obtained Bulls from Pope Alexander VI that in effect redrew the map which had been agreed in 1479. War with Portugal was now a distinct possibility but diplomacy was allowed to triumph and at Tordesillas in 1494 a new treaty was signed which partitioned the Atlantic along a line of longitude running 370 leagues west of Cape Verde in Africa. Seas and countries to the east of this line were to be Portuguese while west of the line Castile was to enjoy sovereignty. As longitude could not be exactly calculated there was plenty of room for dispute and for some time Portugal was to claim that the regions of Arctic Canada lay on its side of the line. These claims would eventually be abandoned but the bulge of South America, that later became Brazil, was found to lie clearly in Portugal's half of the world.

The Tordesillas agreement was remarkably successful in keeping the peace between Castile and Portugal and enabled them for nearly a century to exclude other Europeans from directly participating in the exploitation of the New World and the commerce of Asia. Still more remarkable, however, were the implications of the treaty for international law and for Europe's claims to overseas sovereignty. Two European nations were now claiming sovereignty in lands not yet discovered, let alone occupied and conquered. By this treaty the 'Spanish and Portuguese domesticated overseas expansion by defining their overseas jurisdictions as extensions of the realms of Castile and Portugal'.[19] Moreover, 'the Iberians claimed jurisdiction over the oceans, as well as extra-European lands, and thereby politicized maritime space in a historically new way.'[20] At the time it was signed the existence of mainland America was not known and the agreement may have been framed simply with the idea of settling in advance claims to new groups of islands that might be discovered. However, once Castilians located the mainland of central America and the Portuguese discovered the coastline of Brazil the treaty was interpreted as covering vast mainland territories which were not only unexplored but were densely populated with non-European peoples. Europe was in effect claiming dominion over the world, a dominion which the papacy underwrote by extending to Castile the privileges that Portugal enjoyed in the church outside Europe.

Tordesillas averted war and laid the juridical foundations for Iberian expansion, but at the same time Isabella had set in motion the dispersal of the Iberian Jews – the Sephardic diaspora. Jews expelled from Castile crossed into Portugal, where the influx precipitated a crisis. The Portuguese Crown decreed that the Jews must either convert or leave and large numbers now abandoned the Iberian peninsula and were to be followed over the next century by many of those who had initially converted. The Sephardic diaspora was to take people of Jewish origin to northern Europe, to Africa, the islands, Brazil and Spanish America, where they played a large part in creating the networks of finance and commerce that made European expansion possible.

In 1495, in the middle of these events, Dom João II died and was succeeded by his cousin. The new king not only reinstated the Braganza family in their titles and estates but brought about a significant shift in Portuguese politics. Like so many of his predecessors Dom Manuel planned a union of the Crowns of Portugal and Castile. The first stage was to be his own marriage to the eldest daughter of Isabella, a marriage which carried with it the requirement that Portugal expel all Jews from the kingdom. The marriage duly consummated, it was agreed that the boy born of the union would be brought up in Castile and would be recognized as heir to both kingdoms. Manuel was now firmly tied to Castile and Portugal followed the Castilians, who had conquered Granada in 1492, in renewing the bid to reconquer North Africa for Christianity. Manuel's reign was to see a marked revival of Portugal's Moroccan ambitions and a concentration of military resources on North African warfare.

Meanwhile, although Columbus, Pinzón and others were steadily revealing the extent of the lands discovered in the West, which were still believed to be part of Asia, Portugal was doing nothing to follow up Dias's discovery. According to the historian João de Barros, 'there were many different opinions expressed but the majority were against the discovery of India because, apart from the fact that it would bring with it many obligations, it would so weaken the strength of the kingdom that it would lack even what it needed to maintain itself.'[21]

Dom Manuel's concern to conclude a satisfactory agreement with Castile, and the disturbances consequent upon the expulsion of the Jews, may explain why no attempts were made to send out further exploratory voyages and when a small fleet of four ships was eventually got ready, it seems to have been more a gesture to appease the political faction headed by Dom Jorge than a considered policy of the Crown.[22] The king invested relatively little in the expedition and one of the ships was provided by the Marchioni bank. Vasco da Gama, an unknown knight of the Order of Santiago, together with his brother Paulo, was appointed to the command but, in contrast to the large and expensive embassy dispatched to the Congo in 1491, the fleet sailed very ill-prepared for the diplomatic mission it would have to undertake.

Between 1497 and 1499 Vasco da Gama successfully completed the first sea voyage from Europe to India, which he achieved by making use of the knowledge of the circulating wind system of the south Atlantic. Just as Columbus had made excellent use of the knowledge of the trade winds which the Portuguese had acquired during a century of navigation between Europe and the islands and fishing grounds of the North Atlantic, so Vasco da Gama brilliantly exploited Dias's discovery that to round the southern end of Africa a ship must not follow the west African coast southwards, battling into constant head winds, but from the Cape Verde Islands had to steer south-westwards into the Atlantic to pick up the southerly trade winds. Vasco da Gama's successor Pedro Álvares Cabral followed the same route but, steering more to the west, struck the coast of Brazil in 1500.

Conclusion

Columbus's voyage had shown that the route to the New World was relatively short and straightforward and seamen from Portugal, Italy and even England were soon making landfalls in the New World. Portugal's route to the south Atlantic and into the Indian Ocean was far more complex and required an intimate knowledge of islands, winds and currents. Although Italians and Germans were anxious to invest in Portuguese trading fleets, none of them attempted to make independent voyages, and for a generation or more the Portuguese were the only Europeans who knew how to navigate these waters.

Portugal's commercial voyages to West Africa and the long-distance voyages to Brazil and India enabled the Portuguese to acquire not only vast experience of the winds and currents of the oceans but also an intimate knowledge of thousands of miles of coastline which they laboriously plotted onto sea charts and from sea charts onto world maps. Although the hunger for geographical knowledge, which had spread throughout western Europe, meant that the information acquired by the Portuguese was soon widely disseminated, the Portuguese remained Europe's leading maritime pilots and cartographers for most of the sixteenth century. Without any great academic institutions or traditions of learning, the Portuguese had made the greatest contribution to the scientific knowledge of the world since Roman times and in so doing had launched the process of economic and scientific globalization. Although its seamen had a lot of practical experience of Atlantic navigation there were few intellectual resources on which to draw when it came to the more complex aspects of navigation, cosmology or geography. It used to be thought that Dom Henrique had created a School of Navigation but there is no contemporary evidence for this. The royal chroniclers apart, few Portuguese recorded their experiences during the fifteenth century and the exploration of Africa did not generate a Portuguese geographical literature until a century later. Portugal's expansion was firmly rooted in the experience of practical seamen and in the ambitions and ideals of a class of knights and squires who served the great princes of the blood and the higher nobility.

The maritime expansion of Portugal had not been achieved by an advanced capitalist economy. Fifteenth-century Portugal was a poor country with a small commercial class which had little disposable capital. Most of the voyages were privately financed by the nobility, by rich merchants like Fernão Gomes or by Italian merchant banks. Until the discovery of the gold markets of the Mina coast, the profits of the voyages mostly came from slaving. Though these profits tempted many to undertake individual voyages they were not great enough to cause the rich commercial cities of Italy or the northern European kingdoms to compete with the Portuguese. Indeed the willingness of the Portuguese to allow Italian and later German banks to invest in land and commercial voyages not only explains how Portugal's expansion was financed but also why, the Castilians apart, no other European state mounted a challenge to Portugal's claims to the extra-European Atlantic world.

The role of the royal family was indeed of critical importance. It was Dom Henrique who was instrumental in obtaining Papal Bulls which gave a legal framework for overseas enterprise. The Casa da Guiné, later expanded to deal with Elmina and the commercial establishments in the East, provided essential oversight of the crown's interests in the trade of Africa and the islands, and during the reign of Dom João II the crown's direct involvement in maritime enterprise can be seen at all levels from the dispatch of embassies to African kings and the building of Elmina to the organization of the voyages of Cão and Dias. This direct participation of the crown, even though it was at times intermittent, has no parallels in Europe of the time and goes far to explain the long-term success of Portugal's enterprise.

4

The First European
Maritime Empire

The Estado da Índia

During the sixteenth century the Portuguese created a worldwide commercial empire stretching from the China Sea and the Indian Ocean to Brazil and Angola in the South Atlantic. This empire, which was not challenged by any other European state for a hundred years, made a profound long-term impact on the economy and culture of Europe and initiated changes in the relations of Europe with the rest of the world, which can today be recognized as the beginnings of globalization.[1]

After Vasco da Gama returned to Lisbon in 1499 from his successful first voyage to India, the king, Dom Manuel I, realized that great profits could be earned from direct voyages to India. War between Venice and the Turks had put a premium on the value of spices imported into Europe and the sea route round the Cape was not only far beyond the reach of Turkish power but enabled greatly increased quantities of spices to be imported. A second fleet was quickly organized, this time consisting of fourteen ships. To equip such a fleet was beyond the resources of the Crown, so Italian and German banks were allowed to invest in the voyage. Its commander, Pedro Álvares Cabral, lost four of his ships in storms (including one captained by Bartolomeu Dias), and engaged in open warfare with the ruler of Calicut (now Kozhikode), the principal pepper trading port of the Malabar coast. Although the voyage produced spectacular profits it showed something of the problems that would be faced by fleets sent annually from Portugal. The ships had no secure base in which to re-equip and carry out repairs and, because of the violence employed by the Portuguese on their early voyages, they now had to contend with a hostile reception in many of the trading ports in the Indian Ocean. Having to fight wars in the East had not been foreseen and raised major issues of supply and manpower. Moreover, the Portuguese were not well supplied with goods with which to buy

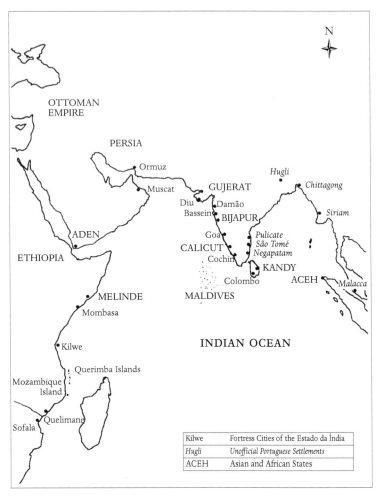

N

OTTOMAN
EMPIRE

PERSIA

Ormuz
Hugli
Muscat
GUJERAT
Chittagong
Diu
Damão
Bassein
BIJAPUR
Siriam
ADEN
Goa
Pulicate
CALICUT
São Tomé
ETHIOPIA
Cochin
Negapatam
KANDY
Colombo
ACEH
Malacca
MELINDE
MALDIVES
Mombasa

INDIAN OCEAN

Kilwe

Querimba Islands
Mozambique
Island
Quelimane
Sofala

Kilwe	Fortress Cities of the Estado da Índia
Hugli	Unofficial Portuguese Settlements
ACEH	Asian and African States

THE ESTADO DA INDIA, 16TH TO 17TH CENTURIES

Indian spices as the eastern markets required little that Europe could produce except bullion, which, until the opening of the gold trading factory at Elmina, had always been in short supply in Portugal.

Two more voyages (by João da Nova and Vasco da Gama) merely highlighted these problems and it appears that by 1504 the Portuguese court even contemplated giving up the India voyages altogether. Instead the decision was taken to put the whole enterprise on a totally new footing, a decision which was to provide a template for future European empires and for European maritime supremacy throughout the world. Plans were drawn up to create a new kingdom for the Crown of

Portugal, which would be administered by a viceroy and would be governed from a permanent base in the Indian Ocean. Dom Francisco de Almeida was sent out in 1505 with a large army and fleet to establish this new Estado da Índia (State of India).

The Estado da Índia was a truly revolutionary concept in state building. When it was created the Portuguese did not control any territory in the Indian Ocean, indeed, they had no sovereign territory of any kind nearer than Elmina and the Cape Verde Islands. However, the Tordesillas treaty had purported to divide the world between the Portuguese and Castilians and, on the basis of what had been agreed in that treaty, Dom Manuel now declared himself to be sovereign of the sea. The Estado da Índia would have as its sovereign territory the Ocean and the king added to his title 'Lord of the Conquest, Navigation and Commerce of Ethiopia, Arabia, Persia and India'. This new domain was to operate in much the same way that a land-based state operated. People wishing to cross the Portuguese 'territory' would have to obtain a pass (a *cartaz*), would have to comply with restrictions on what and whom they could carry, would have to adhere to the Crown monopolies in certain goods and would have to pay taxes to the ruler in the form of customs payments on goods carried. To enable this state to function the Portuguese would not only maintain an armed war fleet but would establish bases at strategic points on the Ocean's rim.

The first viceroy not only established the structure of the new state but began the process of further expansion by sending missions to Malacca and Sri Lanka. He also won a decisive naval victory over a coalition of enemies which confirmed the overwhelming superiority of Portuguese ships in naval warfare in open waters. However, it was his successor, Afonso de Albuquerque, who fully grasped the strategic significance of the geography of the Indian Ocean. He seized and fortified bases which controlled the narrow sea passages that gave access to the Ocean. By his death in 1515 the Portuguese dominated the straits of Ormuz and Malacca and the Mozambique Channel. Only the Gulf of Aden remained outside Portugal's direct control. These pinch-points, which were heavily fortified with the latest European fortress-building technology, enabled the Portuguese to make the maximum use of their limited manpower to control and tax maritime trade between India and the Far East and Mediterranean. They were to the Indian Ocean what the king of Denmark's control of the Skagerrak was to the Baltic.

In establishing the Estado da Índia Portugal had demonstrated the importance of sea-power. Portugal's ocean-going *naus* could carry heavy

Alfonso de Albuquerque. A posthumous portrait painted in Goa.

artillery (the largest guns were up to four metres in length) and had an armament much heavier than any ship they encountered in the East.[2] Moreover the *naus* could also be used to transport soldiers and supplies which gave the Portuguese armed forces a flexibility and manoeuvrability which allowed them to dominate the coastal regions of the Indian Ocean. They were able to make many of the coastal rulers tributaries or allies of the Estado da Índia and in this way gained privileged access to local markets and to the resources needed to maintain the empire.

From the start the Estado da Índia was conceived as an enterprise in which all the participants would be paid servants of the Crown and the trade, like that of Elmina, would be conducted on the king's account. The trade in pepper, gold and horses would be royal monopolies to

A sea battle before Ormuz between Portuguese and Persians, 1607.

which were eventually added cinnamon, cloves and ivory. Private trade was to be strictly limited and the soldiers, clerks and seamen were all to live within the royal fortresses under rules set out in detailed *regimentos*. The juridical foundation of the Estado da Índia was to be found partly in the terms of the Tordesillas agreement but also in the Papal Bulls which had granted to the Portuguese Crown rights over the Church, and hence all Christians east of the Tordesillas line.

The rise of the informal empire

The Estado da Índia never worked as designed. Private trade rapidly grew out of control and large numbers of Portuguese left royal service to settle in neighbouring Asian and African states as freelance traders or mercenaries. No effective blockade could be maintained in the Gulf of Aden and the captains of the fortresses and ships were only too willing to take bribes to allow Indian merchants free passage with contraband goods. By the middle of the sixteenth century the costs of maintaining the fleets and fortresses persuaded the Crown to begin the process of leasing its monopolies to the fortress captains and selling the rights to the monopoly voyages. The model of crown monopoly capitalism, which had been successfully pioneered at Elmina in West Africa, was being replaced by a restricted form of private capitalism. However, this was not the joint-stock capitalism later developed by the English and Dutch, but an older form of short-term capitalism in which a consortium of wealthy individuals financed the temporary monopoly held by a fortress or ship's captain. At most these consortia had only three years to realize their profits and usually only a single voyage.

As the Estado da Índia evolved away from the original concept of a tightly controlled royal monopoly, so its range increased. Portuguese traders penetrated the Zambesi valley and the gold-bearing regions of Zimbabwe; Portuguese forts were built in Bahrein and Basra to exploit the pearl fisheries and the caravan trade reaching the Gulf ports; the Portuguese dominated the western coast of India from Diu in the north to Calicut in the south from a dozen fortified towns; settlements were built in the Bay of Bengal while colonies of Portuguese traders and mercenaries were to be found in Pegu and Arakan; on the Coromandel coast there were Portuguese towns at São Tomé (Chenai/Madras) and Negapatnam; in Sri Lanka the Portuguese controlled the port-city of Columbo and from there extended their control over the kingdom of Kotte; the islands of the Moluccas as well as Timor and the lesser Sunda Islands had Portuguese communities protected by missions and forts. However, the area where this expansion was most impressive was in the China Sea, where Portuguese interlopers obtained permission to settle at Macao in 1556 and from there spread to Japan, establishing a treaty port at Nagasaki in 1571.

The Portuguese in Japan. A Japanese *namban* screen.

Most of this expansion took place beyond the formal confines of the Estado da Índia. For example, east of Sri Lanka the viceroy only had direct control over Malacca and the fort at Ternate in the Moluccas. Such important Portuguese settlements as São Tomé de Meliapor, Hugli, Macao and Nagasaki were independent commercial settlements over which the viceroy in Goa had only indirect influence. This expansion of the 'informal' empire was greatly facilitated by the rivalry of the missionary orders (Dominicans, Jesuits and Augustinians) who constantly sought new mission fields, often preferring to work beyond the interference of the Portuguese captains and viceroys. However, their converts (by the end of the sixteenth century there may have been over a million Christians in the countries east of the Cape of Good Hope) were bound to the Portuguese crown through the *padroado real*. This authority over the church had the effect of extending the influence of the Portuguese crown into areas where the writ of the viceroy in Goa did not run.

A model for a maritime empire

The Estado da Índia created a model of maritime commercial empire that was later adopted by the Dutch, English and French even though these had no religious aspirations and operated through monopoly companies rather than crown monopolies. Initially the Dutch sought to take over the structure of the Portuguese empire as a whole, attacking Malacca and Mozambique between 1605 and 1608 and making a concerted effort to capture all the Portuguese colonies in the South Atlantic between 1624 and 1641. However, this was only partly successful and in the end the Dutch built their own commercial empire centred on Batavia. The model established by the Portuguese was one of commercial enterprise supported by naval power which set a precedent for Europeans trading in the East. Access to markets was to be obtained by political pressure and military supremacy rather than by peaceful commercial competition. Moreover, following the Portuguese precedent, this naval supremacy was to be used to manipulate the market. The Portuguese had tried to use political pressure in Malabar and Sri Lanka to obtain pepper and cinnamon at prices below the current market rate but they had only sought direct control over the distribution of these spices – the means by which the product reached the European market. Once landed in Lisbon the Portuguese depended on the distribution networks of the Italians, Germans and Netherlanders to sell their goods. Indeed, until the mid-1540s Portugal depended on its factory at Antwerp not only for the sale of spices but for raising finance and for the purchase of silver and armaments. The Dutch widened the scope of these monopolistic ambitions and extended their control over the production of spice in Asia and over its marketing in Europe. Europe's eventual dominance in world trade was not achieved by the operation of the 'free market' but always depended ultimately on protection, the use of force and the armed backing provided by the state for the activities of merchants. In this way the model of empire adopted by the Portuguese early in the sixteenth century remained substantially unchanged till the nineteenth century.

Travelling and describing the world

If the Estado da Índia created a template for subsequent European maritime empires, it also produced radical change in Europe's relations with Africa and Asia. Prior to Vasco da Gama's voyage, Europe's relations with the East had been very restricted. The open roads, which had briefly existed in the thirteenth century and which had allowed missionaries and merchants to travel along the Silk Road as far as Beijing, had closed with the decline of the Mongol empire. In the fifteenth century commercial contacts were maintained by the Venetians through intermediaries in Egypt and the Levant with only a few hardy individuals, among them Dom João II's spy Pero da Covilham, making their way as far as India. Apart from delegates from eastern churches who attended the Church Councils in the fifteenth century, few Asians or Africans made the journey to western Europe.

The opening of a direct sea route meant that large numbers of Europeans could now travel to Asia and that Asians could make the voyage to Europe. First-hand information about Asian and African countries now began to enter directly or indirectly into the intellectual bloodstream of Renaissance Europe. During the fifteenth century the Portuguese had apparently shown little interest in the peoples with whom they came into contact. There are very few first-hand accounts of any Portuguese voyage to Africa and it was left to the official chroniclers Zurara, Rui de Pina and later João de Barros to collect information and organize it into a presentable literary form. Indeed Álvaro Velho's 'diary' of the first voyage of Vasco da Gama is the earliest first-hand account of any of the voyages written by a Portuguese. Early in the sixteenth century, however, a number of important accounts of Africa and the countries of the Indian Ocean were put down on paper by Portuguese who had served in the East – among them the substantial reports compiled from first-hand experience by Duarte Pacheco Pereira, Duarte Barbosa and Tomé Pires, as well as many lesser accounts. These, however, remained in manuscript form and were not made public. It was left to Germans and Italians to publish the first detailed accounts of the extra-European world.

The same was apparently true in the field of map-making. The Portuguese made very accurate sea charts and in the sixteenth century compiled *Roteiros* or sailing guides for use in the Indian Ocean and Red Sea. Portugal also had a thriving industry producing high quality and artistically decorated maps of the different continents. Fine Portuguese maps were acquired as luxury items by European monarchs or nobles, like the famous Cantino map which was clandestinely acquired in 1502 for the Duke of Ferrara, and were seen and copied by cartographers in Italy and the Netherlands. However, the Portuguese did not directly publicize their cartographical knowledge and did not develop an industry to engrave and print the latest maps.

The first Portuguese to make a serious effort to collect together and publish the mass of ethnographic and geographical knowledge that was being accumulated by the officials of the Estado da Índia and their agents was João de Barros. In 1532 he received an official appointment in the Casa da Índia and from that time became an assiduous collector of information, building up a network of informants that reached to India and East and West Africa. 'It seemed necessary to do what your honour desired of me, namely, to search for men who had formerly been in Bisnaga; for I know that no one goes there without bringing away his quire of paper written about its affairs', wrote one anonymous inform-ant to Barros.[3] His *Da Asia* was not just a chronicle of warlike deeds but a vast compendium, an encyclopaedia almost, of the knowledge the Portuguese had acquired. The first volume appeared in 1552 and from that time a succession of works by Portuguese authors made the extent of Portugal's global empire known to the rest of Europe. Diogo do Couto took it upon himself to continue Barros's work, his first volumes appearing in 1602. In 1563 Garcia d'Orta, a New Christian doctor, had published his *Coloquios dos Simples e Drogas . . .,* a work of major medical and botanical importance, and in 1569 appeared the first European work on China entitled *Tractado em que se côtam muito por estenso as cousas de China.*[4] These works were followed by many more.

The dissemination of information was systematized in the second half of the century by the missionary orders, especially the Jesuits, whose propaganda spread information about the exotic mission fields in Africa and the East through Europe. Works on Asian and African languages and religions were published along with medical and botan-ical treatises, geographies and manuals of navigation. Soon poetry and autobiography were added to the literary genres as well as the dramatic reportage of shipwreck narratives, many of them written by survivors. Portugal and Portuguese writers became by far the most important contributors to this flowering of geographical knowledge in late six-teenth-century Europe, for the information on which it was based originated from the Portuguese settlements in the East and from the missions operating under the *padroado real.*

This information was hungrily assimilated and digested by other Europeans who found in it not only useful practical information with which to plan commercial strategies of their own but a vision of societies with values and manners different from their own, against which to measure western civilization. By the beginning of the seventeenth cen-tury Dutchmen like van Linschoten, Englishmen like Richard Hakluyt and Samuel Purchas and Frenchmen like François Pyrard had collected and collated the geographical knowledge available in Portuguese writings. Knowledge was power and this source of power was passing rapidly from the hands of Portugal into those of other Europeans.

If Portuguese agents in the East provided the flow of information about Asia that was rapidly transforming Europe's view of itself and of the world, and if Barros and others of the early chroniclers were producing a triumphalist literature that interpreted 'the activities of greedy predators as the agents of Christianity and civilisation',[5] they also spelled out the deep moral misgivings that many perceived in the widening gulf between the professed ideals of Christianity and the plundering of the Asian seaboard which marked so much of their activities. The *Peregrinação* (Pilgrimage) of the aspiring Jesuit Fernão Mendes Pinto, which was written in the 1570s (the decade which saw the publication of *Os Lusíadas* of Luís de Camões) and published in 1614, provided a fierce critique of Europe's conduct towards the non-European world. Pinto first used the device, which was to be copied by writers of the Enlightenment like Montesquieu in his *Lettres Persanes*, of using fictional Eastern characters to voice the most bitter criticisms of the conduct of his countrymen. In Pinto's narrative a Chinese hermit confronts Portuguese pirates with the words

If thou art hungry for more silver – as is apparent from thy greedy look – to cram into the insatiable pouch of thy infernal appetite, thou shalt find enough in the other buildings around here on which to gorge thyself to the bursting point. And perhaps that will be a good idea after all, for as long as thou art condemned to hell for what thou has already stolen thou mayest as well go to hell for stealing the rest – for the heavier the burden on thy head, the quicker shalt thou sink to the bottom, as anyone can tell from the evil deeds that bear witness against thee.

And the episode concludes with the hermit's words:

You must try to seek salvation for yourselves, because I can assure you that the earth, the air, the winds, the waters, the people, the beasts of the field, the fish, the birds, the grass, the plants, and everything in creation under the sun will surely rise up against you and attack you so mercilessly that only He who lives in the heavens above will be able to avail you.[6]

If no Portuguese writings achieved the heroic dimensions of those of the Spanish Dominican Bartolomé de Las Casas, their moral critique of European imperialism was no less compelling.

The beginnings of globalization

The worldwide reach of the Portuguese and Castilian empires led to a great expansion of markets, and to a quickening of the economies of Europe and of the maritime states of the East. Ever since the time of the Greeks trade had moved westwards along the Silk Road or across the Indian Ocean to Basra and Suez and from there to the Mediterranean. This trade was primarily in luxury goods. The quantities were small and the prices high to meet the huge costs of transport and protection. The arrival of the Portuguese in the East made little impact on commerce within Asia, for the scale of their activities was relatively modest and they were only one among many trading communities and quickly adopted Asian ways of doing business. However, their arrival revolutionized the trade between Asia, Europe and the Atlantic world. Early in the sixteenth century beads from India and cowries from the Maldives were already being traded in West Africa, while a bronze figure of a Portuguese soldier, cast in Benin in the late sixteenth century, is apparently holding a musket of a type made in Japan. The Portuguese *carreira da Índia* greatly facilitated the emergence of global markets for Asian products as well as the volume of goods that could be transported. Spices now began to arrive in Europe in greater quantity and circulated among a wider group of consumers at a lower price. Other eastern commodities, many of them new to the European market, also began to arrive – luxury items like diamonds, fine furniture and *objets d'art*, but also drugs, porcelain, cotton fabrics and tea. In the course of the seventeenth century these transformed the taste and the material culture of Europe, so that by the eighteenth century Europeans themselves were producing porcelain and making cotton cloth.

In exchange for eastern commodities Europe had to export increasing quantities of silver. It was able to do this because of the discovery of vast silver reserves in the Americas. From Potosí and the Mexican mines silver was transported by armed warships to Seville from where it entered the European economy, a large amount being remitted to Lisbon for onward shipment to India. Consignments of silver also crossed the Pacific to enter the Chinese economy in payment for the silks that now found a market in America as well as Europe. At the same time silver production in Japan began to expand, largely as a result of the stimulus given to it by the Portuguese, and eventually reached about half the level of American output. For approximately eighty years after 1550 the Portuguese were the main agents for trading Japanese silver and for the transport to Japan of the cargoes of silk from Canton.

The contractors who operated the Portuguese crown's pepper monopoly were major traders in silver, while Portuguese New Christian bankers maintained an international financial network extending from the Netherlands to the Iberian peninsula, India and South America. It was the Portuguese who acted as the vital intermediaries by whom the silver of America and Japan injected liquidity into the global economy and the Spanish silver real was made the world's first currency of international exchange.

By the 1590s globalization had reached the point at which it was possible for a merchant to travel round the world, trading from one lucrative market to the next. Francisco Carletti, a Florentine merchant, sailed from Seville in 1594.[7] He bought slaves in the Cape Verde Islands for sale in Spanish America, visiting Cartagena, Lima and Mexico City. From Acapulco he made a 66-day crossing of the Pacific to the Philippines, smuggling bullion with the connivance of the captain. From there he went to Japan and then Macao where he bought a cargo of silk. Shipping this via Malacca to Goa, he entered into an agreement with a Gujerati merchant to sell the silk in northern India. From Goa he returned by sea to Europe. Carletti's remarkable trading voyage showed the extent to which maritime commerce was already organized on a global basis. World-wide networks of shipping, finance, market intelligence and commodity broking were already in place.

By the time Carletti sailed there was also an international language in which commercial dealings could be conducted. In maritime Asia and Africa Portuguese had become the language which facilitated not only the development of international commerce but also the spread of Iberian legal and religious ideas. Portuguese was understood and spoken in the clove-producing regions of the Moluccas; in Sri Lanka, where on their arrival the Dutch found that they had to use the language of their enemies to be understood; in coastal India; and down the African coast, where shipwrecked *fidalgos* found African chiefs who could speak to them in their own language. In Dutch-controlled areas of Indonesia 'all attempts by the authorities to spread the use of the Dutch language and stem the flood of the Portuguese language notwithstanding, Portuguese became the lingua franca of Batavia'.[8] It was spoken by the so-called Mardijkers (locally recruited soldiers, workmen and artisans) and by the Luso-Indian wives of the Dutch settlers. Portuguese remained the language of trade on the West African coast until the nineteenth century. Portuguese Creole dialects took root in Sri Lanka, Malacca and South India as well as

Guinea and the Atlantic archipelagos of Cape Verde and São Tomé, where they are still universally spoken.

Globalization was not limited to economic or scientific matters. The most important way in which it manifested itself was in the spread of new food crops and domestic animals. It had been Portuguese practice to take with them domestic animals as well as seeds and cuttings to be propagated in regions where they settled. Food crops that were familiar in Europe were introduced into the Atlantic Islands, the New World and Asia – these included vines, citrus, wheat and sugar cane. To Brazil the Portuguese introduced bananas, ginger and the oil palm. In return a wide range of American food crops were brought to Europe and Africa, including tomatoes, papaya, sweet potatoes and squashes. However, it was maize, potatoes and cassava which brought about the radical transformation of the diet, and hence the size of the sustainable population, in both continents – indeed it has been claimed that the dissemination of new food crops by itself accounts for the 'global demographic growth since 1492'.[9] Maize, being relatively resistant to drought and to the depredations of birds and insects, proved to be hugely important in Africa and spread also into southern Europe, while the potato became the staple crop of much of northern Europe and fuelled a population explosion in countries like Ireland and Northern Germany. Tobacco was another commodity which the Portuguese were instrumental in spreading to Asia, Africa and Europe and which, by the seventeenth century, had become a staple of world commerce as well as the drug of choice among all classes of European and Indian society.

There is one final area in which the Estado da Índia had a profound influence on the history of Europe and its relations with the rest of the world. The treaties signed between Portugal and Castile (Alcaçovas in 1479, Tordesillas in 1494 and Saragossa in 1529) had resolved territorial disputes between the two kingdoms but had gone much further than was customary for such treaties. They had also partitioned and allocated lands which had not yet been discovered, let alone settled, and which were the domains of other rulers. However, these treaties were still more revolutionary as they purported to establish sovereign rights over the oceans. It was this that enabled Dom Manuel to declare himself 'Lord of the Conquest, Navigation and Commerce of Ethiopia, Arabia, Persia and India' and to act as sovereign over the Indian Ocean. These exclusive claims by the Iberian sovereigns, expressed by the Latin phrase *Mare Clausum,* were not, of course, accepted by the rulers of Asia and Africa, nor by other European countries. Early in the seventeenth century the Dutch challenged the Portuguese claims and laid down the principles of the 'freedom of seas' – *Mare Liberum* – which became widely accepted for the next two or three centuries. The treaties between Portugal and Castile had sought to create a structure of international law to cover the oceans and to regulate international relations. This newly developed international law initially reflected the interests of just two European kingdoms and was underwritten by the head of the Catholic church but it proved to be the beginning of the pretensions of Europe (and later of the US) to regulate the affairs of the rest of the world.

Early in the seventeenth century Portugal's leadership in world trade and in the global distribution of scientific knowledge had been overtaken by other Europeans. The Dutch and the English with their stronger navies, their greater economic resources, better commercial organization and more dynamic intellectual culture would relegate Portugal to a minor role, but the whole impetus of European expansion, with its incalculable importance for the rest of the world, had for a century been almost exclusively Portuguese.

5

The Union with Spain and the Armada, 1578–89

The road to disaster

Following the discovery of Brazil and the sea route to India the Portuguese had embarked on a heady period of overseas expansion which was to involve them in conflicts of major importance in the East. The arrival of the Castilian fleet, commanded by the Portuguese renegade Fernão de Magalhães, in the Moluccas in 1521 led to a stand-off with Castile that was only resolved in 1529 at the Treaty of Saragossa when the Portuguese 'bought off' Castilian claims with a substantial payment to Charles v, and yet another royal marriage – this time a double one with Charles and Dom João iii marrying each other's sisters. Conflict with the Turks was not so easily resolved. With the Ottoman conquest of Egypt in 1517 the Portuguese came face to face with a major military state which had significant sea power and the same global reach as themselves. The ensuing struggle for supremacy in the Indian Ocean was to lead to Portuguese fleets sacking Suez, to armies being sent to Ethiopia and to two hard-fought and desperate sieges of the Portuguese fort at Diu in 1538 and 1546. It was only in the 1550s that the Portuguese finally gained the upper hand and destroyed Turkish sea power in the Indian Ocean.

Such armed confrontations could only be sustained because Portugal did not participate in any of the wars resulting from the religious conflicts and the rivalry of Habsburg and Valois in western Europe. Not that it was entirely unaffected. As the so-called Italian Wars between Spain and France spilled over into the Caribbean, Portugal faced increasing numbers of French interlopers, many of them Protestant, trading and even settling along the coast of Brazil. These, however, were successfully expelled in the 1560s. English and French interlopers also appeared on the coast of Guinea but, remarkably, there was no attempt to challenge Portugal's supremacy over the route to India. Because the

Portuguese did not face any major challenge from other Europeans, the defence of their coastal and island settlements in the Atlantic was largely neglected. In the Netherlands the situation was rather more serious. Since 1515 the distribution of the spices arriving on the ships of the *carreira da Índia* had been entrusted to the royal factory in Antwerp. However, warfare in the Channel and along the borders between France and the Spanish Netherlands interfered to such an extent with Portugal's commercial operations that the Antwerp factory had to be temporarily closed in 1545.

Portugal's ability to keep out of European wars was to a large extent due to the fact that the kingdom had become a client of the Habsburg empire of Charles v. After centuries of conflict between Castile and Portugal a permanent basis for peace had been established at the treaties of Tordesillas (1494) and Saragossa (1529). These treaties laid down distinct and mutually acceptable spheres of influence overseas, while Portugal brought its policies with regard to the Jews increasingly into line with the Castilians, agreeing in 1495 to expel all unconverted Jews and in 1536, somewhat reluctantly, to establish the Inquisition in Portugal. Portugal moved even closer into the orbit of Spanish power through a succession of dynastic marriages which linked the royal houses in an unhealthily close matrimonial alliance. The young king Sebastião, who came to the throne after the death of his grandfather Dom João iii in 1557, descended from six generations of first-cousin marriages, the last three being with Infantas of Spain. As the young king was only four years old when his grandfather died, Portugal was ruled for five years by his Spanish grandmother Caterina, the aunt of Philip ii of Spain. Portugal was close to becoming a satellite of Spain.

One consequence of the long years of peace was that Portuguese institutions failed to keep pace with developments elsewhere in Europe. The large income earned by the crown from the pepper monopoly and the gold trade of Elmina removed the need to create the kind of fiscal bureaucracy that was emerging in other European states. The kings of Portugal did not depend, as other monarchs increasingly did, on being able to raise taxes and did not evolve the means to collect or administer them. Portugal also failed to modernize its armed forces. In the East it relied on its heavily gunned warships and scientifically designed fortresses but for its manpower it increasingly depended on Asian mercenaries. In the North African fortresses an archaic mode of warfare prevailed as raids by mounted men on Moroccan villages alternated with siege warfare, the fortresses relying on relief arriving by sea. Some military reforms were undertaken during the early years of Dom Sebastião's reign but these did little more than provide for a system of mobilization for home defence. The evolution of European armies which had seen Swiss pikemen and German *landsknechts* and finally the formidable Spanish *tercios* dominating the battlefields of Europe found no echo in Portugal. When an armed force was needed the king, like his medieval predecessors, had to rely on the nobility and their retainers.

Ironically, it was this disastrous military unpreparedness of Portugal that was to thrust the kingdom once again onto the centre of the European stage.

During the 1560s and '70s there was a marked revival of crusading sentiment in Portugal. This was most clearly reflected in literature – in the 1550s João de Barros had published the first three volumes of *Da Asia*, his great chronicle of Portuguese conquests in the East, which was closely followed in 1557 by Bras de Albuquerque's *Comentários do Grande Afonso de Albuquerque*, which revived memories of the achievement of the early conquistadores in the East. Then in 1571 appeared Camões's epic poem *Os Lusíadas* with its apotheosis of Vasco da Gama and its celebration of the heroes of early Portuguese history. This focus on military heroics had a contemporary resonance with the epic defences of Diu in 1546 and Mazagan in 1562 – though the lesson to be learned from these events was that Portugal was now clinging onto its possessions by desperate defence rather than showing any capacity to seize the initiative.

How unprepared Portugal was for undertaking any significant enterprise on a European stage, which had changed so radically since the fifteenth century, was tragically revealed in 1578. The young king, Dom Sebastião, had 'come of age' in 1567 at the age of fourteen. Suffering from unspecific but serious physical and mental disorders he showed no interest in sex or marriage and displayed symptoms not unlike those of autism, being locked into a world of his own imagination and apparently unable to respond to what people were saying to him. Whatever physical disorder he was suffering from did not lessen his energy and the king embarked on a strenuous physical regime, gathering round him like-minded but immature young men who encouraged his worst excesses. This was also a moment for the Jesuits, who in the person of Luís Gonçalves had provided the young king with a tutor and confessor to establish their ascendancy. Jesuit influence can be seen clearly in the forward policy adopted in Africa as soon as the young king came of age. Armed expeditions were sent to the Congo, to East Africa and to Angola, in all of which the desire of the Jesuits to conquer lands in the name of the Cross was evident.

Dom Sebastião planned to undertake a crusade in Morocco and in 1571, the year that the charter for the conquest of Angola was signed and the year which saw Francisco Barreto sail up the Zambesi to conquer the mines of Monomotapa and avenge the death of the Jesuit martyr Gonçalo da Silveira, the king made a visit to Tangiers and accompanied a number of raids into the Moroccan countryside. Returning to Portugal, he set about planning his Moroccan crusade. The Pope and Philip II of Spain were approached for support and mercenaries were engaged in northern Europe, but the bulk of the forces that Sebastião gathered were untrained Portuguese levies from the provinces and noble estates and a regiment of *fidalgo* volunteers. Under the command of the inexperienced young king, now aged 24, this large, straggling army, which with its camp followers numbered between 15,000 and 20,000 people, landed at Arzila (Asilah) in July 1578 and set out to meet the forces of the Sultan of Fez. Poorly equipped with cavalry and artillery the army was surrounded and annihilated at Alcazar el Kebir on 4 August 1578.

The young king disappeared in the battle and, although his body was eventually identified, taken to Ceuta and buried, rumours began to circulate almost at once that he had escaped the slaughter and had gone into hiding.

The Portuguese succession crisis

As a consequence of this disaster, Portugal was faced with a deepening crisis which soon affected the whole of Europe. The military disaster was of a magnitude to shatter Portuguese national morale. Coming at a time when foreign interlopers like Drake were increasingly active in Portuguese waters, when the Portuguese had been driven from Ternate in the Moluccas and when Francisco Barreto's army had been destroyed in East Africa, the ability of Portugal to defend itself, let alone mount any credible action overseas, was laid bare. However, it was not just the military consequences which made Alcazar el Kebir signify the end of an era. The defeat resulted in the collapse of an ideology, of a whole mindset that had extolled the virtues of the crusader for ever fighting the infidel across the world, Don Quixote embattled in rusty, antiquated armour outfacing the monsters and ogres of legend. From this time the celebration of heroics is replaced by the spirit of pessimism in Portuguese writing about their empire. Defeat, disaster and shipwreck characterize the literature of the end of the century. As the Portuguese searched their souls for the reasons why God had deserted them, the empire was increasingly celebrated through epics of defeat rather than victory.

Hundreds of Portuguese soldiers from the families of the nobility were now prisoners in the hands of the Moroccans awaiting ransom, while the kingdom had passed into the hands of Cardinal Henrique, the aged former head of the Inquisition who, as brother of Dom João III, was the last legitimate male member of the house of Avis. The Cardinal was childless and ailing and the kingdom, lacking credible leadership, was faced with an imminent and seemingly inevitable succession crisis.

In 1383, almost exactly two hundred years earlier, Portugal had faced a similar situation on the death of Dom Fernando.

If the disaster of Alcazar el Kebir produced a crisis for Portugal, the consequences for the rest of Europe were scarcely less serious. Although Portugal had played little part in European affairs, the kingdom was widely perceived as possessing a vastly rich and extensive commercial empire. What would happen to Portugal's worldwide empire on the death of Cardinal Henrique now became a topic of wide speculation. There were three possible claimants to the throne. The first was Dom António, the Prior of Crato (the titular head of the Order of the Hospitallers) who had fought at Alcazar el Kebir. He was the illegitimate son of Dom Luís, the brother of Dom João III. (Here the parallel with the equally illegitimate Dom João, head of the Order of Avis, who had successfully contested the Crown in 1385, is striking). However Dom António's mother was believed to have been a New Christian (in other words, a Jewess in the eyes of many orthodox Portuguese). Although the Prior of Crato had considerable popularity in Portugal and was seen (as João of Avis had been in 1385) as the anti-Castilian candidate, he was bitterly opposed by Cardinal Henrique who was determined to thwart his plans to succeed. The second possible claimant was Caterina, a niece of Dom João III who was married to the Duke of Braganza. Although it was through her that the Braganza dukes were to claim the throne in 1640, she made it clear that she would not contest the succession when the Cardinal died. This left Philip II of Spain, son of Dom João III's sister, whose first wife had also been a Portuguese princess. Philip considered his succession a foregone conclusion and in this he was secretly supported by Cardinal Henrique, even though the latter went through a formal process of summoning a cortes and appointing a commission of lawyers to examine the claims to the succession.

The prospect of Philip II uniting the two worldwide empires under his personal sovereignty represented a dramatic readjustment of the political balance in Europe. When Charles V had abdicated in 1555 his lands had been divided, the German inheritance going to his brother Ferdinand and the Spanish and Burgundian kingdoms to Philip, who between 1554 and 1558 had briefly added England to his dominions. Now an empire even greater than that of Charles was in prospect. A union of Spain and Portugal would bring under one ruler the two halves of the world that had been divided at Tordesillas. The flow of silver from the mines of Japan and America, which paid for a rapidly expanding global commerce as well as Spanish armies in northern Europe, would now all be controlled from one centre.

Still more important, Philip would now possess the Azores and the coastline of Portugal, which would enable him to dominate the sea lanes of the north Atlantic. This union of the Crowns seemed to threaten the security and even the survival of the Protestant states of northern Europe. The revolt in the Spanish Netherlands, which had gathered momentum in the 1560s, had by the end of the 1570s reached a stalemate. Spanish forces had made some headway in reconquering the south, especially after the appointment in 1578 of the Duke of Parma as the commander of Spanish forces, but they were seriously hindered by the growing instability of France in their rear and by an almost complete loss of control of the sea. The rebel Sea Beggars had seized control of the most important ports in the Northern Netherlands in 1571–2 and had effectively stopped all Spanish shipping in the Channel, in which they were enthusiastically supported by English privateers. As a result Spain's forces had to be supplied and paid by keeping open a tortuous overland route from Italy. If Philip became king of Portugal he would control Lisbon, the greatest natural harbour on the Atlantic coast of Europe, as well as the shipyards of Portugal (and India). He would have a great opportunity to rebuild his sea power and wrest control of the Channel from his enemies.

It had been the successful interloping expeditions of Hawkins and Drake in the 1560s and early '70s that had convinced Philip of the need to improve the defences of his Atlantic empire. A squadron of small galleons had been organized in 1570 to guard the silver *flota* but in 1578, when the future of Portugal was first thrown into doubt, Spain still had only very limited naval resources and tended to rely on its

Mediterranean war galleys. The Portuguese on the other hand had a fleet of nine royal galleons in home waters, as well as galleys and the galleons and carracks that were employed on the *carreira da Índia*. Moreover control of the Azores would provide Spain with a safe half-way stopping point for the silver *flotas*, which would limit the ability of English and French pirates to interfere with the arrival of American treasure.

In January 1580 Cardinal Henrique died, leaving the succession undecided and the kingdom in the hands of five '*governadores*'. Both Philip and Dom António immediately claimed the throne. António, like his predecessor João of Avis, appealed for foreign aid and tried to rally Lisbon to his cause. Although he had vociferous support among the lower orders in the capital, his only real military assets were the nine royal galleons, which were part of the prize Philip hoped to secure. Writing in February from Lisbon the correspondent of the Fugger Bank was deeply sceptical of António's chances since

> They [the Portuguese] have not a single soldier in Portugal who has ever seen any fighting or would know how to lead properly. They have no arms for they lost them all in the African war. They have no money and there is fearful scarcity in the country. Moreover the plague is raging everywhere. Yet, with empty hands, they think themselves strong enough for the Spaniards.[1]

Philip's response was to dispatch the aged Duke of Alba with an army of 20,000 men to occupy Lisbon while the Marqués of Santa Cruz sailed with a squadron of galleys to secure control of the sea and the Portuguese royal galleons. There was to be no repeat of Aljubarrota. First at Setúbal and then at Lisbon the Portuguese galleons were isolated and forced to surrender, while Santa Cruz landed men at Cascais to seize the Tagus forts. At Alcântara immediately outside Lisbon the levies raised by Dom António, which included freed slaves and prisoners released from jail, were scattered by Alba's troops and Philip II was proclaimed king in Lisbon. Philip's successful acquisition of the Portuguese galleons (one is strongly reminded of Napoleon's attempt, in that case unsuccessful, to gain control of the Portuguese navy in 1807) was the first move in a prolonged battle for the control of the Atlantic and the Channel. At stake was the security of the silver shipments to Spain and the control of the Channel ports which might sever the links between England and the Netherlands.

The battle of the Atlantic

Dom António, defeated at Alcântara, made his way to France and to England, an escape that Philip blamed on Alba. In England he was received by the Queen, who realized that the existence of a pretender to the Portuguese throne would give her the kind of diplomatic and propaganda leverage that Mary Queen of Scots gave her Catholic enemies, while in France Dom António obtained practical help from Catherine de Médici and was allowed to recruit ships and men in French ports to help him secure possession of the Azores.

If the union of the crowns of Spain and Portugal was to bring Philip the strategic advantages and increase in naval and military power he hoped for, he would have to prevent Dom António raising the standard of revolt in the Portuguese dominions and he would have to gain rapid control of the Azores which, as Drake and Hawkins had realized, could provide an effective base for Dutch, English and French sea raiders. This became urgent when news arrived that only two islands in the Azores, São Miguel and Santa Maria, had recognized Philip and that the island of Terceira had declared for Dom António.

Philip's first move was to try to win over as many of the Portuguese as possible. Through promises and bribery he had already secured the support of many leading Portuguese but it appears he was pushing at an open door, for the nobility and business class in Portugal all favoured a Castilian succession and there was little enthusiasm for a war in support of an impoverished independence. At the Cortes that was summoned in April 1581 to Tomar (the ancient seat of the Templars and of the Order of Christ) Philip was proclaimed king and put his name to a wide-ranging document that guaranteed the autonomy and privileges of the Portuguese. He also confirmed his willingness to ransom the sons of the Portuguese nobility still held captive in Morocco. The Tomar agreement, which appeared to underwrite Portugal's separateness as a kingdom and which prevented its total absorption into the Castilian monarchy, gave Philip what he wanted in the short term – control of the Portuguese harbours and maritime resources.

With Portugal apparently acquiescent, the importance of Lisbon to Philip's plans became apparent. It had been in the harbour of Lisbon that eight hundred ships had assembled to take Sebastião's army to Morocco. Now, with the Duke of Alba dead, the king took up residence in the city and issued orders for eight new galleons to be constructed in Portuguese shipyards and for the great *São Martinho*, which had been built in 1574, to be overhauled. Lisbon was designated as the principal naval arsenal of Spain (*a principal praça d'armas navais d'Espanha*).[2] Meanwhile a new governor was sent to the Azores, though his attempts to land in Terceira ended in farce as the islanders stampeded cattle into his soldiers' encampment. Philip now moved methodically towards launching his first deep-sea armada, which aimed not only at occupying the rebel islands in the Azores but at securing control of the Atlantic from the English and Dutch. Early in 1582 soldiers were dispatched to the Azores and a naval engagement took place off Ponta Delgada. Then in July Santa Cruz at last set sail from Lisbon in command of an armada of twenty-seven ships, with the *São Martinho* as his flagship, a reinforcement of twenty ships from Cadiz having failed to join him because of bad weather.

Santa Cruz reached the Azores on 21 July and was immediately confronted by Dom António's fleet of sixty sail, mostly French, under the command of Philip Strozzi, who had with him 6,000 volunteers and mercenaries. For three days the two fleets manoeuvred, failing to damage each other with their cannon, before the French launched an assault on the Portuguese galleon *São Mateus*. The battle which followed lasted five hours and ended in a complete Spanish victory. Ten French ships were captured or sunk with the loss of 2,000 men. Santa Cruz lost no ships but suffered 224 killed. Although he was not strong enough to attack Terceira, in a striking display of the efficacy of the union of the Crowns, he returned victoriously to Lisbon escorting the Portuguese ships of the *carreira da Índia* and the *flota* from the Indies.

This battle in the Azores was the first major sea battle between ships mounting broadside batteries and, it has been claimed, the only major sea battle to have been fought in mid-ocean until the battle of Midway in 1942.[3] However, to those familiar with the naval warfare of the seventeenth and eighteenth centuries what is striking is how little damage the gunfire caused. The *São Mateus* apparently received 500 hits without being fatally damaged.

The following year another armada was assembled and equipped in Lisbon. It consisted of a total of 62 ships (including 5 galleons and 12 war galleys) and carried 8,800 troops. Although a fleet of fifteen French and English ships with 1,000 soldiers was sent to try to reinforce Terceira, they failed to make contact and three deserted. Santa Cruz reached Terceira on 23 July and his army easily occupied the island, executing the leaders of the rebellion. Once again the flagship, the *São Martinho*, returned to Cadiz loaded with trophies. It was then that Santa Cruz, now granted the title of *Capitão-General do Mar Oceano,* proposed to Philip the plan for an armada to be sent against England.

Santa Cruz's victory and the suppression of the revolt in the Azores seemed at the time a decisive assertion of Spanish power. The French had been humiliated and Dom António effectively wiped from the political map. Work began on the massive fortress on the island of Terceira that would guard the anchorage of the *flota*. Moreover, this victory suddenly seemed to make possible the control of the Channel and an invasion of England.

In 1583 Philip was presented with Santa Cruz's proposal for a large army to be shipped directly from Portugal by sea for the invasion of England. Philip was reluctant to press ahead with the plan primarily for financial reasons but events gradually convinced him of both the necessity and the feasibility of the scheme. His determination was strengthened when he heard of the death of the heir to the French throne in 1584, which raised the spectre of the Protestant Henry of Navarre eventually becoming king of France. Then in 1585 Parma captured Antwerp which seemed to promise a rapid victory in the Netherlands. The same year Drake's raid on the Caribbean once again raised fears that the flow of silver might be interrupted. However, detailed plans for an invasion of England were only drawn up in 1586 after Santa Cruz and Parma had both been further consulted. According to the final plan a fleet would assemble in Lisbon and, having secured control of the Channel, would escort Parma's army across the Channel to invade England. All eyes now turned to Lisbon, where the great armada was to assemble and where its equipment and resources would be gathered.

The importance of Lisbon had become increasingly clear as year after year not only were new galleons laid down in its shipyards but armadas were assembled and equipped to send to the Azores or to escort ships arriving from the Indies or the East. Lisbon's superiority over other Iberian ports became clear in May 1587 when Drake sailed into the harbour of Cadiz and set fire to the assembled merchant ships without the shore defences or the galley fleet being able to prevent him. When Drake left Cadiz, and before occupying Sagres, he briefly reconnoitred Lisbon, possibly with the aim of repeating his success. However, he realized that Lisbon was too well protected by forts and by natural obstacles. Indeed, as subsequent history was repeatedly to show, although Lisbon could be blockaded and was vulnerable to an assault from the landward side, it could not be attacked from the sea.

Philip had begun to assemble his warships in Lisbon in January 1586, when an invasion of England was still very uncertain. The most immediate task was to protect the shipping coming from the East and from the Indies, and in April of that year an armada consisting of six Portuguese galleons and eighteen other vessels was made ready and, after a number of changes to its orders, successfully escorted home the carracks coming from India. Another fleet had meanwhile been assembled in Cadiz to be sent to the Caribbean. The year 1587 had been intended for the invasion of England but in April Drake attacked the harbour of Cadiz and remained for five weeks off the coast of the Algarve shutting down all movements by sea. So, instead of setting out for the invasion of England, Santa Cruz sailed from Lisbon for the Azores early in July with thirty-two vessels, twelve of them Portuguese galleons and led once again by the *São Martinho*. In August the Indies fleet reached the Azores and Santa Cruz now escorted a vast fleet of ninety-three ships back to Lisbon and Cadiz, leaving some ships in the Azores to meet the Portuguese carracks from India. Both fleets returned to Lisbon in September to find conditions in the city considerably altered.

The Armada and its fate

Lisbon had been chosen for the point of assembly of the armada for the invasion of England partly because of its extensive and secure anchorage, partly because of its geographical location and the fact that its immediate hinterland could provide much of what was needed for the fleets, and partly because it already had a well-organized naval administration which included shipyards, armouries and warehouses, each under the administration of *comissários dos armazéns*. Lisbon also had two powder mills and five forges for casting cannon with a nominal capacity for producing 300 guns a year. Philip, however, was not satisfied with the working of these installations and established a new royal gun foundry and powder mill, though this only came into production at the end of 1587 and was not able to provide enough ordnance to equip a fleet of the size that Philip was planning to assemble. As a consequence cannon suitable for use on board ship were taken from the coastal fortresses of Portugal or were brought up from wrecks, while some arrived from as far as the island of Terceira. As soldiers and seamen gathered in Lisbon, two hospitals were established to deal with outbreaks of disease – particularly typhoid – while a hospital ship was prepared to accompany the Armada.[4]

As the armada was assembled extreme tension arose between the citizens of Lisbon and the soldiers, seamen and royal officials. Lisbon's water supply was not adequate for the ever-growing fleet, while the building of the royal gun foundry led to strong local hostility. However, it was the constant arrival of soldiers from Spain who were billeted in the city, and the soaring prices of food, that led to fighting in the streets between Castilians and Portuguese, including some nobles.

Philip had ordered Santa Cruz's fleet to be overhauled and ready to sail by the end of October 1587 and to speed matters along had agreed to pay the costs of repair to the Portuguese galleons from the Castilian treasury. However, throughout the autumn the shortage of seamen, anchors, artillery and especially money meant that the preparations could not be completed. In February 1588 Santa Cruz himself fell victim to the typhoid epidemic and died, unmourned by the Portuguese, to whom he had appeared cruel and arrogant. In March the Duke of Medina Sidonia was appointed to succeed Santa Cruz, his apparent reluctance to take command probably being a manoeuvre to extort more time and resources from an increasingly anxious king. Meanwhile soldiers were recruited from Portugal to add to the complement in the ships.

At the heart of the fleet that gradually assembled in Lisbon in 1587 and 1588 were the royal galleons of Portugal. Indeed as Augusto Salgado, the latest Portuguese historian of the Armada, has pointed out, it is impossible to imagine the Armada of 1588 being viable without the Portuguese contribution. The Crown of Portugal supplied nine galleons, the largest being the *São João* (700 tonnes), two *zavras* and four royal galleys, as well as a large number of smaller caravels and supply boats. The flagship of the Armada was the now veteran *São Martinho*, which had accompanied Dom Sebastião to Morocco and had already served three times as the flagship of Spanish armadas in the Atlantic.

The *felicissima armada* eventually sailed from Lisbon at the end of May 1588.

The story of the Armada does not need to be told again. The tight organization of the fleet prevented the English ships (which probably exceeded those of the Armada in total numbers and firepower) doing any serious damage until the fleet reached the Low Countries, where it found that Parma's army was not ready. Then, having been forced out of its anchorage by fireships and scattered by a storm, Medina Sidonia gave the orders for the fleet to return around the north of Scotland and the west of Ireland. On this journey twenty-one ships were lost but the majority (one estimate says five out of six) of the ships of the Armada returned safely, though hardly gloriously, to the Iberian peninsula. Six of the nine royal galleons of Portugal returned including the *São Martinho* which had borne much of the battle. Most of the ships took refuge in Santander and Corunna where next year the *São João*, having survived all the tribulations of the expedition itself, was burned by its crew to prevent it falling into the hands of an English fleet which had occupied and plundered the lower town. Among the slaves who escaped when their galley was driven ashore on the coast of France was the first of the false Sebastians who had briefly raised a flicker of popular opposition to the Castilian takeover of Portugal.

The spectacular defeat of the Armada, mostly by storms off the Irish coast, made little difference to the longer-term struggle to control the sea passages between America and Europe. Assembling the Armada had been a great feat of organization and determination on the part of Philip II but it had never had any realistic chance of success. Parma was a most reluctant participant and the 17,000 men he was prepared to release for the campaign (who were mostly German mercenaries and English renegades) would have had no chance of military victory if they had been landed in England. Medina Sidonia understood this quite well. From Corunna he had written to the king:

> I recall the great force your Majesty collected for the conquest of Portugal, although that country was within our own boundaries, and many of the people were in your favour . . . How do you think we can attack so great a country as England with such a force as is ours now?[5]

On events in the Low Countries the defeat of the Armada made less difference than the unfolding drama in France where first the Duke of Guise and then the king himself were assassinated and the throne was claimed by the Protestant Henry of Navarre.

After the Armada

On hearing of the disaster that had overtaken the Armada Philip's immediate plan was to refit the fleet and to embark on a large-scale ship building programme. In 1589 a Spanish fleet, again with the *São Martinho* as flagship, was ready to put to sea, though plans for another invasion of England in 1590 had to be abandoned. In 1591 Santa Cruz's brother, Alonso de Bazan, achieved an important symbolic victory over the

English, forcing the surrender of the *Revenge* which had been captained by Francis Drake in the battles against the Armada. The English meanwhile had suffered a disaster almost as significant as that of the Armada itself – and once again the site of the drama was Portugal.

Once the dispersal of the Armada became known Elizabeth and her council had determined to search out and destroy the surviving ships in the ports of northern Spain where they had taken refuge. A force of 12,000 men was to be assembled which was then to aid Dom António regain the Portuguese throne. In short Elizabeth and her admiral and commander were going to retaliate in kind, destroy Philip's fleet and attempt an invasion of Philip's dominions. Although the Duke of Medina Sidonia had won two months' delay in 1588, he had eventually obeyed Philip's instructions to the letter against his own better judgment. Elizabeth was not so fortunate and her commanders from the outset determined to make the attack on Portugal their priority against her specific instructions. The English 'armada', consisting of 83 ships, left on 17 April, made no attempt to attack the Spanish and Portuguese ships in Santander and San Sebastian and wasted two weeks burning and looting Corunna, which had no strategic or economic value. On 17 May 6,000 troops were landed at Peniche and marched on Lisbon, but without Dom António being able to arouse the Portuguese population to support his cause. The English army camped for a week (22–29 May) before the walls of Lisbon, but when Drake failed to sail into the Tagus to support them they withdrew to Cascais and re-embarked on 3 June. The fleet was then dispersed by bad weather and most of the ships made their way lamely back to England by the end of June.

Nothing had been achieved and the opportunity of destroying the surviving ships of the Armada had been lost, for some fifty Spanish vessels had been at anchor in Santander 'all unrigged and their ordnance on the shore and some 20 men only in a ship to keep them'.[6] Drake had not even attempted to reach Santander and he had not dared to sail into the harbour at Lisbon as he had done at Cadiz two years earlier. Once again the security of Lisbon's great natural harbour had been demonstrated.

In 1596 and 1597 Philip sent two more armadas against England, each of which was forced by storms to turn back. However, Philip's priority in the naval war had always been to secure the flow of silver from America to Seville and in this he emerged with a decisive victory. The Azores remained in his hands and all the English attempts to seize the islands or waylay the *flota* failed. The great fortress at Angra on the island of Terceira remains to this day as the symbol of Spanish power and success in this first battle of the Atlantic.

The *São Martinho*, surely the greatest fighting ship of its age, accompanied Alonso de Bazan to the Azores in 1591 but no longer as flagship. It appears finally to have gone out of active service in 1593.

6

The Portuguese Restoration and the General Crisis of the Seventeenth Century

The Union of the Crowns

Philip II of Spain's armies had conquered Portugal in July 1580 and Philip had been formally recognized as king by the Cortes that met at Tomar in April 1581. Later he is supposed to have said in reply to a question about his title to the Portuguese throne – 'I inherited it, I conquered it and I bought it.' Although the pretender Dom António had considerable support among the lower classes and even the lower clergy, this never coalesced around an effective leader and the latent hostility to Castile found expression primarily in the growing underground cult of Sebastianism – the belief in mysterious prophecies that promised the return of Dom Sebastião as the *encoberto* (the hidden one), a sort of messiah, who would bring salvation to Portugal.

Philip meanwhile had consolidated his grip on Portugal. He himself took up residence in Lisbon and remained there for two years, apparently contemplating moving the capital of his dominions to that city. Concerned primarily with gaining control of Portugal's harbours and naval resources, he signed a constitutional agreement at Tomar which had already been outlined in secret negotiations with Cardinal Henrique and which guaranteed Portugal a wide degree of autonomy. By this agreement Philip promised that he would observe the traditions of the Portuguese monarchy and that he would only be represented in Lisbon by a member of the royal family (that is, not by some Castilian nobleman like the Duke of Alba). Portuguese laws would remain in force and the Cortes would always be summoned to meet in Portugal. All Portuguese would keep the offices they held in church and state and these positions would only be held by Portuguese in future, although Portuguese would be eligible for appointment to offices elsewhere in the Spanish dominions. The privileges of towns would be maintained and the nobility would keep their *moradias*, or pensions, from the crown.

The Portuguese would continue to control the trade with India but the borders between Portugal and Spain would be open to commerce. Portugal's separate identity as a kingdom would be guaranteed by the creation of a new Council of Portugal, the Portuguese language would continue to be used in administration and the arms of Portugal would continue to appear on the coinage. This agreement secured the consent of the nobility, clergy and business classes and brought Philip the acquiescence of the majority of the population. When Dom António reappeared with an English army in 1589 there was no rising in his favour.

Later writers were to refer to the Union of the Crowns as the 'Babylonian captivity' and were to attribute to it the disasters that overtook Portugal's overseas empire, but historical developments are seldom so monocausal and the sixty years of the union with Spain have to be seen in a wider context. Philip's accession to the Portuguese throne was, from one perspective, the inevitable consequence of repeated dynastic marriages between the royal families of the two countries, which had certainly been intended on both sides to bring about a union of the crowns. Indeed, for a brief period after the birth of Dom Manuel's son Miguel in 1498, Aragon, Castile and Portugal had all acknowledged the same heir apparent to their thrones. So, by Philip's accession, the union, so devoutly wished by Dom Manuel, had been realized and there were many in Portugal who stood to gain from it. The higher nobility and clergy could now look for lucrative offices in the service of the Spanish monarchy, while businessmen found new opportunities to trade with Spain and to have direct access to the great commercial centre of Seville. Silver from Seville could flow into Portugal and from there to India, while Portuguese financiers could begin to exploit opportunities in the Spanish Indies. At Tomar Philip had agreed to provide for the defence of the *carreira da Índia* and a vast programme of fortification was undertaken to protect the coasts of Portugal and the islands. Many of these fortifications (for instance in Cidade Velha in the island of Santiago and Setúbal) still carry the name of Filipe. And there were unexpected gainers. New Christian banking and merchant families found that they were in less danger from the Inquisition as Philip needed their services and was ready to grant far-reaching exemptions and amnesties. The career of the great Diego Velázquez, the grandson of Portuguese Jews, who was born in Seville in 1599, was to be a living illustration of the opportunities that were now open to Portuguese and New Christians alike. Reforms were undertaken to the administration of Portuguese finances and a revised law code, the Ordenações Filipinas, was promulgated.

On the other hand Portugal was now at the very centre of the war to control the Atlantic. Lisbon and the Azores were prime targets for English, Dutch and French attacks and the other relatively undefended Portuguese colonies were also vulnerable. Drake sacked Cidade Velha in the Cape Verde Islands in 1582 and again in 1585; the Dutch attacked São Tomé in 1599 and in 1617 the Moroccans, usually in loose alliance with the Protestant countries on the basis that 'my enemy's enemy is my friend', devastated Madeira, carrying off nine hundred people as slaves. In the 1590s the first large Dutch and English fleets headed for the spice islands and challenged Portugal in the Indian Ocean. Moreover the Portuguese were now suffering unprecedented losses at sea. Forty-five per cent of all Indiamen returning to Portugal from the East were lost in the decade 1590–1600.[1]

By the early seventeenth century Portugal had begun to reap some benefits of the Union. In 1604 peace was made between Spain (and Portugal) and England, and in 1609 a twelve-year truce was signed with the Dutch. Although this did not bring about an end to hostilities in the East, Portugal had already survived the early Dutch attacks – Malacca had not fallen and Mozambique Island had beaten off two determined Dutch assaults. The Estado da Índia now staged a remarkable recovery and the first two decades of the century were to see its trade reach still greater levels of prosperity while Portuguese forces expanded their territorial control in Sri Lanka and East Africa.

The Thirty Years War

It was the Thirty Years War which was to drag Portugal and Spain into a conflict that ultimately destroyed Spain's power in Europe and Portugal's commercial empire in the East, leading finally to the collapse of the Union of the Crowns. At the outbreak of the war (usually thought to have begun with the revolt of the Protestant nobles in Bohemia in 1618) Spain had rapidly achieved a military ascendancy in the Rhineland and the Low Countries, culminating in the famous siege and capture of Breda in 1625. In the years following, the armies of Spain's Habsburg allies overran north Germany and Denmark, raising the possibility that Habsburg control of the Baltic would put an end to Dutch commercial supremacy in the north. By 1628 the Catholic cause championed by Spain had achieved successes far beyond anything Philip II had believed to be possible.

However, in 1621 the Dutch had founded a West India Company, on the model of the successful East India Company (the voc founded in

1602). Its mission was to wage maritime and commercial war on the Spanish dominions in the New World. Although the West India Company had a strong interest in the fur trade and founded a trading settlement on the Hudson river that later became New York, its principal objective was that old dream of Protestant pirates, the interception of the silver *flota*. To this was added a new objective, the capture of the sugar and slave complex of the Portuguese South Atlantic. The former would cripple Spain's finances, the latter would provide the Dutch with a ready-made commercial empire in Brazil, Angola and the Gulf of Guinea. In 1624 a Dutch fleet captured Salvador de Bahia, the capital of Portuguese Brazil, but the city was retaken by a Spanish armada the following year, while a Dutch attack on Elmina also ended in disaster. The Spanish and Portuguese empires appeared strong and durable. However, between 1628 and 1630 the war was to turn against the Spanish and a decade of disasters culminated in the revolutions of 1640 that threatened to destroy the monarchy.

In 1628 the Spanish had embarked on a war with France over the succession to the Duchy of Mantua, a war which the Spanish recognized they could not sustain alongside their struggle with the Protestant states. The same year the Dutch admiral Piet Heyn captured the silver *flota* on the coast of Cuba, predictably causing a crisis in Spanish finances and stalling the prosecution of the war. Two years later, in 1630, a Swedish army, led by their king Gustavus Adolphus, landed in northern Germany and in twelve months reversed most of the gains that the Habsburgs had made since the beginning of the war. The same year the Dutch mounted their second, and this time successful, attack on Brazil. Recife in the north was captured and the conquest of the sugar plantations began. Although Spanish forces defeated the Swedes at Nördlingen in 1634, the following year France formally entered the struggle in alliance with the Protestant states, forcing Spain to fight on two fronts in the Low Countries.

In the East the Estado da Índia was also under increasing pressure. Ormuz had been lost to a combined Persian and English force in 1622 and although the Conde de Linhares, who held the post of viceroy between 1629 and 1635, had responded by undertaking a major overhaul of Portugal's naval capacity, Portuguese forces had suffered a major disaster in Sri Lanka in 1630, while the Dutch maintained an almost continual blockade of Goa. Events were also turning against Portugal in Japan and by the end of the decade Japanese ports were finally closed to Portuguese commerce.

The Portuguese believed then, and have continued to believe, that the Dutch attack on Brazil was a direct consequence of the Union of the

Crowns which involved Portugal in Spain's war in the Netherlands, and that Spain contributed little to the defence of Portugal's overseas empire. However, it seems that during the 1630s it was Spain's commitment to trying to regain Brazil that made peace with France and the Dutch impossible. In other words, it was Portuguese interests that stood in the way of a general peace.

Spain's chief minister, Gaspar de Guzman, Count-Duke of Olivares, had come increasingly to rely on Portuguese bankers for loans and his reform of the Council of Finance in 1626 had enabled him to reschedule the Crown's debts with Portuguese New Christian bankers, though this meant that he had to extend still further their exemption from interference by the Inquisition and relax restrictions on their movements. In 1628 Olivares tried to create an East India Company in imitation of the English and the Dutch which also relied on New Christian investment. The growing alliance between the New Christians and the Crown was unpopular with the majority of the Portuguese population as well as with the aristocracy who looked with deep suspicion on the forces of international capitalism, represented by the rich New Christian banking houses. The loss of the silver fleet in 1628 plunged Spain into yet another financial crisis and as disasters multiplied in the 1630s the Spanish minister saw no alternative but to press ahead, in the face of growing opposition, with plans for a radical overhaul of all the military and financial resources of the monarchy.

The crisis of 1640

Across the Channel in England Charles I, like the Spanish king the personal ruler of a union of separate kingdoms, also faced a lack of resources to fund his army and navy. Although England and Scotland had largely kept out of the Thirty Years War, the fluctuating fortunes of Catholic and Protestant forces in Europe had been closely watched and fears had grown concerning the Catholic tendencies of the court, where Charles's French queen was openly practising Roman Catholicism in the royal chapel and Archbishop Laud seemed to be steering the English church in a popish direction. The attempt to impose Laudian reforms on the Scottish church in 1638 plunged England into a war with Scotland – an island version of the greater struggle on the continent. It was Charles's inability to pay for this war that led to his attempts to place his finances and military forces on a new basis – a basis which involved raising taxes and soldiers in Ireland for use in his other kingdoms. Attempts to enforce common, centrally decided policies, and in particular war taxation, on the different Stuart kingdoms moved the British Isles inexorably towards civil war.

In the eyes of insular British historians these events have little to do with the social and political turmoil on the Continent but that is not how contemporaries saw it. After the suppression of the popular revolt in Portugal by Spanish forces in 1637, Olivares apparently 'held it up, in a conversation with the British ambassador, as a model for Charles I to follow in his dealings with the Scots'.[2]

Spain, like Britain, was a dynastic state in which separate kingdoms with their own laws and institutions were united solely by having a common sovereign. It was tension arising between the different components of these segmentary monarchies, exacerbated by religious issues, that had caused the original revolt of the Netherlands and which was to cause the revolt of the Scots against Charles I. France suffered similar fragmentation, for the *pays d'état* and the Huguenot enclaves were as jealous of their local autonomy as the different kingdoms of the Spanish Crown. In all three states financial pressures were leading governments to attempt drastic measures which appeared to threaten regional autonomy and treasured liberties. Taxation in the kingdom of Castile had always been the 'Crown's traditional mainstay'[3] and had formed the largest part of the royal revenues. In Portugal, by contrast, taxation had been relatively light and the government had always been more dependent on the profits derived from the royal trade monopolies. Olivares's plans, first presented to Philip IV in 1624, involved levying direct taxation to finance a national system of defence to which the Portuguese would have to contribute, a project known as the Union of Arms. In 1628, after failure to get local estates to consent to the higher defence contributions, Olivares began to impose these directly in the different regions of the monarchy.

During the 1630s the strains of constant warfare began to take their toll, not least on the finances of those involved. In both France and Spain ministers tried to enforce new taxes and extend others – notably taxes on salt. Higher taxes led to outbreaks of social revolt in the affected regions, while poor harvests exacerbated the civil tensions as labourers and peasant farmers were caught between the competing demands of the state, landlords and a burgeoning capitalism that was suffering the chill wind of a depression. It was not only the poor who rose in violent protest but the provincial elites who bitterly resented the encroachment of central government. In 1632 an insurrection occurred in

Vizcaya and in France there were serious outbreaks in 1634, 1636–7 and in 1639 when bands of *nu-pieds* in Normandy fought with the royal army.

Olivares, 'a man whose thought processes tended more to vigour than coherence',[4] hoped to impose the Union of Arms on a Portugal which was exhausted by seemingly endless war and affected by a sharp downturn in the European economy. In the last decades of the sixteenth century plague had become endemic in Portugal and, as there was considerable emigration to Brazil and the Spanish Indies, the country now began to suffer from demographic decline. Although Portugal had been spared the worst consequences of Spain's disastrous financial policy and the debased copper *vellon* had not been introduced there, the uncertain climatic conditions of the 'little ice age' had led to a succession of bad harvests and vintage failures. Commercial life had also been considerably disrupted by the outbreak of war in 1618 and still more by the Dutch invasion of northern Brazil, which had been especially damaging for the commercial classes of Portugal because, with the exception of the royal monopoly over Brazilwood, trade with Brazil was free.

The growing social tensions could be felt in popular hostility towards the New Christians and in continuing manifestations of Sebastianism. Outbreaks of anti-Castilian feeling were also becoming more common. In 1611 a crowd had attacked the viceroy's palace in Lisbon and, when eventually Philip III had visited Lisbon in 1619, twenty-one years after coming to the throne, in order to get the Portuguese Cortes to recognize his son as heir to the throne, he had had to wait at Belem for the arrival of Spanish warships and an escort of soldiers before entering the city. With Portugal increasingly required to raise money for its own defence and that of its empire, fresh indirect taxes were now being directly imposed from Madrid to fund the general war effort and these led to further unrest. In 1629 there were civic protests in Lamego and Porto, the latter amounting to a full-scale tax riot, and trouble in Lisbon, Santarém and Setúbal. Following the Dutch capture of Pernambuco in 1630 'voluntary contributions' were levied on Portugal, on rich and poor, clergy and laity alike, in order to win back the city from the Dutch. After 1633 government officials were required to donate half their emoluments (although the Crown's ministers refused to join in this demonstration of patriotism) and Portuguese recruits were also demanded for the Spanish regiments. In 1636 there were riots in Vila Real, and early in 1637 in Lisbon against new taxes levied on fishermen.

In 1637 rioting broke out in Évora against the collection of new taxes with the burning of tax and court records. The Spanish believed that agents of Richelieu were involved and there is clear evidence that Richelieu, through his consul Jean de Saint-Pé, was trying to make contact with groups in Lisbon who were believed to be plotting a revolt against Spain. The outbreak, however, had all the characteristics of a spontaneous popular outburst, encouraged by officials of the town council but motivated by ideas of a moral economy that was being eroded by the necessities of war. The rioting spread throughout the south of Portugal and there were rumours of a mysterious young man, known as *manuelinho,* appearing as leader of the revolt – another manifestation of the messianism that was always liable to appear when the wider population was stirred to political action. What began as opposition to further taxation soon threatened to become something much more serious – 'the popular movement was anti-fiscal in its origin but rapidly became nationalist and anti-Castilian.'[5] To Olivares's anger the Portuguese nobility appeared reluctant to take any action, and Spanish troops were eventually sent to suppress the revolt. As António de Oliveira put it, 'the members of the "seigneurial class" (clergy and nobles) had a two-faced attitude towards the Crown: of support when it would benefit them; of opposition when their privileges were infringed by the Monarch.'[6] They now became concerned that, if the demands from Spain for money and men continued, there would be further outbreaks and disturbances that would have serious consequences for the whole social order in Portugal.

In 1639 Spain suffered a disastrous and debilitating defeat when a large armada commanded by Oquendo and Hoces was comprehensively defeated by the Dutch admirals de With and van Tromp off the English coast with the loss of sixty ships. Philip II had recovered within a year from the defeat of the *felicissima armada* in 1588 but Spanish sea power was not to recover from the Battle of the Downs. In this battle Olivares had lost the principal means of maintaining his authority in Portugal, while the Portuguese were left to face Dutch sea power alone. The same year a French fleet appeared off the coast of Spain and was rumoured to be heading for Portugal, which had been left defenceless and exposed.

In the summer of 1640 revolt broke out in Catalonia. Initially this was a popular rising against the billeting of the royal army in the province but it soon became a widespread rebellion against Castilian overrule and the burdens of the war. The murder of the viceroy, Conde de Santa Coloma, on 7 June made it clear to Olivares that he had a full-scale rebellion on his hands.

The Lisbon *coup d'état*

By 1640 a significant section of the Portuguese church and nobility had become thoroughly alarmed at the deterioration of the fortunes of the monarchy. The war in Europe was going badly, seriously affecting the commercial economy of Portugal, and there seemed to be no way of stemming the losses in Brazil and in the Estado da Índia. Among the lower classes anti-Castilian feeling was rising and had reached danger-ous levels in the outbursts which had occurred in Évora and across the country in 1637. It was widely believed that the Spanish Crown was plan-ning to undo the agreement that had sealed the Union of the Crowns at Tomar, and was plotting nothing less than a *coup d'état* to establish the Union of Arms, which meant Castilian dominance, in Portugal. Af-ter the revolt of 1637 Philip IV is supposed to have told a delegation of Portuguese notables summoned to Madrid that he now considered the Tomar agreement at an end.

It is not clear when the idea of breaking away from Spain began to take shape in Portugal but in the late 1630s it started to appear an increasingly attractive option. Many of the elite believed that if Portu-gal broke away from Spain the attacks of the Dutch on their colonial possessions would cease, commerce with the Netherlands would be restored and Portugal would be free to conclude advantageous alliances with Spain's enemies. Meanwhile, the popular cult of Sebastianism remained focused on the return of the messianic figure of Dom Sebastião, who would free Portugal from foreign bondage, a concept that had its echoes in some educated circles in the revival of interest in the Bandarra prophecies and the ideas of establishing the 'Fifth Monar-chy'. In Sebastianism 'a nostalgia for a past golden age and the feeling of national humiliation felt by a people in the face of a foreign occupa-tion' came together with 'the messianic aspirations of a community unable to decide its own destiny'.[7] At a more mundane level there were those who looked forward once again to having a king who would dis-pense patronage from a court in Lisbon. These discontents were reported back to Richelieu by his consul in Lisbon and were certainly secretly encouraged by the Cardinal's agents, who promised money and support to any dissident person or group.

However, it was the revolt in Catalonia that concentrated minds both in Madrid and Lisbon, and brought matters to a head, just as later, in 1820, it was a revolution in Spain that was to kick-start a correspon-ding movement in Portugal. When orders arrived from Madrid for the

Seventeenth-century cavalier (in tiles) from the Fronteira Palace, Lisbon.

Portuguese nobility to join the army gathering against Catalonia, many were persuaded of the need to action. Rumour spread that 'this last summons for the nobility to attend the king, was only a specious pretence to force them out of their own country, lest their presence might prove an obstacle to some cruel design which was doubtless on foot'.[8]

Olivares's resentment at what he saw as the unwillingness of the Portuguese nobility to contribute financially and militarily to the war effort went back at least to the early 1630s. He had long doubted the loyalty of some of the Portuguese nobility and had tried to deal with the problem by placing his own men in charge of Portuguese affairs both in Lisbon and in the Council of Portugal. He had also planned to forestall the possibility of the Duke of Braganza assuming the leadership of an anti-Castilian movement and in 1634 had sent a member of the royal family, Margaret of Savoy, a person who would outrank Braganza, to act as viceroy in Lisbon. He had tried to lure the duke away from Portugal by offering him the governorship of Milan but the appointment had been refused. In 1639 Braganza was offered the still more prestigious post of viceroy of Naples. Again he turned it down.

It was the Duke of Braganza's ancestry (he was the great-grandson of Dom João III) rather than his ambition that made him dangerous. 'His birth, his riches, his title to the Crown, were not criminal in themselves, but became so by the law of policy', as the Abbé Vertot put it in his famous *History of the Revolutions of Portugal*.[9] His grandfather had declined to contest the throne with Philip II in 1580 and, although seditious rumours had surrounded his father Theodosio, João, who had succeeded to the dukedom in 1630, was not preparing to head any rebellion. He was a studious and cultured man and had not countenanced anti-Castilian plots, notably in 1637 when crowds urged him to lead a revolt against Spain. He was an accomplished composer and musician who liked a quiet life. A French agent left a description of him, after he became king:

> He is of medium stature and of an extremely strong and robust constitution to which his previous way of life has greatly contributed. For when he was Duke of Braganza he spent the greater part of his time hunting of which he was passionately fond. When he was at his palace of Vila Viçosa he diverted himself with music at which he is very skilled, and which is the sole past time he pursues. He himself composes most of the pieces that are sung in the chapel where the services are performed with greater ceremony than anywhere else in Christendom.[10]

Because Braganza showed so little indication to lead a revolt, Richelieu appears to have toyed with the idea of supporting the candidature for the Portuguese throne of the grandson of Dom António, the Prior of Crato. The plotters, for their part, considered approaching other noblemen of royal descent or even of declaring a Republic, and it may have been that, added to the urging of his wife Luisa de Guzman, sister of the Duke of Medina Sidonia, which eventually persuaded the duke to accept the crown.

As soon as information about the Évora rising reached the rest of Europe speculation focused on the importance of the Duke of Braganza and in a letter written that year Hugo Grotius had observed that 'those who . . . wish to foment the beginnings of a revolt ought to give aid and support to the Duke of Braganza'.[11] Soon after the outbreak of the revolt in Catalonia Olivares appointed the duke *Governador Geral de las Armas*, ostensibly to organize the defences of Portugal against an attack by the French which was considered imminent.[12] The Abbé Vertot thought that Olivares planned to have him arrested when he left his ducal seat of Vila Viçosa to make a tour of the country's fortresses, but it is more likely that it was a last-minute attempt to secure the duke's loyalty by giving him a high command. Either way it had the effect of giving Braganza a quasi-viceregal profile in the country.

The plot to overthrow Spanish rule was concocted by members of the minor nobility. It is not certain that the Duke of Braganza knew exactly what was being planned, though some of his followers certainly did and his business agent in Lisbon, João Pinto Ribeiro, was one of the leaders. (One thinks of the situation in April 1974 when junior army officers plotted the *coup d'état* against Caetano without General António de Spínola, the man who was to become president of the new republic, having any direct part in it.)

On 1 December 1640 a small group of armed men entered the viceregal palace in Lisbon and arrested Margaret of Savoy. There was no resistance but, unlike the coup in April 1974, there were a few casualties. Miguel de Vasconcellos, the unpopular secretary to the viceroy, and one of his assistants were murdered, but proposals to do away with the strongly hispanophile Archbishop of Braga were abandoned because of the outrage this would cause.[13] Margaret of Savoy was forced to sign orders to the Spanish garrisons to hand over their fortresses and then took refuge in a convent. Braganza himself hurried to Lisbon where he was declared king on 7 December and crowned a week later as Dom João IV. One by one the towns of Portugal accepted the new regime and the three Spanish galleons in the Tagus and all the fortress garrisons (except those at Angra in the Azores and Ceuta in North Africa) surrendered. As nearly as possible it was a bloodless coup in which popular support and the Lisbon crowd had played little role beyond that of noisy but peaceful acquiescence. Portugal once again had its own *rei natural* – its native king.[14]

There are interesting comparisons to be made with the earlier occasions in 1383–5 and 1578–80 when a Castilian takeover of Portugal had seemed imminent. On the previous occasions, most of the upper nobility and senior churchmen had been strongly pro-Castilian and rallied to the Castilian cause. This class had either gained or hoped to gain substantially from a union with Castile, already had family alliances with Castilian nobles and were, in cultural terms, largely 'Castilianized'. In 1640 also many of the principal nobles of Portugal, including Braganza's own brother, remained loyal to Spain. An example was Dom Francisco de Melo, who commanded the Spanish army of Flanders and, after the victory over the French at Honnecourt in 1642, was made a grandee of Spain. The higher clergy, led by the Archbishop of Braga and the Inquisitor, Dom Francisco de Castro, also supported Philip, though here there was a notable exception as the Archbishop of Lisbon was a strong supporter of the revolt. There was some hesitation in the empire as well and it was not until later in the year that Salvador da Sá, governor of Rio, declared for the new king.

However, it was not just family ambition that attached the great nobles to the Castilian cause, but fear of popular revolt. All three of these moments of crisis for Portuguese independence had been accompanied by popular turbulence and it was undoubtedly fear of social revolution that made so many of the upper class cling to the security promised by a union with a powerful neighbour. However, the fear of popular insurrection played differently in each case. In 1383–5 popular insurrection against Leonor Teles and her Castilian associates was cleverly manipulated and controlled by the small group of noble supporters of João of Avis. In 1580 the fact that Dom António had so much popular support which he was prepared to mobilize finally convinced the propertied classes to turn their backs on him and to welcome Philip of Spain. In 1637–40 the dangerous insurrection of 1637 convinced the plotters of the 1640 coup to proceed without any attempt to raise popular participation in the revolt.

In 1640 it was the local town authorities, the minor nobility, the lower clergy and, most importantly, the Jesuits who were the initial supporters of the Restoration but, after the defeat of an attempted counter-coup in October 1641, in which the Archbishop of Braga, the Inquisitor and some leading nobles were involved, Dom João was able to win back most of the old noble families to support Portugal's independence. However, like his contemporary Charles I of England, who had tried to fend off the hostility of Parliament by sacrificing his chief minister, Strafford, João was forced to give way to the demands of the Cortes that his principal adviser, the secretary Francisco de Lucena, be tried for treason and executed. More fortunate than Charles I, Dom João's sacrifice of Lucena calmed the hostility of the Cortes and consolidated his rule.[15]

The Portuguese Restoration in a European context

Events in Portugal and Catalonia are often spoken of in the same sentence. However, they were very different in character. In Catalonia the revolt was led from below with the nobility and the town authorities joining in as it gathered momentum. There was considerable disorder and violence. In Portugal the coup was carried out by a small group of nobles and was accepted in the country with no disturbance and with little resistance offered by the Spanish garrisons in Lisbon or elsewhere.

The revolt of Portugal and the restoration of an independent Portuguese monarchy was in some ways the final blow to the universal empire that Philip II had tried to create, but in other respects was of only marginal importance. Philip and Olivares had been taken by surprise by events in Catalonia and had underestimated the extent of the revolt and the threat of direct French intervention in the peninsula. The immediate response was that an army was needed to bring the rebellious province to heel. Garrisons were withdrawn throughout Spain and orders were issued for the Portuguese nobility to raise troops for service in Catalonia. The immediate impact of the revolt in Portugal crippled Spain's ability to achieve a swift reconquest of Catalonia (some Portuguese units of the royal army deserting to the French) and in this way contributed to the disaster at Montjuic two months later on 26 January 1641. However, probably the most serious consequence of the Portuguese revolt was the blow to Spanish morale. Philip and Olivares had apparently had no doubts about Portugal's loyalty – 'Olivares appearing to be carelessly confident that the principle of the obligation of the various kingdoms to help each other would apply'[16] – and they had no ready response to such a bitter blow to the unity of the monarchy. Although Catalonia was eventually reconquered and brought back under Spanish rule, Portugal was not.

It has long been recognized that in the years 1639 to 1643 the Spanish monarchy faced a crisis that not only brought it close to defeat in Europe but that threatened its very existence. Disasters seemed to hit the monarchy from all sides – the defeat of the Spanish fleet at the Battle of the Downs in 1639, the revolts in Catalonia and Portugal in 1640, the rout at Montjuic in 1641 and the crushing defeat of Francisco de Melo by the French at Rocroi in 1643. The separation of the Portuguese monarchy from that of Spain also separated the two maritime empires. The Atlantic was once again divided between Spain and Portugal but no longer on the friendly terms that had existed before 1580, and Spain was denied the use of Lisbon as a base for its Atlantic fleet. This wrote a conclusive end to Philip's narrative of maritime power.

In Europe the Portuguese revolt seemed to promise a new alignment of anti-Spanish forces. The Portuguese government believed that it would soon have to face a major military assault from Spain with a desperate lack of military and financial resources. Portugal had no army to speak of, no frontier defences in good repair and a fleet that was badly weakened by the struggle with the Dutch. Foreign assistance seemed the only hope and Dom João IV immediately sought an alliance with the Dutch, who agreed to a truce in Europe and even sent some warships to protect Lisbon. However, no agreement was reached on a cessation of hostilities in Brazil, where the Portuguese refused to recognize the Dutch conquests, and there was to be some time before any truce was registered in the East. In the meantime, before any peace could be finalized in Europe, the Dutch commanders stepped up their attacks and in 1641 took Luanda, São Tomé and Malacca. Moreover, before commercial contacts could be normalized, the Dutch demanded extensive commercial concessions in Portugal, including freedom of worship and the exclusive right to lease ships to Portugal.

Dom João also sought a formal alliance with France, which had encouraged the revolt. However, the French were to prove reluctant to make any commitments to the new regime and it soon became apparent that the French considered Portuguese independence to be something over which bargains could be struck in any general European peace agreement. In 1642 a treaty was signed with England allowing Portugal to recruit ships and men and granting the English the same privileges as the Dutch. However, 1642 saw the outbreak of the Civil War in England which made the treaty of little value.

The Portuguese revolt had its own particular causes and local logic but it was also symptomatic of a wider resistance to what Geoffrey Parker has called 'War Absolutism'. In all of the major European states the demands of central government for extraordinary taxation and the conscription of soldiers was leading to the same cycle of events. The resistance of provincial assemblies, chartered towns and constitutionally separate provinces (often led by the local elites and supported by popular uprisings) was met by increasingly direct measures from the centre which were seen as attempts to suppress local liberties and install a new centralised absolutism. In the Spanish monarchy local resistance had been successfully overcome, until the outbreak of the Catalan revolt. Revolt then spread to Portugal and in 1644 to Sicily and Naples. In France

Richelieu had been relatively successful in crushing provincial outbreaks and palace plots, which were seldom coordinated enough to threaten his government. After his death, however, France slipped into the chaos of the Fronde. More unexpected, but in retrospect not so surprising, the Dutch, who never seriously feared a centralized absolutism, also suffered from war exhaustion and between 1645 and 1648 saw their hold on Brazil loosened and Angola lost altogether, while in the 1650s their power at sea was successfully challenged by that of a resurgent republican England.

7

Portugal, the Inquisition and the Triumph of English Merchant Capitalism

The Inquisition as an historical problem

The Inquisition has, one way or another, haunted the collective memory of Europeans and has become a near obsession for those writing the history of early modern Spain. Almost exactly contemporary with the Holy Office in Spain, the Inquisition was established in Portugal and the coterminous existence of the two bodies, even though the Portuguese Inquisition has until recently been much less studied, provides fruitful opportunities for comparison and the testing out of hypotheses.

The Inquisitions of Spain and Portugal have appeared to historians in many different guises. In the sixteenth and seventeenth centuries, they were usually seen, both by their supporters and their enemies, as institutions set up to guarantee the purity of the faith and the orthodoxy of the faithful. Protestants saw them as aimed against themselves and in return incorporated them as one of the pillars of the black legend of Spanish infamy alongside the genocide of Indians in South America. For Jews the Inquisitions have always been primarily an example of institutionalized anti-Semitism directed to the extirpation of Iberian Jewry. However, as fashions in historiography have changed so have interpretations of the Inquisitions: they have been seen as examples of self-perpetuating bureaucracies dedicated above all to their own survival; as bodies institutionalizing the interests of the landed aristocracy in its struggle with mercantile capital; as instruments of social control aimed at elements in the lower orders who through their beliefs (including witchcraft and popular medicine) and practices (often involving sex and gender issues) posed a threat to the established social order. Followers of Foucault have seen in the Inquisitions the 'theatre of punishment' taken to extraordinary lengths of theatricality, while others have seen them primarily as a form of intellectual and cultural censorship. Over and above all this, much of the history of the Inquisitions unfolded in

Auto-da-fé of the Inquisition held in front of the royal palace.

a context of bitter conflicts of jurisdiction within the Church itself, conflicts which clearly determined much of the history of the Holy Office.

More speculatively the Inquisitions can be seen as popular institutions (in the sense that they received widespread popular support),
which continued to define an essential element of Spanish and Portuguese nationalism, while in Portugal the Inquisition was the body
principally responsible for the long-term economic backwardness of the
country and indirectly for the much-resented English ascendancy.

In spite of the voluminous literature on the two Inquisitions, and
the depth of the research now being carried out into their extensive
archives, at least one fundamental contradiction remains to be resolved.
The Inquisitions appear to have been thorough and highly organized
investigative bodies with draconian powers of confiscation and punishment, and throughout their three hundred years of existence their
principal objective was undoubtedly the rooting out of Judaism and
Judaic practices from Iberian religion and society. However, although the
Spanish Inquisition was largely successful in this, the Portuguese Inquisition seems to have been notably unsuccessful. Although even approx-
imate figures are not available for something that is by definition
clandestine, it seems that by the middle of the seventeenth century,
after a hundred years of apparently vigorous persecution, there were,
or the Inquisition claimed there were, more Judaizing New Christians

(the term commonly used in Portugal for converted Jews and their descendants) than ever. And the same was apparently the case a hundred years after that, when the New Christian community were eventually accorded full citizenship rights and freedom from persecution. Indeed, as Francisco Bethencourt has written, 'brutal external pressure led to a greater cohesiveness within the *converso* community, strengthening its ties of solidarity in the face of a hostile society'.[1] So why was such an apparently formidable body so ineffective in achieving its primary objective and, if the activities of the Inquisition were so much to be feared, why did so many New Christians continue to reside in Portugal and Spain and to do business there? At the very least this contradiction highlights the inability of the Inquisitions to act on a consistent basis.

The foundation of the Inquisition

The Portuguese Inquisition was institutionally quite separate from that of Spain, but in many respects the Spanish Inquisition was its godparent. In the Middle Ages papal inquisitions had been established to counter the spread of heresies like those of the Cathars but they had seldom concerned themselves with converted Jews and no papal inquisition had ever been established in the Iberian peninsula. The foundation of the Holy Office by Ferdinand and Isabella between 1478 and 1481 has, therefore, always been seen as a radical departure from the medieval concept. Founded originally to investigate the infiltration of converted Jews into Spanish society, and the subsequent infection of Catholic orthodoxy by heretical Judaic beliefs and pratices, the Inquisition assumed an important role for the monarchy as its jurisdiction covered all the Spanish kingdoms and its close links with the Crown (which appointed the Inquisitor General) made it in many respects a powerful political arm of the state.

Secret informants (familiars) denounced suspects who were never told who their accusers were or what the accusations against them might be. Prisoners were held incommunicado, were not allowed to call witnesses in their defence and were urged to confess their own crimes and to reveal their accomplices. Torture was used to extract confessions if they were not forthcoming voluntarily. Denunciations were frequently concerned only with the words uttered by the accused and not with any demonstrable activities on their part. Those found guilty were punished at lavishly spectacular public ceremonies known as *autos da fé*. The Inquisition also issued certificates of 'purity of blood' to those seeking honours and offices in church and state and was entrusted with the censorship of publications. When the Portuguese Inquisition was established it replicated these practices almost exactly. The methods employed by the Inquisition have been imitated by the secret police of so many modern regimes that, by extension, the Inquisition itself has been seen as the secret police force that enabled the Spanish Monarchy to operate effectively in a land that was institutionally deeply divided and socially anarchic.

At first the Spanish Inquisition had not been concerned with professing Jews, only those who had converted (*conversos*), but eleven years after its foundation it persuaded Ferdinand and Isabella that the expulsion of all Jews from Spain was essential if secret Judaic practices were to be eradicated. Spain was not alone in seeking the expulsion and conversion of Jews, as anti-Semitism was on the increase throughout Europe, linked ironically with the advance of Islam in the form of Turkish conquests, but it was never clear whether the real objective was to expel the Jews or achieve their conversion.

At the time of their expulsion in 1492, Spain had the largest community of Jews in Europe (possibly as many as 80,000) so that the decision to expel the whole community had a significant impact on society. Between 1492 and 1497 a confused situation arose. About half the Spanish Jews decided to leave the country while the other half underwent formal conversion and were allowed to stay. Of those who decided to leave, many subsequently returned and converted while a large number crossed the frontier into Portugal. Here Dom João II allowed 600 Jewish families to settle permanently while others were given the temporary right to stay. Those who remained after the grace period were to be enslaved and their children taken into Christian custody.

With the accession of Dom Manuel in 1495 Portugal came under pressure to bring its policies more into line with those of Castile. This was made a condition for the royal marriage between Isabella's daughter and the king which, it was hoped, would lead to an eventual union of the Crowns. As a result, in 1497, Dom Manuel, who had begun his reign by freeing those Jews who had been enslaved, ordered all Jews who would not convert to leave the country. Once again large numbers underwent formal conversion and the king, who clearly wanted to stop as many Jews as possible from leaving, promised that for twenty years those who converted would not be molested by the authorities (a promise eventually extended to 1534), which almost amounted to a guarantee that during this time there would be no Portuguese Inquisition. Indeed it has been argued that Dom Manuel wanted the New Christian population to remain and took active measures to prevent its departure. Perhaps with some exaggeration, António José Saraiva, the most controversial Portuguese historian of the Inquisition, wrote, 'the king of Portugal was firmly decided to prevent the Jews leaving the country' and refused to send back Spanish *converso* refugees. 'For D. Manuel, the more Jews the better.'[2] The full significance of this policy of accommodation can be appreciated when it is set against the ferocity with which the Spanish Inquisition was prosecuting and burning *conversos* across the border in Castile.

In fact, throughout the history of the persecution of their religious minorities Spain and Portugal often operated in counterbalance with each other. Energetic activity on one side of the border was frequently accompanied by a limited toleration on the other when the activity of the Inquisition could even appear to be dormant. A strange example of this occurred early on. In 1497 Dom Manuel, who had shown a marked tendency to try to accommodate Jews fleeing from Spain, decided to expel the remainder of the Moorish population from Portugal but these were allowed to settle, and indeed were welcomed, across the border in Isabella's Castile.

The Sephardic diaspora

Although estimates of the numbers involved in these expulsions and migrations vary from tens to hundreds of thousands, in total they came to constitute what has been considered the second great Jewish diaspora – that of the Sephardic Jews. The expulsion decrees had two major consequences – large numbers of Jews in Spain and Portugal now converted to Christianity, greatly swelling the population of *conversos* (more usually known in Portugal as New Christians) and hence enlarging the scale of the '*converso* problem'. The second consequence was the departure of large numbers of Iberian Jews initially to Italy and North Africa but later to Northern Europe and the Portuguese overseas territories. This latter trend is of considerable importance. In 1509 Dom Manuel granted special privileges to Jews who left Portugal to settle in the North African *praças* (garrison towns),[3] while the Portuguese settlements in the islands and on the West Coast of Africa also became a favoured destination for New Christians. Not all of these were voluntary exiles and there is a story that as many as two thousand Jewish children were sent to São Tomé to restart the foundering settlement in the island. Later many were to settle in Brazil where they played a major part in the development of the sugar industry and from where many moved to mainland North America to settle in the Dutch and English colonies.

This Jewish diaspora took place at a time when large numbers of Christian Portuguese were also leaving for the islands and other destinations overseas and when significant numbers of slaves were being shipped from mainland Africa to help people Portugal's overseas settlements. These three streams of migrants were to merge to form the societies of the Portuguese Atlantic (the Atlantic Islands, coastal West Africa and Brazil) with their distinctive Creole cultures, languages and social formations.

The foundation of the Portuguese Inquisition

By the 1530s the *conversos* had been largely eliminated as a cohesive and influential social group in the Spanish kingdoms and the Inquisition, its initial ferocious energy having burnt itself out, was increasingly concerned with rooting out other manifestations of heresy like Illuminism, Erasmianism and Lutheranism and was also turning its attention to issues of witchcraft, sexual deviancy and popular medicine. In Portugal, meanwhile, the New Christians had become increasingly entrenched in all the institutions of the kingdom and pressure to set up a Portuguese Inquisition had begun to mount. Although discussions with the Papacy began as early as 1531, it was only in 1547 that the Holy Office eventually assumed the form under which it was to operate for the next two hundred years. During the sixteen-year struggle to establish the Inquisition the political and juridical issues that were to surround its controversial history were clearly articulated. The Papacy wanted to retain ultimate control in order to prevent it adopting the secret practices of the Spanish Holy Office, which, even in the sixteenth century, were recognized as being against natural justice. In this it had the backing of a well-organized New Christian lobby. The kings of Portugal were equally determined that the Inquisition should be a national institution without direct papal control. When the statutes of the Inquisition were finally approved it was on the basis of a compromise. The Inquisitor General, who would appoint the other Inquisitors, would be nominated by the king and instituted by the pope, an arrangement which meant that, in practice, the Inquisitor was largely independent of both.[4]

One notable difference between the Portuguese and Spanish Inquisitions was that the former operated with only four separate tribunals while the latter had no fewer than twenty-one. In Portugal the Inquisition had branches in Évora, Coimbra and Lisbon, the Lisbon branch having jurisdiction over all the Portuguese settlements in the Atlantic. In 1560 a fourth office of the Inquisition was set up in Goa which had jurisdiction over all Portuguese settlements in the East. In 1622 it was proposed to create a separate Holy Office in Brazil but the plan was never put into effect either then or subsequently.[5] The Lisbon tribunal never had the manpower or resources to maintain a continuous presence outside Portugal with the result that the Portuguese Atlantic settlements, although they were never entirely free from inquisitorial interference, were allowed to develop a large degree of religious and cultural pluralism.

The Spanish and Portuguese Inquisitions in comparison

Immediately after its foundation the Portuguese Inquisition processed some very high-profile cases – the humanist Damião de Gois, the cobbler prophet Gonçalo Annes Bandarra, who gave birth to the Sebastianist legend, João da Costa, the rector of the University of Coimbra, and in 1549 George Buchanan, the Scottish humanist, were all investigated. However, the Crown interfered directly to give some protection to the New Christians and both the Regent Caterina and Dom Sebastião, once he became king, allowed the New Christians to purchase immunity from molestation. Nevertheless, between 1547 and 1580 the Portuguese Inquisition punished 1,998 people with 220 death sentences (11 per cent), most of them people accused of Judaizing, and in the next twenty years (1581–1600) became still more active, sentencing 3,200 people with 221 death sentences (6.9 per cent).

By contrast the Spanish Inquisition was entering a period when the surviving *converso* communities were left largely unmolested. In its first forty years of existence the Spanish Inquisition had focused its attention almost exclusively on the *conversos* with the consequence, as already noted, that many fled the country or crossed into Portugal. By 1540 it had shifted its emphasis to a concern with heresy more generally and a preoccupation with Islam. Between 1540 and 1559 only 5.9 per cent of all cases were people accused of Judaizing, with the result that numbers of Portuguese New Christians began moving to Spain to get out of reach of the Portuguese Inquisition. After the publication of the Tridentine decrees the Spanish Inquisition changed its focus yet again, now concerning itself more with sorcery, blasphemy and sexual crimes than with heresy as such. Between 1540 and 1700 27 per cent of its cases were concerned with blasphemy, 24 per cent with Islam, 10 per cent only with Judaism, and 8 per cent with Lutheranism; the rest were accounted for by sorcery, sexual offences and offences against the Inquisition itself.[6]

The activities of the Inquisitions outside the Iberian peninsula also show marked disparities. The Spanish set up tribunals in Mexico and Lima in 1569–70 and Cartagena in 1610, and then under strict instructions that converted native Americans were not to be investigated. In all 2,000 cases were investigated, but only 20 per cent of these were alleged Judaizers.[7] In New Castile only 40 per cent of all the cases that came before the Inquisition from 1480 to 1770 were concerned with heresy (of all kinds).[8] The Goan Inquisition by contrast was set up in 1560 and was extremely active until its investigations were curtailed by Pombal in 1774, when an inventory of its records showed that it had carried out more than 16,000 trials – an average of 75 a year. Re-established after Pombal's fall, its final abolition occurred in 1812 when the British, who occupied Goa during the Napoleonic Wars, insisted on its abolition as one of the conditions of the new commercial treaty signed with Portugal in 1810. Most of those who appeared before the Goa tribunal were poor Indians who had submitted to conversion, often with little or no instruction[9] – the Frenchman Charles Dellon recorded that at the 1674 *auto da fé* the only two people executed were 'a man and a woman [who] were black Native Christians, accused of magic, and condemned as Apostates; but, in truth, as little sorcerers as those by whom they were condemned'.[10] The Goa Inquisition played its part in the creation of the 'black legend' of the Inquisition as Dellon's account of the Goa tribunal, translated into many languages, was by far the most popular and widely read account of the Portuguese Inquisition's activities.

Brazil was periodically visited by commissions of the Inquisition and also had cases remitted to Lisbon by the ecclesiastical authorities. Around 1,000 cases were investigated, 50 per cent being alleged Judaizers, the most famous of whom was the dramatist António José da Silva, who was executed at an *auto da fé* in 1739. Once again the Portuguese Inquisition emerges as more focused than its Spanish counterpart on persecuting New Christians and, in its pursuit of converted Africans and Indians, less amenable to royal control.

The Union of the Spanish and Portuguese Crowns in 1580 offered important new commercial and financial opportunities to the New Christian business community in Portugal. Access to Spanish silver enabled it to play an increasingly important part in overseas commerce within both empires and to establish its members as rivals to the Genoese bankers who had traditionally financed the Spanish government. The Spanish Crown recognized the importance of not alienating such an important group and in 1604 was instrumental in obtaining a Papal pardon for all past Judaizing offences, for which the New Christians paid the substantial sum of 1.8 million ducats. Purity of blood examinations were suspended and New Christians were allowed to travel freely within the Spanish empire. Persecution of *conversos* continued but at a comparatively restrained level – between 1560 and 1614 only 5.5 per cent of those tried by the Inquisition in Spain were accused of Judaizing. This averages less than 33 a year spread between the 21 tribunals and such figures represent a level of risk that *conversos* were presumably prepared to live with. Throughout the seventeenth century the risk remained roughly the same. Between 1615 and 1700 an average of 38 cases were tried in Spain each year – although the influx of Portuguese New Christians during the period of the Union of the Crowns appears to have revived the concern about crypto-Judaic practices. Indeed it has been claimed that in the seventeenth century the term Portuguese became synonymous with 'Jew' in Castile. Such tolerance was increasingly resented in Portugal, where the Inquisition continued to exploit a powerful strain of popular anti-Castilian as well as anti-Jewish nationalism.

After the disastrous loss of the silver *flota* in 1628 Philip IV turned increasingly to the Portuguese New Christian bankers to provide finance for his European wars. In 1628 the Crown had tried to create an East India Company to take over the pepper contracts and provide an effective response to the Dutch and English Companies. New Christian capital was needed to make a success of the scheme but this prompted a boycott by other potential investors. The Crown itself had to take up unsubscribed shares and in 1631 the affairs of the short-lived company had to be wound up. The Inquisition in Portugal and its noble backers now found itself increasingly at odds with royal policy.

The aristocratic coup, which restored the independent Portuguese monarchy in 1640, led to a confused alignment of forces. The Inquisitor General, Dom Francisco de Castro, was among those who actively opposed the restoration of Portuguese independence and who plotted a countercoup to reimpose Spanish rule. Ironically the restoration was also opposed by many New Christians who had loaned money to the Spanish Crown and who feared the consequences of losing Spanish protection. The Abbé Vertot, in his history of the Portuguese Revolution, commented drily that this was 'perhaps the first time that ever the Inquisition and Synagogue went hand in hand together'.[11]

The Restoration not only saw a revival of Inquisition activity in Portugal but witnessed increasing conflict between the crown, supported by the Jesuits, and the Inquisition, with its formidable backing from the nobility and from popular sentiment. The crown wanted to continue the policy of the Spanish kings and enlist New Christian support for various commercial and industrial enterprises. To attract New Christian money the king repeatedly promised immunity from prosecution and confiscation of assets by the Inquisition. The first crisis was precipitated by Dom João IV's decree of 1649 forbidding the confiscation of property of those who invested in the Brazil Company, which had been strongly promoted by the Jesuits. The Inquisition vigorously opposed this measure.

In 1670 a similar situation arose when the regent Dom Pedro tried once again to float an East India Company. The Inquisition responded by creating an anti-Semitic panic and arresting António Vieira, the most eloquent Jesuit defender of the New Christians. The matter reached Rome, where Jesuit influence resulted in papal orders being issued for Inquisition trials to be suspended for seven years between 1674 and 1681. Dom Pedro, who had been trying to promote a number of new industrial enterprises backed by New Christian money, but who was still only regent for his deposed brother, eventually backed down fearing a noble coup which might oust him from power. The Inquisition then proceeded against a number of New Christians who had been involved with the new industrial enterprises that Pedro had been promoting.[12]

The Inquisition had triumphed in its duel with the Crown and the Papacy and experienced a period of renewed activity under Dom João V, who became king in 1706. However, its ideology and its activities were becoming increasingly anomalous in the Europe of the Enlightenment and after the Lisbon earthquake Sebastião de Carvalho (the first minister better known as the Marquês de Pombal) forced through a package of reforms which abolished all distinctions between New and Old Christians and destroyed the archives relating to inquests into purity of blood. The last *auto da fé* was held in 1768 and in 1771 the Inquisition was limited to dealing with cases of witchcraft and blasphemy, special permission having to be obtained to carry out any executions.

Understanding the Inquisition

The Portuguese Inquisition was very similar in structure and cultural ethos to its larger Spanish counterpart, yet there were always important differences in timing and emphasis. Their histories are closely linked but

never run entirely parallel. In the whole history of the Portuguese Inquisition between 1536 and 1794, 40,026 cases were investigated or 160 a
year divided between the three tribunals. 760 *autos da fé* were held and
31,353 persons were penanced – an average of 125 a year. Of these 1,254
were executed – an average of five a year divided between three tribunals. However, averaging these figures disguises periods of much
greater activity. For example, between 1633 and 1640 the average rose to
285 persons penanced each year.[13] In contrast, between 1680 and 1821 the
numbers sentenced by the Portuguese Inquisition averaged only 35 a
year and a study of the tribunal of Évora shows a dramatic fall off in
accusations after 1690.[14] In marked contrast to the situation in Spain, the
Portuguese Inquisition continued to target New Christians. Of accusations before the Évora tribunal between 1660 and 1821 81.5 per cent were
for Judaizing practices, the numbers almost equally divided between
men and women. Bigamy, blasphemy and sorcery were the only other
categories of note.

The Inquisitions in Spain and Portugal both acted in a spasmodic
way. There were periods of intense activity and periods when the institutions were much less active. What is the explanation for this? One reason undoubtedly lies in the financial problems of the Inquisition. The
Holy Office was expensive to run and the *autos da fé* were costly to
mount. It has been claimed that in New Castile the vigorous persecution of the early days led to the flight of all *conversos* of substance so
that, in order to survive, the Inquisition had to turn its attention to other
categories of offender and to invade the jurisdiction of other courts by
reclassifying a wider range of crimes as heretical. Shortage of money
'is what impeded the prosecution of more important crimes', concluded Jean-Pierre DeDieu.[15] Throughout its history the Portuguese Inquisition also was seriously short of money, in spite of its practice of
confiscating the goods of the accused. Failure by secular authorities to
support its activities severely limited their scope. When the commission
of the Inquisition arrived in Madeira in 1591 the town council (*câmara*)
of Funchal refused to contribute to its expenses and 'did not show itself particularly receptive to the visit', as the powers of the Inquisitors
were bound to conflict with local jurisdictions.[16]

It has often been suggested that the Inquisition deliberately targeted
the wealthy and had to maintain the flow of New Christian prosecu-
tions and confiscations in order to replenish its coffers and to sustain itself. As António José Saraiva wrote, 'the function of the tribunal of the
Holy Office was not to destroy Judaisers but to manufacture them',[17]

and he prefaced one of his books with a quotation from the Portuguese statesman Dom Luís da Cunha who wrote in 1735:

> The proceedings of the Inquisition, instead of rooting out Judaism multiplies it . . . Just as in the Calcetaria there is a building where money is made, so in the Rossio [where the headquarters of the Lisbon Inquisition was located] there is another in which they make Jews.[18]

Carl Hanson summed this up, 'it is indeed ironic that the Portuguese Inquisition depended on its despised victims for its very survival.'[19] Lack of sufficient resources is undoubtedly one reason why so few inquisitorial visitations took place in the islands and Brazil and consequently why heretical practices were allowed to flourish there.

The second reason why the Inquisition tended to act in a spasmodic fashion was because its activities were more reactive than proactive – it tended to respond to contemporary events and changing perceptions of the problem of heresy. It could be stimulated into action by challenges to its authority, by occasions when New Christians appeared to be particularly active in public affairs, or by 'scares', when the anti-Semitism which was rife in Portuguese and Spanish popular culture surfaced in response to some incident like the sacrilegious robbery in the church in Odivelas in 1671.

If the Inquisition could rouse itself to mount impressive displays of power and even to challenge the Crown itself, its routines were focused on more subtle exercises in power and influence. The investigations into the purity of blood of those seeking office or honours continued until the time of Pombal in the mid-eighteenth century and allowed the Inquisition to wield extraordinary influence in church and state. Saraiva was typically sceptical about the way this operated. According to him there was never any systematic attempt to exclude all people with New Christian ancestry from office as virtually the whole of Portuguese society could have been excluded if a search were to be made too far back into their families. What was important for

> the Inquisition and for the group of which it was the instrument was the existence of discrimination itself, that is of a process by which certain sectors of the Portuguese population could be excluded from positions of authority and from feudal rents.[20]

In other words purity of blood was a weapon that could be used as and when required to exclude certain groups and individuals.

The Inquisition was always as much concerned with wider aspects of social control as with heresy. Its role in censorship allowed it to interfere in the intellectual and academic life of Portugal and to exert influence over publishing and the use of propaganda while its investigations into sexual offences, cults, witchcraft and popular medicine made it the arbiter of manners and what was deemed acceptable in society. Francisco Peña wrote in 1578, 'we must remember that the primary goal of the trial and the condemnation to death is not to save the soul of the accused but to contribute to the public good and intimidate the multitude.'[21]

The powers of the Inquisition were systematically extended as it widened its definition of heresy to include ever more categories of offence – sexual deviancy, sorcery, popular medicine, blasphemy, the misconduct of priests and even criticism of the Holy Office itself. However, with offences so widespread and so ill-defined, its powers could not be exercised consistently or with any degree of comprehensiveness.

So the story of the Inquisition is one of periodic purges and spates of feverish activity culminating in the impressive *autos da fé* which were intended as displays of power to which even the king had to subject himself. Charles Dellon, who took part as a penitent in an *auto da fé* in Goa in 1674, described how the procession of penitents was

> led through the principal streets, and [was] everywhere regarded by an immense crowd which came from all parts of India, and lined all the roads by which we passed; notice having been given from the pulpit in the most distant parishes, long before the Act of Faith was to be celebrated.[22]

It has been suggested that under cover of the drive for religious orthodoxy the Inquisition was really an instrument of aristocratic power which could be used against all those who threatened the dominance of the landed aristocracy and the old Christian families who benefited from control of state resources. Again and again the Inquisition went into action to prevent the crown building an effective alliance with New Christian merchants and bankers and to force it to abandon its experiments with capitalist enterprise. Moreover there is no doubt that the purity of blood accusations could be, and were, used to prevent the social advancement of men and women from the merchant classes. Saraiva even went as far as to claim that the New Christians were not crypto-Jews at all but a social class of merchants, bankers and businessmen who were threatening the dominance of the landed aristocracy.

However, the net of the Inquisition was thrown much wider to catch others than wealthy merchants. An analysis of those accused by the Évora tribunal after 1660 shows that the largest groups were agricultural labourers and textile and leather workers. Only 250 (less than 10 per cent) were categorized as merchants. When the Inquisition sent a commission to Madeira in 1591, as well as alleged Judaic practices, it found itself dealing with fifteen or so cases of blasphemy (*soltura de lingua*) among the Spanish soldiers of the garrison.[23] However, if the victims of the Inquisition were drawn from all classes of society, a disproportionate number were single – 52.5 per cent of those accused by the Évora tribunal were either unmarried or widowed. This figure, of course, included priests and other religious, but it suggests that those without close kin were particularly vulnerable.[24]

The Inquisition became an established bureaucracy dedicated to defending its power and influence in the face of numerous enemies. At different times it had to face determined attempts to limit its operations from the crown (both the Spanish and the restored Portuguese crown) and the New Christian community but also from enemies within the church. On two occasions in 1546 and between 1674 and 1681 the papacy tried to inquire into the Inquisition's practices, and on the second occasion ordered the suspension of trials. In the seventeenth century the Inquisition also found itself at war with the influential Society of Jesus. The Jesuits were not opposed to the Inquisition in principle, indeed Francis Xavier had recommended that a tribunal be established in Goa and the Jesuits routinely took a central part in the ceremonies of the *autos da fé*. In the seventeenth century, however, sources of conflict multiplied as the Jesuits came under attack for their opposition to Indian slavery, for their missionary methods which were held to be unorthodox, for their support of the New Christians and for the admittedly strange views of their most famous preacher, António Vieira, who was arrested by the Inquisition and examined under suspicion of heresy. These conflicts were fundamentally religious 'turf wars'. The Jesuits fought to protect their privileged position in the mission field and tried to enlist the crown and the papacy in their defence. The Inquisition increasingly represented the interests of those who, for whatever reason, found themselves in opposition to the Jesuits. The Jesuits backed the Braganza restoration while the Inquisition opposed it; the Jesuits strongly supported the creation of the Brazil Company and persuaded the Crown to suspend confiscations of New Christian wealth which was bitterly opposed by the Inquisition; the Jesuits also persuaded the papacy to undertake an inquiry into the practices of the Inquisition. This rivalry continued into the eighteenth century until ended by Pombal who used his quasi-dictatorial powers to emasculate the Inquisition and to abolish the Jesuits altogether.

In the eighteenth century the Portuguese Inquisition became increasingly focused on the prosecution of 'sorcerers', many of whom were practitioners of popular medicine, but who included fortune tellers and dispensers of love potions and other popular remedies. In June 1787, long after the teeth of the Inquisition had been drawn with respect to the New Christians, William Beckford complained that as he was being driven in his coach about Lisbon he was nearly upset into

> sandy ditches amongst rotten shoes, dead cats and negro beldames who retire into such dens and burrows for the purpose of telling fortunes and selling charms for the ague. The Inquisition too often lays hold of these wretched sibyls and works them confoundedly.[25]

From 1600 to 1774 the Inquisition in Portugal investigated 818 people accused of practising different forms of magic. In the rest of Europe trials of this kind would have been common in the first half of the seventeenth century and would have declined sharply in the eighteenth. In Portugal the trend was exactly the opposite. From being little concerned with magic and sorcery early in the seventeenth century, the Inquisition stepped up its investigations and trials between 1715 and 1760. Timothy Walker examined 442 cases, broadly defined as magic, that were tried by the Inquisition between 1668 and 1802 and came up with some startling figures. Whereas there were only 3 cases between 1668 and 1680, there were 62 cases in the five years 1716–20, a third of whom were healers.[26] In absolute terms these numbers are tiny – just one or two cases each year heard by each of the three tribunals – but the trend is interesting enough to suggest a significant change in the character of the Inquisition in the eighteenth century. It is also perhaps notable that none of those accused of these crimes was executed.

The officials and familiars of the Inquisition had always been drawn largely from the educated upper classes. In the late seventeenth century Portugal began to be influenced by the French Enlightenment and although many scientific and secular works were banned by the Inquisition this did not prevent the educated classes in Portugal, and even the Inquisitors themselves, obtaining these works and being influenced by them. One aspect of the Enlightenment that became increasingly influential in Portugal was medicine and it has been argued that it was enlightened and progressive medical practitioners who were behind the increased activity shown by the Inquisition against popular healers and diviners. In other words the Inquisition, with an irony that must have made its traditional supporters somewhat uneasy, increasingly became an instrument for the propagation of progressive, scientific thought.

The Inquisition and the English dominance in Portugal

In the century which followed the 1640 Restoration the English mercantile community in Portugal and Madeira grew in size and prosperity and by 1750 was in a position to supply industrial goods to Portugal's colonies and to dominate its overseas trade. During this time Portugal became in effect an economic and political dependency of Britain. However, the second half of the seventeenth century was also the time of the greatest struggle between the Portuguese Crown and the Inquisition over the rights of the New Christians. The Crown's repeated attempts to protect New Christian merchants from prosecution and confiscation were countered, in the end effectively, by the Inquisition with the net result that more and more New Christian families, which had been relatively secure during the period of Spanish rule, moved their capital and frequently themselves abroad, contributing materially to a renewed Sephardic diaspora. This exiled Portuguese mercantile capital was welcomed in the Netherlands, France, Britain and the New World, and contributed substantially to the economic development of these countries.

While the battle between Inquisition and Crown continued, the newly independent kingdom had struggled to survive on the international stage and Dom João IV hastily signed treaties of alliance with Sweden, England and the Netherlands. The first of these, the treaty with England, signed in 1642, established the broad terms for an alliance, allowing the Portuguese to raise troops and hire shipping in England and containing a clause that no Englishman would be molested for his religious beliefs. In 1654 a second treaty was signed with the Commonwealth government. This extended the religious privileges to include a right to hold religious services in private houses and immunity from prosecution by the Inquisition for possessing bibles or religious books. It also protected the debts that prisoners of the Inquisition might owe to English merchants and allowed the English to have their own burial ground. This treaty also made formal provision for the appointment of a Judge Conservator to hear cases involving the English merchants.[27] Although the English did not obtain all they wanted, and in the 1660s actually had their consul summoned before the Inquisition, these treaties in effect protected the English merchant community from prosecution and confiscation. These privileges were also enjoyed by Dutch and other foreign merchants in contrast to the native New Christian mercantile community which had no effective protection and was increasingly persecuted.

The privileges of the English community were confirmed by a third treaty in 1661 which also offered Portugal military aid and in 1703 two more treaties, the Methuen Treaties, confirmed England's position as the dominant trading partner of Portugal. Portugal now became the principal purveyor of wines to Britain while all tariffs against English woollens were removed. Portugal also agreed to join the war against Louis XIV and became dependent on British military protection for itself and its colonies. By the first decades of the eighteenth century Britain's rapidly growing trade surplus with Portugal was covered by gold remittances and British merchants were buying up vineyards in the north of Portugal and establishing their financial control over Portuguese foreign commercial transactions.

As the New Christians were harried into exile, their place was taken by the equally hated but securely protected Protestant British who constituted a capitalist class, dominated by heretics and far more alien to Portuguese interests than the much maligned New Christians.

Conclusion

Although condemnation of the Inquisition is as imperative in Anglophone intellectual circles as condemnation of the slave trade, this moral righteousness can obscure an understanding of the institution. The Inquisition survived in Portugal just short of three hundred years and was an active and independent body for 250 of these. Such longevity in any institution indicates a high degree of flexibility and adaptability as well as a consistent level of popular support. There is no way the Inquisition would have weathered the attacks on it by the Crown, the Jesuits and even the papacy if it had not had strong support across a wide spectrum of Portuguese society. So, although when seen from one point of view it was a tyrannical institution repressing the population, from another it can be seen to have articulated national sentiment. By constantly defining and identifying heretical practices and dissident sections of the community it went a long way towards defining and solidifying the national identity of Portugal. In condemning the Inquisition as a peculiarly wicked Iberian institution the enemies of Spain and Portugal were tacitly recognizing how important this institution was to a sense of Iberian national consciousness. Although not escaping periodic social unrest, Portugal during the period of the Inquisition's existence had nevertheless remained a remarkably cohesive society. This changed in the early nineteenth century which saw the country slide into endemic civil war at a time which coincidentally saw the abolition of the Inquisition.

Although the total numbers of persons tried by the Inquisition over 250 years ran into tens of thousands, when reduced to annual averages this actually breaks down into quite small numbers tried and even smaller numbers executed. In return Portugal was spared the horrors of witch burnings, pogroms and religious wars. Francisco Bethencourt was able to state emphatically that 'the witch-craze which affected most of central and western European countries from the middle of the sixteenth century to the middle of the seventeenth century did not occur in Portugal.' Indeed there was 'a clear attitude of cultural rejection on the part of the religious elite'.[28] As the Inquisitor in Shaw's *Saint Joan* put it,

> the heretic in the hands of the Holy Office is safe from violence
> ... Before the Holy Inquisition existed, and even now when its
> officers are not within reach, the unfortunate wretch suspected
> of heresy, perhaps quite ignorantly and unjustly, is stoned,
> torn in pieces, drowned, burned in his house with all his inno-
> cent children, without a trial, unshriven, unburied save as a dog
> is buried.[29]

The Inquisition may have been religious intolerance institutionalized, but it prevented social breakdown, indiscriminate popular violence and ethnic cleansing, for although the New Christians of Portugal were the constant target of the Inquisition these persecutions were never severe or persistent enough to destroy the New Christian community on a permanent basis.

The British view of their own history is one in which royal absolutism was resisted and eventually curtailed by Parliament and the Courts – strong aristocratic institutions with popular backing. In Portugal royal absolutism was not effectively opposed by the Cortes, which by the eighteenth century had ceased to meet at all. Instead it was the

Inquisition which again and again articulated the opposition of the aristocracy to the policies of the crown, and it was able to do this because of the wide popular support which it enjoyed. Although the Inquisition can hardly be classed as a democratic institution, its opposition to royal absolutism was certainly as effective as the opposition mounted by privileged corporations in other European countries of which the British aristocratic parliament is a prime example.

8

The Lisbon Earthquake, the Enlightenment and Crisis Politics

In 1962 the economist Milton Friedman, wrote, 'only a crisis – actual or perceived – produces real change. When that crisis occurs, the actions that are taken depend on the ideas that are lying around.'[1] In this way natural or man-made disasters have opened the way for what has been called 'disaster capitalism'. In the eighteenth century the catastrophe of the Lisbon earthquake created the conditions for the emergence of a strong man who used the contemporary ideas which were 'lying around' to take control of the Portuguese state, to redistribute its resources and to reorder its institutions – in short to provide opportunities for the ideas of modernization and capitalism to bring real change not only to Portugal but, arguably, to the whole of Europe.

The politics of survival

After the restoration of Portugal's independence in 1640, the kingdom faced an uncertain future in a Europe that had become increasingly predatory. In the sixteenth century Portugal had largely avoided involvement in European wars, establishing close relations with Castile secured by royal marriages and bilateral agreements to resolve colonial disputes. This strategy would no longer suffice in the seventeenth century. Spain remained an irreconcilable enemy and only grudgingly recognized Portugal's independence in 1668. At the same time the Portuguese overseas territories were falling prey to the Dutch. Between 1640 and 1663, when the Dutch finally made peace in the East, Portugal lost all its possessions in Malaysia, Malabar, Kanara and Sri Lanka with the inevitable consequence that it was almost entirely excluded from the spice trade on which its eastern empire had been founded. The Dutch had also tried to capture Brazil and the Portuguese possessions in western Africa but after prolonged warfare Portugal regained control of Brazil, Angola and São Tomé, although it was forced to recognize that it had permanently lost its trading posts on the Gold Coast and at Arguim.

Faced with this precarious position the Portuguese had to find allies elsewhere in Europe. For the rest of the seventeenth century policy vacillated between seeking an English or a French alliance. As Louis XIV built his formidable new army and consolidated his power in western Europe, largely at the expense of Spain, the Portuguese saw France as a natural ally. Both countries had a common enemy and Dom João IV and his supporters remembered the promises of aid that had been so freely given by Richelieu prior to 1640. The French alliance, however, remained elusive and always beyond Portugal's grasp. While the war between France and Spain continued the French saw the future of Portugal as something with which to bargain at the conference table, with the result that Portugal's independence was not guaranteed either in the Westphalia treaties of 1648 (to which Portugal was not admitted as a party) nor in the Treaty of the Pyrenees in 1659. In 1665, however, a royal marriage was negotiated which brought a French princess, Marie de Savoie, to Portugal and moved Portugal briefly into France's diplomatic orbit. When the mentally retarded Portuguese king, Afonso VI, was removed from power by an aristocratic coup in 1667, Queen Marie, with French encouragement, obtained an annulment of her marriage and transferred her matrimonial favours to the king's brother, the regent Pedro.

However, the French alliance did not prosper. Portugal and France never established strong commercial ties, for the wines which were Portugal's principal export were of no interest to France and, in spite of the considerable investment made by Colbert in the French navy, France was never in a position to offer the maritime protection that Portugal and its colonial possessions needed. More seriously from the Portuguese point of view, after 1668 France began to develop close relations with Spain which were intended to lead either to a union of the Crowns or to a French protectorate over Spain and its vast empire.

Meanwhile, after peace had been made between France and Spain in 1659, Portugal had to face a more determined Spanish attempt at reconquest and continued to fear for the remainder of its empire. In this context the English alliance gradually came to appear the more advantageous option. This alliance, of course, had its origin at the time of the Hundred Years War but it had become inoperative while Portugal had been in effect part of the Spanish monarchy. Dom João IV had approached the

English for recognition and help soon after the break with Spain but the recognition obtained in the 1642 treaty brought little benefit for Portugal as England became embroiled in a civil war which lasted for the next ten years. At one stage the civil war threatened to engulf Portugal itself when in 1650 the parliamentarian admiral, Robert Blake, blockaded Prince Rupert and his royalist fleet in the harbour in Lisbon. Eventually Dom João IV signed a treaty with the Commonwealth government in 1654 which gave considerable commercial advantages to the English as well as immunity from the attentions of the Inquisition. However, it was the Anglo-Dutch war of 1652–4 rather than the treaty which brought most advantage to Portugal. Dutch defeat at sea prevented any last-minute attempt to relieve the garrisons in Brazil, which finally surrendered to the Portuguese in 1654.

In 1661, following the death of Dom João IV in 1656, the queen mother, who acted as regent, arranged a dynastic marriage between her daughter Caterina and Charles II of England. By this marriage treaty England received the Portuguese colonies of Tangiers and Bombay together with a dowry of two million *cruzados*, in return for which England, for the first time, provided guarantees for the continued independence of Portugal and its empire. English regiments duly took part in the defence of Portugal against the Spanish invasion that followed. In retrospect the three Anglo-Portuguese treaties can be seen to have fastened the grip of the English on Portugal, although they did not confer on England any privileges which were not also conferred on the Dutch and French. In the end it was not the treaties so much as the growth of strong commercial ties that was to bind the English and Portuguese so closely together. During the wars between England and France and their allies, which began in 1688 and were to continue with scarcely a break until 1713, embargos on importing French wines made the English turn to Portugal for their supplies. In 1678 only 120 tuns of Portuguese wine entered the port of London but during the War of the League of Augsburg this quantity rose to an annual average of 5,490 tuns. Imports steadily increased and in the 1740s 13,550 tuns were imported annually.[2] The wine trade brought prosperity to the English commercial houses which were then able to profit from the flow of gold from Brazil which began in the early eighteenth century and which greatly stimulated the market for consumer goods in Portugal.

The second factor which consolidated England's dominance was the crisis of the Spanish succession. Carlos II of Spain died childless in 1699, leaving his kingdom and empire to the grandson of Louis XIV. Portugal was prepared to accept this arrangement but, as a Grand Alliance built up to challenge this settlement and to promote the alternative claims of an Austrian archduke, the Portuguese found themselves faced with a cruel dilemma. If Portugal remained neutral or sided with the Franco-Spanish forces, not only Portugal itself but its whole empire would be at the mercy of the powerful English and Dutch fleets. However, if Portugal sided with the Grand Alliance its coasts and colonies would be protected at sea but it would be open to invasion across its land frontiers from French and Spanish armies.

In 1703 any doubts in Portugal were settled by the British naval victory at Vigo and Portugal acceded to the Grand Alliance, signing a new commercial treaty, one of the shortest and most famous treaties in the history of European diplomacy. Unlike the lengthy and wordy treaty of 1654, the 1703 Methuen Treaty had only three short paragraphs. One of these guaranteed that Portuguese wines would be admitted to Britain at a third less duty than those of France, while the other seemingly innocuous clause simply promised 'to admit, for ever hereafter, into Portugal the woollen cloths, and the rest of the woollen manufactures of the Britons, as was accustomed till they were prohibited by laws'.[3]

The Methuen Treaty by itself changed little but seen in the wider context of the privileges already granted in the earlier treaties, the war and the flow of gold from Brazil, it set the seal on Portugal's dependency. Dom Pedro now finally abandoned his attempts to develop import-saving manufactures which had been so vigorously opposed by the Inquisition. It was far simpler and less controversial to allow consumer goods (of which textiles were the most important) to enter Portugal from Britain and for these to be paid for by the export of wines for which Britain now provided a protected market. Had this been an equal exchange the benefits to Portugal would have been considerable but the trade balance rapidly tilted in Britain's favour and between 1730 and 1755 Britain had an average annual trade surplus of £773,000. Payments to cover this gap were made in gold which was regularly, if illegally, remitted to Britain on board the warships that visited the Tagus. Captain Augustus Hervey, whose amorous adventures in Lisbon throw interesting light on the nature of the contemplative life in Portuguese convents, records in his journal three visits to Lisbon in September 1748, September 1752 and April 1753: on the first occasion he sailed with 80,000 *moidores* on board, on the second with 30,000 and on the third with 63,533.[4] As it was technically illegal to export gold from Portugal, British firms established in Portugal were encouraged to invest their growing profits in purchasing Portuguese land, in providing loans to support new vineyards and various other Portuguese enterprises and in financing Portuguese trading houses operating in the colonies from which British merchants were excluded.

During the War of the Spanish Succession Portugal was briefly a major theatre of war as allied armies landed in Lisbon and advanced into Spain, occupying Madrid in 1706. Thereafter the allied cause in Spain faltered and Portugal's main preoccupation became the defence of its frontiers. Lisbon, however, became the main supply base which allowed the British navy to operate in the south Atlantic and the Mediterranean with greater freedom and effectiveness. For the rest of the century, Lisbon became the British navy's forward base in return for which it was understood that Britain would guarantee Portugal's security from a Franco-Spanish invasion. British warships were constantly to be found in the Tagus and the influence of the navy complemented that of the British Factory in maintaining Britain's dominance in Portugal.

There were two consequences of this alliance that are seldom commented upon. Throughout the eighteenth century the French, British and Spanish fought a series of colonial wars, raiding each other's colonies and seizing and exchanging islands, fortresses and mainland territories. The vast Portuguese overseas empire, bigger in territorial extent than any of the others, was left out of this struggle for colonies. Apart from two French raids on Rio in 1710 and 1711 and the almost continuous rivalry between Portugal and Spain to control the mouth of the Río de la Plata, the Portuguese empire was not in contention in the European wars. Yet the Portuguese control of Madeira, the Azores and the Cape Verde Islands meant that Lisbon could dominate the main Atlantic sea routes while the vast backlands of Brazil and the wealth derived from its mines and plantations equalled or surpassed the wealth of the mainland colonies of the other European powers.

The second significant consequence of the alliance was that, alone among the European monarchies of the eighteenth century, Portugal did not build up its armed forces or its naval strength and therefore did not benefit from the huge consumer market provided by large armies and fleets. If this meant that Portugal remained unnecessarily dependant on Britain for defence, it should have released resources for investment in infrastructure, for in the first half of the eighteenth century vast wealth flowed into the country from Brazil. It has been estimated that between 1735 and 1756 between 11 and 16 tons of gold arrived every year and that in the course of the century a total of 1000 tons of gold reached Portugal. However, this wealth, where it remained in the country, was largely spent on the building and embellishment of churches, on the construction of the royal palace of Mafra and on Dom João v's attempt to turn Lisbon into the pre-eminent centre of Catholicism in Europe after Rome itself. The Church indeed became a sort of standing army and the resources of Portugal were mobilized to support 200,000 clerics rather than 200,000 soldiers.

Disaster and revolution

By 1750 Portugal, safe under the patronage of Britain, had receded from the consciousness and concern of most of Europe. It neither threatened its neighbours nor was threatened by them and, although the papacy welcomed the flow of Brazilian gold that resulted from Dom João v's piety and Italian artists benefited from the commissions for religious works of art, few in Europe concerned themselves with a kingdom which came to be almost a byword for backwardness. Fewer still gave more than a passing thought to the Treaty of Madrid signed in 1750 between Portugal and Spain which broke through the old boundaries set at Tordesillas in 1494 and created the vast territory of modern Brazil, giving Portugal half the South American continent and a territorial empire far larger than that of either France or Britain. And although the passing of Dom João v and the succession of his son Dom José in 1750 was duly noted, no one outside the diplomatic corps was much concerned with the appointment to the post of Foreign Minister, shortly before the new king's accession, of a relatively undistinguished former diplomat called Sebastião José de Carvalho e Melo, a man already in his fifties.

Then, on All Saints' Day (1 November) 1755 Lisbon was struck by a major earthquake. The epicentre lay off the coast of the Maghreb and many towns in Morocco and southern Portugal suffered damage. However, it was the central areas of the city of Lisbon that experienced the full force of the earthquake and the subsequent tsunami. The shocks came in three bursts lasting nine minutes in all, with aftershocks continuing for the next two months and numbering 500 in all. There had been previous earth tremors recorded in Lisbon, three in the sixteenth century and two in the eighteenth century (in 1724 and 1750), but the scale of the 1755 earthquake was such that from the start it was felt to be an event of uncommon significance. The earthquake seriously affected the low-lying centre of the city (the Baixa) and the region of the Bairro Alto. The Alfama

The Lisbon earthquake and tsunami.

district clustering around the castle of São Jorge survived relatively intact. The earthquake was followed by a tsunami which briefly inundated the Baixa and by numerous fires which broke out in collapsed buildings and which burnt for a week. Altogether possibly 10–15,000 people lost their lives, the highest ranking being the Spanish ambassador who was hit by his own carved coat of arms falling on his head as he fled his home. Four-fifths of the buildings in the city were badly damaged or totally destroyed, including the royal palace, the Casa da Índia, the headquarters of the Inquisition and the newly completed opera house. Only five of the sixty-five convents and monastic houses in Lisbon remained habitable. However, the sturdy Romanesque cathedral withstood the tremors, as did the aqueduct, the *aguas livres*, which had been the great engineering achievement of Dom João v's reign.

No European capital, except possibly London in the Great Fire, had suffered a similar catastrophe and although Europe was poised on the eve of yet another war, the event attracted unprecedented attention, not least from the literati and from natural scientists who faced the challenge of providing a credible explanation. The sheer volume of writings about the earthquake was unmatched by that relating to any other comparable natural phenomenon and served to make Portugal and its affairs the centre of attention for educated and scientific Europe. In Portugal, however, the event was not just a catastrophe providing inexhaustible subject matter for sermons, poems and pamphlets, it provided the catalyst for radical political and social change.

It is now recognized that a major natural disaster sweeps away not only fixed assets in the form of buildings, homes and businesses but can shake to their foundations established institutions and ways of doing things, providing opportunities for entrepreneurs to commandeer national resources and usurp the functions of government. In the aftermath of the earthquake a number of key figures in the king's entourage rose to the occasion but it was the Foreign Minister who soon emerged as the man with the energy and administrative ability to plan what was an unprecedented relief operation. Immediate action had to be taken to maintain civil government and prevent looting, to dispose of the dead and prevent the outbreak of disease and to provide food and water to the thousands of refugees who were trying to survive in tented cities beyond the area of ruins. Once these problems had been addressed, valuable property had to be retrieved and secured and decisions had to be made about clearing the ruins and reconstructing the city. Carvalho and his assistants were granted exceptional powers by the king and a form of martial law was imposed not only in Lisbon but throughout the kingdom. Thomas Chase, who had himself been badly injured, wrote an account of the earthquake and how the problems it caused were tackled.

> The King sent directly to the nearest garrisons for his troops; upon whose arrival order was restored and butchers and bakers were dispersed about, to provide for the people, who were not permitted to remove farther from the city without passes. The common people were immediately forced by the soldiers, with swords drawn, to bury the dead bodies, the stench becoming so noisome that bad consequences were apprehended from it. The judges were likewise distributed in different parts of the city, with orders to execute on the spot all who were found guilty of murder or theft. It was said, before we left the place, that there were above eighty bodies hanging upon gibbets round about the city. The ships were several of them searched, and not allowed to quit the harbour without permission. All the heart of the city, the richest part of it, was burnt; but the suburbs, which are very large, escaped, and have since been repaired.[5]

After the Great Fire of London plans had been drawn up for a radical redesign of the old city but these had succumbed to the vested interests of property owners and London was largely rebuilt on the old street pattern. In Lisbon consideration was given to abandoning the old city and building a wholly new one on greenfield sites further down the Tagus – after all, thirty years earlier Goa, the second city of the Portuguese world, had been abandoned and a new capital built at Panjim nearer the sea. However, Dom José was persuaded by Carvalho that the ruins of Lisbon should be cleared and the city rebuilt, and that the opportunity should be taken to plan a model city according to the latest rationalist ideas of town planning. Portugal, steeped in tradition and with the powerful interests of the aristocracy and the Inquisition usually able to stifle any new initiatives, was the last place where one would have expected radical town planning to occur. That it did was the result of a political revolution which, in the wake of the disaster, swept away corporate privilege and the opposition of vested interests.

Carvalho was the man who led this revolution and who drove forward the rebuilding of the city. It was to be his finest and most lasting achievement. Most European cities had grown up within a defensive circle of walls which had cramped their growth, or around hilltop fortifications with narrow and steep winding streets. Lisbon had indeed grown up in just this way. The rebuilding of the city had to break free from these traditional constraints. Carvalho had served as ambassador in Vienna, where he had met and married his second wife, and the rebuilding of Lisbon was entrusted to skilled military engineers, at least one of whom, Karl Mardel, came from Habsburg Hungary. Austrian military architecture informed the plans for the new Lisbon, which was laid out in a strict grid pattern with uniform parallel streets leading from the great riverside Praça do Comércio to the Rossio. The buildings were uniform in design and were built around specially designed wooden frames, since it had been noticed that it was the wooden buildings of the city that had best withstood the earthquake. After the great earthquake which struck southern Sicily in 1693, the ruined towns with their convents and palaces had been rebuilt in a lavish baroque style which celebrated the power of the church and the aristocracy.[6] In contrast, the new city of Lisbon was consciously designed as a bourgeois city to reflect the rationalism and order of the Enlightenment. The sober streets and squares were intended to provide business premises and city centre apartments, not convents and aristocratic palaces.

The rebuilding of Lisbon continued over a twenty-year period and culminated in the unveiling of a giant bronze statue of Dom José in the Praça do Comércio in 1775.

The Lisbon Earthquake: having a good argument

The educated and wealthy who frequented the literary salons of Europe, the 'chattering classes', liked nothing better than a good argument. Although the popular hold of religion was still generally strong throughout Europe, the influence of theology and the power of the church over the educated had begun to slip. The intellectual battlefield was hard fought and by mid-century the debates that had been precipitated by the scientific work of Newton and Leibniz, and by David Hume in his 1748 *Essay on Human Understanding,* had begun to burn themselves out. An event like the Lisbon earthquake opened a new front in this intellectual war of attrition between revelation and reason and posed old questions in a new and very dramatic form. A catastrophe on this scale goaded the *philosophes* and the religious traditionalists to try once more to gain possession of the commanding heights in the battle of ideas.

An English merchant who was an eyewitness of the earthquake recorded that 'for the first few Days the Natives seemed entirely taken up with Acts of Devotion and Repentance: Every Road and every Field were filled with People at Prayers, or in Processions.'[7] One group within the church reflected this popular mood by calling publicly for repentance, organizing processions and interpreting the event as God's punishment not only for the traditional sins of the ordinary man but for Portugal itself, the land which had been specially chosen by God for his work and which had fallen by the wayside. 'Would to God,' wrote the

The Praça do Comércio, rebuilt after the earthquake.

Jesuit Malagrida, 'we could see as much determination and fervour for this necessary exercise [repentance] as are devoted to the erection of huts and new buildings!'[8] Reactions such as these ran counter to the direction taken by Carvalho and his team, who had from the start determined to take a practical approach to the catastrophe and to rally the efforts of the city to deal with the crisis. The earthquake was to be treated as a natural phenomenon and the destruction of the city as calling for rational and scientific solutions. Calls for repentance and religious observance to ward off a repetition of the divine wrath, calls which were supported not only by the religious orders but by political opponents of Carvalho, soon came to be seen as scarcely veiled political discourse and as direct opposition to the government. What was apparently a religious and philosophical argument was soon to assume a violent political dimension.

Elsewhere in Europe the earthquake stimulated a wide-ranging philosophical debate about man's relations with nature. The randomness of the destruction and the huge loss of human life once again posed questions about whether there was intelligent design in the universe or a moral hand at work in human affairs, whether God, if he existed, could be considered to be good and just. These questions were famously and brilliantly posed in Voltaire's novel *Candide, ou l'optimisme* which appeared in 1759 and has remained a bestseller ever since. In this work Voltaire combined burlesque and biting satire with a racy narrative and a serious philosophical purpose. It was a literary masterpiece with which few philosophical or religious traditionalists could hope to compete.

The earthquake, and the tsunami that followed, also stimulated a significant scientific discussion about the causes of such phenomena. Views ranged from a sensible theory that air and water trapped beneath the earth's crust overheated and exploded, to more far-fetched ideas that the newly discovered force of electricity was to blame. If earthquakes could be understood, then perhaps they could be predicted and their impact lessened. Like Halley's predictions about the regular reappearance of comets, this idea represented a further major encroachment of science into a territory which had traditionally been inhabited by religion and magic. This advance of scientific prediction was assumed to be inevitable, although two hundred and fifty years later, while earthquakes can be measured and understood, they still cannot be predicted nor their human impact lessened.

Political revolution

Natural catastrophes, as has been noted, provide unique opportunities for change and an earthquake on this scale, laying low a whole capital city, was, not surprisingly, followed by a political earthquake of comparable proportions. Portugal was the first European state to experience such a revolution, heralding an age when revolutions were to sweep away ancient institutions and whole state systems throughout the European world. Portugal was not the most likely candidate to lead Europe into revolutionary change. Economic backwardness and the safety valve of emigration to the colonies, coupled with the solidity of its traditional institutions and the existence of the Inquisition, a well-tried secret police system, seemed to have created conditions that made revolution impossible. Indeed revolution would not have occurred without the catastrophe of the earthquake.

Prior to 1755 Portugal had been dominated economically by the British and intellectually by the institutions of the church – the Inquisition, the Patriarchate and the Jesuits with their control of the education system. The aristocracy was co-opted by being granted a monopoly of high office and by lavish handouts of state wealth which were greatly swollen by the gold and diamonds of Brazil. By 1750 it was believed that the British, the Jesuits and the Inquisition, hardly natural allies given their history, were acting in concert or were at any rate upholding each other's interests. British merchants and the Jesuits in Brazil were thought to be working together to sabotage Carvalho's economic policies. The French writer Pierre Ange Goudar blamed the state of Portugal alike on the Inquisition which had stifled the country's independent economic growth and the British who had been allowed to take economic control – 'The gold mines of Brazil belong entirely to England . . . This country [Portugal] is full of English millionaires'.[9] When his book, *Relation historique du tremblement de terre . . .*, was banned by the Inquisition in October 1756 it was believed that this had been at the instigation of the British.

Gradual change had already been taking place, however, which weakened the structure that the earthquake was finally to overthrow. The scientific and rationalist ideas of the Enlightenment had begun to spread in Portugal, not least among the Inquisitors themselves, while hostility towards New Christians was on the wane and no longer served to hold Portuguese society together. Fashionable salons met to discuss French ideas and increasing numbers of Portuguese went abroad either as exiles from the Inquisition or to seek an education and find employment in France, Britain or Austria. In 1750 most of Portugal's leading intellectuals were, or had been, diplomats or so-called *estrangeirados*. In particular the Austrian influence, channelled through Dom João v's Austrian Queen, Maria Anna, was all the more influential as it was coming from a country with unimpeachable Catholic credentials which was faced by many of the same problems as Portugal.[10] What was also surprising was the number of competent engineers and administrators who Carvalho was able to mobilize and who provided the cadres for the revolution that he intended to carry out. By 1750 there was a growing consensus among educated and forward-looking men that the modernization of Portugal required that the power of the British, the Inquisition and the Society of Jesus should all be radically reduced.

The earthquake produced a spectrum of apocalyptic responses ranging from those who thought repentance and a return to traditional values was the only way to appease an angry God to those who saw the destruction of Lisbon as a wake-up call for fundamental change. The earthquake was clearly a warning but a warning about what? Goudar, two hundred years before Milton Friedman, saw the earthquake as an ideal opportunity to bring about revolutionary change – 'I say that Portugal can derive great advantage from this misfortune.' The political revolution that followed the earthquake did not come from below, from the *povo*, but, like the subsequent revolution in France, was a bid for power by an increasingly confident middle class that had been denied office and influence by the structures of the old order. It was Carvalho who harnessed and directed this revolution and who, unlike his French successors, was not consumed by the forces he unleashed. It was a revolution that was played out in full view of a Europe which, in spite of the Seven Years War, remained fascinated by the unfolding of the events that followed the earthquake.

Since entering the government Carvalho had been pressing for major changes to Portugal's economic policies. He had already created one large monopoly company to handle trade with Maranhão and Para. This company, and a second one which was created for Pernambuco, was designed to exclude the private commercial agents through whom the British had dominated the trade of Brazil. It was also designed to direct investment towards the colonies and was part of a radical plan to develop the Brazilian interior – the *sertão*. As Jorge Borges de Macedo wrote, 'the first phase of Pombal's government marked the triumph of commercial monopolists, the incorporation of large commercial companies and the annihilation of the small-scale free commerce of the *comissários volantes*'.[11] The directors of these companies came to form a commercial elite that operated through the newly created Junta do Comércio and provided capital and a protected market for the Royal Silk Factory that became the flagship of a series of new state-sponsored industrial enterprises. The farming of the royal monopolies like tobacco were also granted to members of this group.

'A new administration has from six to nine months in which to achieve major changes,' wrote Friedman in 1984,[12] and the earthquake provided Carvalho with the opportunity to strike a still greater blow at the economic dominance of the British. In September 1756, while the streets of Lisbon were still being cleared of rubble, he established the Companhia Geral da Agricultura das Vinhas do Alto Douro, which was to oversee the quality and marketing of Portugal's principal vintages. This provided protection for a narrow group of Portuguese vineyard owners who benefited at the expense of the small producers who were often financed by the British. It was designed to prise British fingers off the main artery of the Portuguese economy and, just as the Brazilian Companies protected Portuguese merchants against the small-scale traders who had worked closely with the British, this measure was designed to transfer capital resource into the hands of native Portuguese entrepreneurs. That Carvalho was able to take these measures while maintaining intact the alliance with Britain on which Portugal's security depended is a significant indication of his political skill.

Carvalho, who had been forming policies to promote economic nationalism ever since taking office in 1750, had seized the opportunities presented by the earthquake to promote the interests of a new group of entrepreneurs to whom major state resources were transferred and who were granted what were in effect near monopolies in commerce, agriculture, marketing and industry. This was real disaster capitalism at work.

As the rebuilding of Lisbon got under way, and the process of placing a new technocratic elite in control of the capital began, Carvalho proceeded to initiate what soon turned into a reign of terror against his opponents, the old ruling class made up of the leading aristocratic families and the Society of Jesus. It has never been satisfactorily explained whether this attack was opportunistic and was designed solely to strengthen Carvalho's personal position, or whether it was part of a carefully planned policy to bring about fundamental social change. However, in seizing the opportunity to attack such a formidable alliance,

Carvalho demonstrated a clear sense of direction and purpose. Ever since 1750, when the Treaty of Madrid had transferred large tracts of mission territory in what is today southern Brazil to Portuguese control, the Jesuits had opposed Carvalho's policies and had used their influence at court to try to undermine his position. When the earthquake struck the Jesuits were among the clerics who tried to use the event to strengthen their influence. Carvalho began to see them as the formidable opponents they were and considered that the sermons and pamphlets of the Italian Jesuit Gabriel Malagrida lay at the root of the problem. In the background there was the realization that the Jesuits effectively controlled education in Portugal and had strong commercial and financial ties with the British which could thwart the implementation of Carvalho's bourgeois revolution.

That Carvalho was presented with an opportunity at the same time to destroy the influence of the great noble families of the court and the Jesuits was fortuitous. That he was able to exploit this opportunity was down to his own political skill and his ability to manipulate public opinion. The attempt on the king's life that took place on 3 September 1758 was followed by the arrest of numerous Jesuits and members of the nobility. A special tribunal, a foretaste of the French Comité de Salut Public, was created to try the prisoners and the official defence advocate, Eusébio Tavares de Sequeira, later told the tribunal that rehabilitated the Távora family that he had heard Carvalho dictate the sentence to the judge even before any defence had been offered.[13] In February 1759 the public executions took place which fascinated and horrified Europe and which continue to be described in every history of Portugal. The execution of the members of the Aveiro and Távora families was a secular *auto da fé*, a theatrical event designed to instil terror and cow further opposition. The publicity given to the cruelty of the executions may well have influenced the French revolutionaries to devise their 'humane' beheading machine. Carvalho took care publicly to justify his measures, and pamphlets were published in many European countries by order of the tribunal setting out the evidence for the crime and the verdicts.[14] This propaganda was largely successful and the lasting effect of this show trial can be contrasted with the mishandling of the trial of the 'Gomes Freire' conspirators in 1817 which, instead of strengthening the government, outraged public sentiment and paved the way for the revolution of 1820.

The executions were accompanied by the imprisonment or exile of many members of the leading aristocratic families and by the decision to abolish the Society of Jesus and to nationalize its assets. Guilherme de Oliveira Santos, who made a special study of the Távora trial, concluded that

> the real target of the trial was not the nobility but the Company of Jesus. Because, in the suspicious mind of the dictator, it was the disciples of Saint Ignatius who were the soul of the conspiracy . . . the *fidalgos* being only puppets which they manipulated as they thought fit.[15]

Orders went out to Brazil, India and Africa and during the autumn of 1759 those Jesuits unable to escape were arrested and sent back to Portugal. It seems likely that Carvalho would have conducted another series of show trials and executions but Dom José apparently intervened to prevent this, with the result that the older Jesuits were all imprisoned and the younger ones sent into exile. The Jesuits remained in prison until Carvalho fell from power on the death of Dom José in 1777.[16] By that time most of them had died. Huge amounts of Jesuit property were seized, the moveable property and slaves were auctioned and the lands and fixed assets were transferred to the Crown. The Jesuit Colleges were taken over by the state to form the core of a secular state system of education. This massive secularization of church property was comparable to Henry VIII's dissolution of the monasteries or the confiscations that took place during the French Revolution.

There was, however, to be one more show trial and Carvalho circumvented royal opposition by using the Inquisition. After three years in prison Malagrida was tried by the Holy Office for heresy, garrotted and burnt at an *auto da fé*. This was the last execution carried out by the Inquisition, which was shortly after 'reformed' by Carvalho. Paulo de Carvalho, the minister's brother, was appointed as Inquisitor General and, after the execution of Malagrida, the powers of the Inquisition were dismantled. Censorship was entrusted to a new censorship board, confiscated property was transferred to the treasury and all records of purity of blood investigations were destroyed. As part of his 'bourgeois revolution' Carvalho removed all official distinctions between Old and New Christians, bringing to an end more than two hundred years of persecution. The Holy Office survived but its remit was limited to dealing with minor cases of heresy, magic and freemasonry.

The impact of this Portuguese revolution in the rest of Europe was soon apparent. Carvalho paid a great deal of attention to propaganda and to disseminating his ideas. Just as the French Declaration of the Rights of Man rapidly spread the ideas of the French Revolution throughout Europe, so Carvalho's propaganda against the Jesuits provided the rationale for the action that was taken first by France, then by Spain and finally by the papacy against the Society of Jesus. This action was followed, as in Portugal, by attempts to create secular systems of education. In Portugal the educational revolution was focused on the radical reform of Coimbra University, which was designed to remove clerical influence and introduce a modern curriculum which would reflect national priorities. Kenneth Maxwell considered 'the new curriculum and the provision of the laboratories was exceptionally advanced for the epoch'[17] and Carvalho himself rated his reform of the university among the most important of the changes he introduced. The new curriculum deeply influenced a new generation of educated Portuguese and Brazilians, preparing the way for the radical politics that would transform both countries in the early nineteenth century.

Conclusion

Carvalho's revolution had placed a new class of educated bureaucrats and entrepreneurs in positions of influence throughout Portugal. Their lasting influence can be seen not only in the reconfiguration of Lisbon as a bourgeois commercial city but in such model examples of urban renewal as the building of Villa Real de Santo António in the Algarve. However, the extent to which Portugal was permanently changed by this revolution can be questioned. Like the French revolutionaries in the 1790s, Carvalho attacked the aristocracy and the church but did little else to alter the conservative base of society. The world of the Portuguese peasant, like that of his French counterpart in 1789, changed little as a result of events in the capital, and the transference of land from the church to rural capitalists, who soon aspired to the position of landed nobles, also produced little change. However, the divisions among the educated elite, between reformers wedded to the ideas of the Enlightenment and those who might be called traditionalists, became ever deeper. As Kenneth Maxwell wrote,

> The great conflict between tradition and innovation was, therefore, unresolved and the inherent incompatibilities between parts of Pombal's reform programme became more obvious

The Marquês de Pombal celebrates the rebuilding of Lisbon and the prosperity of Portugal.

once the dominating and integrating presence of the all-powerful minister was gone.[18]

The social fabric of Portugal began to crumble just as the gleaming limestone fabric of Carvalho's new model city was beginning to emerge from behind its scaffolding.

9
Portugal's Moment of Truth: The French and British Struggle for the Control of Lisbon

Portugal after the fall of Pombal

The death of Dom José in 1777 and the fall of Carvalho, by then known by his recently conferred title of Marquês de Pombal, brought about what appeared to be a restoration of the old order. The surviving Jesuits were released from prison, the remnants of the Távora and Aveiro families were reinstated and Pombal's enemies returned from abroad or emerged from their dungeons. William Beckford, the English multimillionaire who resided in Portugal in 1787–8, described in his diary a round of formal receptions in aristocratic residencies, religious processions and celebrations in the numerous religious houses and a life revolving round the politics of the court, on the face of it little different from the world of the early eighteenth century.

This was not the first attempt in Portugal's history to restore a remembered status quo after vigorous but apparently short-lived efforts from the top to modernize Portugal's antique attitudes and institutions. In 1495 Dom Manuel had restored the Braganzas and their associates who had suffered at the hands of Dom João II the fate later suffered by the Távoras. In 1640 the restoration of the independent Portuguese monarchy had taken place in a heightened euphoria of Sebastianist expectations that the old order before the Union of the Crowns would be restored. Now, with the fall of Pombal, the old nobility returned hoping to undo the effects of the earthquake that their order had experienced at the hands of the all-powerful minister. However, just as the earthquake had destroyed the old Lisbon, Carvalho's revolution had shaken to its foundations the fabric of the aristocratic society. According to Beckford, the Conde de São Lourenço emerged from the eighteen years imprisonment he had suffered at the hands of Pombal but contemptuously refused the honorific post of Chamberlain which he was offered and threw the keys of office which were brought to him into the privy.[1] The old order was not so easily resurrected.

As in France in 1815, the restoration took place on the surface only. The Society of Jesus was not restored nor were the reforms to Coimbra University undone. The Inquisition remained emasculated and the New Christians continued to enjoy their freedom from persecution. Most of those appointed by Pombal retained their offices, including some of his relatives, and the Companhia das Vinhas retained its control of the Douro wine industry. Pombal's police service also survived under the control of Diogo Inácio de Pina Manique whose spies became as all-pervasive as the former familiars of the Inquisition. Perhaps most significantly the British merchant community was not able to re-establish its former influence. As the industries fostered by Pombal gradually established themselves the old British dominance of the economy declined. In particular a cotton weaving industry, which took advantage of the supplies of raw cotton from Brazil and which was not covered by the terms of the Methuen Treaty, began to displace British woollens in the Portuguese market. By the late 1770s Britain's trade surplus with Portugal had been drastically reduced and in the following decade even moved into deficit.

Beneath the surface the rationalist, modernizing ideas that Pombal had promoted continued to bubble like yeast and in Brazil erupted in three conspiracies which alarmed the authorities into staging show trials. The republican plot known as the *inconfidência mineira* was investigated at length by the authorities and culminated in 1792 in a 'ceremony of judgment, a veritable drama in three acts'. 'Tiradentes', the man accused of being the ringleader, was sentenced to be publicly hanged but after this sentence had been given, 'the judge proceeded to the podium and produced a previously drafted letter of royal clemency that he had brought with him from Lisbon'.[2] Long experience of the Inquisition had taught the Portuguese authorities the benefits to be derived from a carefully orchestrated show trial which would demonstrate at one and the same time the severity of the law and the paternal clemency of the king.

In spite of these excitements, after the fall of Pombal, Portugal passed off the radar screen of European concern.

Portugal and the French Revolution

The ideological waves that followed the outbreak of the French Revolution, and which were eventually to build into a veritable tsunami that swept over western Europe, at first seemed to pose little threat to Portugal as Pina Manique's police kept a close watch on any possible signs of sedition. In fact the outbreak of revolution among the slaves in the French Caribbean island of Sainte Domingue in 1793 caused almost more concern to the Portuguese, the British and the newly independent United States than the events in France itself. In Portugal, as in Britain, there was a growing conservative reaction which can be measured through the career of Portugal's most distinguished natural scientist, the priest José Correa de Serra, who, having worked closely with the Duke of Lafões to found the Academia Real das Sciencias de Lisboa in 1779, was forced because of his liberal, scientific and supposedly pro-French opinions to go into exile in 1795.[3]

In 1793 Portugal joined with Britain and Spain in the First Coalition against France and an expeditionary force, commanded by the Scottish general Forbes, was sent to the Pyrenees frontier. This early participation in the war brought no military success but provided the opportunity for some young army officers to fraternize with the French and to absorb some of the heady brew of French ideology. When Spain withdrew from the coalition in 1795 and formed an alliance with the Directory government in France, Portugal found itself in a familiar dilemma, facing the possibility of a Franco-Spanish invasion and dependent on Britain for its defence. However, Portugal and its colonies were not to be allowed to remain on the fringes of European power struggles, as had happened in the eighteenth century, and were soon to be thrust rudely onto centre stage as the control of Lisbon became a major strategic objective for the combatants on both sides with Brazil as the ultimate prize.

In 1794 the Academia Real das Sciências had published Bishop José Azeredo Coutinho's *Ensaio Economico sobre o Commercio de Portugal e suas Colonias*,[4] a book which not only drew attention to the wealth of Brazil but discussed in detail Portugal's position in the world. This work was to prove extremely influential, was translated into English and German, and appeared in many editions up to 1828. The bishop took a long and hard look at Portugal's relations with its colonies and advanced many recommendations about the way this relationship might develop to the advantage of both. However, he also speculated about the future of Portugal's dependence on Britain and pointed out the extent to which Britain was in fact dependent on Portugal. Portugal, through its colonial possessions, was in a position to make itself feared and respected by the rest of Europe, not least through its ability to control the sea routes of the Atlantic which passed through the Portuguese-owned archipelagos of Madeira, Azores and Cape Verde. The Portuguese colonies, which had largely been ignored in the maritime wars of the eighteenth century, were now coming into play.

France had lost most of its colonial empire either to Britain during the Seven Years War or through slave revolt, but as the Revolutionary wars unfolded a new struggle for empire began. After 1794 French armies began the conquest of Europe: the Netherlands and the Rhineland, followed by Venice, Northern Italy and Switzerland. In 1798 the French captured Malta and invaded Egypt. By these conquests they were not only recasting Europe's frontiers and institutions but were devising a strategy to challenge British dominance of the world markets. This strategy involved closing the ports of Europe to British goods and securing the control of the colonies and navies of the various European states. The vast Portuguese possessions in Africa and America made the Portuguese empire the largest in the world in terms of land area and in 1807 the naturalized French geographer Conrad Malte Brun in his translation of John Barrow's *Voyage to Indochina* speculated that the Portuguese empire might, under French influence, free itself from British tutelage and become a rival pole of colonial trade.

> Portugal with a population of 5 million, both inside and outside Europe, would certainly have the means not only to challenge English commerce at every point but even to wage a lively and successful war against England so long as the anglophiles in Lisbon do not join with the capuchins in the task of paralysing and leading astray the policy of the cabinet.

And he went on, in typically purple prose:

> With prudence, energy and the support of France and Spain a Portuguese king could easily carry out this grand project which would cover him with immortal glory and which would place him and his successors on a throne which was less precarious and more brilliant than that of Lisbon. In breaking the sceptre of England's maritime supremacy, this new Manuel would even share the honour of halting, in the middle of its destructive course, the torrent of universal revolution whose blood-stained waves already flow through Europe and which will soon roll like a sea of blood and fire from one pole to the other.[5]

The French were well aware that Britain had traditionally acted to defend Portugal's independence and therefore pursued a strategy of putting just enough pressure on Portugal to force it 'voluntarily' to abandon the British alliance and to seek the protection of France. This pressure could best be exerted through Spain, which would be a willing partner since it would see in this strategy a way of re-establishing its hegemony in the Iberian peninsula. This policy appeared to have some success when Portugal abandoned the coalition and through the French ambassador in Lisbon sought French recognition for its neutrality.

Britain meanwhile was faced with the consequences of a decade of military failure. An army too small, and clearly no match for the Franco-Spanish forces, could not be committed to the hopeless defence of mainland Portugal. Sensing that Britain would not come to Portugal's aid, the Spanish invaded in 1801 and captured the frontier town of Olivença, forcing Portugal to sue for peace and to accept humiliating terms. Britain had left Portugal to its fate and, having already secured control of Goa, had contented itself with the military occupation of Madeira.

The origins of the Peninsular War

After the breakdown of the Peace of Amiens in May 1803 Napoleon planned to administer the *coup de grâce* to Britain by a direct invasion across the Channel. However, unable to establish command of the sea, he was forced in the summer of 1805 to abandon this plan and turned his attention instead to the conquest of central Europe. Between December 1805 and February 1807 his forces entered Vienna, Berlin and Warsaw and forced the Austrians, Prussians and Russians to accept terms. The new Europe that emerged at the Treaty of Tilsit that was signed in July 1807 brought France, Netherlands, Italy and Germany together into what can best be described as the first European Union. Napoleon now controlled most of the European coastline from the Adriatic to the Baltic and had the capacity to rebuild his navy and to operate an effective embargo on British goods. However, for this policy to be successful he needed to bring the Iberian peninsula into his system. Ever since the renewal of the war he believed he could exert sufficient diplomatic pressure on Portugal and Spain to achieve his aims without the direct use of force. Through the influence of his ambassadors in Lisbon and Madrid the Iberian kingdoms could be drawn into Napoleon's empire. Spain could be manipulated through the venal first minister Godoy and Portugal, it was believed, could be bullied and blackmailed into compliance. General Junot was the ambassador appointed to bring Portugal into line.

Once the Treaty of Tilsit was signed Iberian affairs moved higher up Napoleon's agenda. Like Philip II before him, Napoleon had his eyes on Portugal's fleet and on the port of Lisbon, the great natural harbour which the British used as the base for their operations in the Mediterranean and the Atlantic and which was one of the major ports of entry for British commerce into Europe. Beyond Lisbon lay the Atlantic Islands and the vast riches of Brazil. If France could acquire Portugal it might, at a stroke, seize the initiative in Atlantic politics from Britain.

Faced by the evident threat posed by Napoleon's Grande Armée, now released from any wars in central Europe, Britain and Portugal had few options. Britain had already sent a military mission to Portugal that had concluded that the country could not be defended. The only other option was one which had already proved successful in the case of Naples and Sicily and which had been considered many times in Lisbon – that of transferring the capital of the Portuguese empire, along with the royal family and the government, to Brazil. Although French armies might occupy Portugal, the Portuguese monarchy itself would be out of French reach and would no longer be exposed to the sort of pressure that eventually forced the Spanish royal family, taken captive to France, to abdicate its throne.

However, the Portuguese prince regent, Dom João, continued to believe that he could survive by remaining neutral. Apart from the unfortunate war with Spain in 1801, neutrality was a policy that had succeeded ever since Portugal had withdrawn from the coalition against France, so Dom João sought to appease the French by repeatedly declaring that he would close his ports to Britain while secretly telling the British that he was only acting out of *force majeure* and would turn a blind eye to infringements. In 1807 French demands became more explicit and more forceful. The British were to be expelled from Portugal and their property confiscated. The British for their part made it clear that if such an embargo were enforced they would proceed to occupy the Portuguese island of Madeira and possibly other colonies. Then, alarmed at the arrival of a Russian fleet in the Tagus at the end of October (a particularly ominous development since by the terms of the Treaty of Tilsit Russia had become France's ally), they also threatened to impose a blockade on Lisbon. It was a dangerous game of bluff, but Dom João apparently believed until the last minute that he would succeed.

By the late summer of 1807 the affairs of Portugal had become the principal preoccupation of policy-makers in both London and Paris. There were both short- and long-term issues to consider. In the short term France wanted to acquire the warships and dockyards of Portugal and Denmark, which would not exactly achieve parity of naval strength with Britain but would give a realistic opportunity of challenging Britain's naval supremacy in the not too distant future. Britain countered this by a unilateral attack on Copenhagen in August and September 1807 and by intensifying the pressure on Portugal to remove its fleet to a place of safety. However, both France and Britain were developing longer-term strategies. For Napoleon it was increasingly important to close the Iberian ports to British goods and by the summer of 1807 he was convinced that this could only be achieved by putting an end to Portugal's independence. If this could be done by making use of the Spanish, so much the better. If not, then a French army could be sent to do the job. An army under France's former ambassador in Lisbon, General Junot, began to assemble on the Spanish frontier.

Britain rethinks its colonial policy

Britain's long-term strategy was as yet unclear but the events in Portugal were to clarify the issues and usher in a new phase not only of the war but of British imperial history. Early in 1806, still flushed with the naval victory at Trafalgar, an expedition had been sent under Sir David Baird to occupy the Cape of Good Hope. This was easily accomplished and the commodore in charge of the ships, Sir Home Popham, decided on his own initiative to cross the Atlantic and seize control of Buenos Aires and Montevideo at the mouth of the Río de la Plata. This was clearly intended to be a repeat of the easy success that had been achieved at the Cape and was very much in the tradition of the eighteenth-century colonial wars. Britain would annex the conquered territory, which in this case included the whole viceroyalty of La Plata and the Potosí silver mines.

At first the attack was a brilliant success. General William Carr Beresford captured Buenos Aires with hardly a shot being fired and opened the Río de la Plata to British commerce. When the news reached Britain the scandalous fact that the expedition had not been authorized was forgotten in an explosion of patriotic sentiment. This was a blow against the Franco-Spanish combination as massive as that of

Trafalgar and would go a long way towards replacing the markets in Europe which Napoleon had closed. Reinforcements were sent at once under Sir Samuel Auchmuty, Robert Craufurd and John Whitelocke. However, the attempt to conquer the viceroyalty of La Plata rapidly became a quagmire. Beresford and Popham had defeated the Spanish forces but had reckoned without the local patriotic uprising which soon engulfed Beresford's tiny force. Beresford had surrendered by the time Sir Samuel Auchmuty arrived and, although Montevideo was taken by storm, John Whitelocke, who arrived with further reinforcements, was defeated in his attack on Buenos Aires.

Whitelocke was not only forced to surrender but, very wisely, agreed to the total withdrawal of all British forces from the Río de la Plata, which was completed by September 1807. This fiasco for British arms was taking place while Napoleon was completing his conquest of Poland and was forcing Russia to sue for peace. The contrast in the military fortunes of France and Britain could not have been greater.

The surrender of two British generals to colonial forces within the space of nine months was unpleasantly reminiscent of the American War of Independence and prompted the sort of rethink of policy that should have taken place in 1783. However, while Lord Castlereagh, the new Secretary at War, was pondering the lessons of Buenos Aires, events reached crisis proportions in Lisbon. General Junot's army had crossed into Spain in October and proceeded by forced marches to the Portuguese frontier while Spanish troops also mobilized for the long-awaited opportunity to reverse the verdict of 1640. Now thoroughly alarmed, Dom João at last gave the orders to prepare to leave for Brazil while the British fleet under Admiral Sir Sydney Smith hovered beyond the Tagus bar, offering support if the Prince Regent was prepared to leave but threatening Lisbon with the fate of Copenhagen if he did not. The man who could have played a decisive part, the Russian admiral Dmitry Senyavin, sat silently aboard his flagship watching the scene that was unfolding, and did nothing. 'Siniavin', Madame Junot later wrote, 'belonged to a barbarous race,' and she added in her incomparable manner, 'his father was probably one of the number of those who preferred losing their heads to surrendering their beards.'[6]

Amid scenes of considerable chaos the royal family and government crowded aboard nine warships and were followed by fifteen thousand people who crammed themselves into every corner of the vessels, which were ill-prepared to receive them. Adverse winds held up the departure but eventually the ships cleared the Tagus on 29 November just as Junot's advance guard entered Lisbon. The departure of the mad queen, the Prince Regent and the court left Portugal undefended, to be partitioned according to a previously signed agreement between the Spanish and the French. For the first time in its history Lisbon was in French hands and the ports of Portugal were closed to the British. Napoleon, it seemed, had triumphed.

The British meanwhile could also look on these events as a success, for the Portuguese government and the Portuguese colonies were now wholly dependent on Britain. As the fleet proceeded on its two-month voyage to Brazil, Dom João signed the first of two treaties opening the trade of Brazil to the British. Such agreements had been made before but had never been implemented. This one would be different. There was to be no attempt by the British to annex Brazil, as they had attempted to annex the Spanish viceroyalty of La Plata; instead Britain would establish an informal hegemony, becoming the patron and pro-tector of a new kingdom in the Americas. Nevertheless, while the situation remained fluid, the old Adam of colonial annexation raised his head and Britain sent General Beresford to annex Madeira to the British Crown – though in the event the island was handed back to Por-tugal after only three months.

Events had pushed Britain to adopt a new policy towards the South Atlantic. Already in May 1807 Lord Castlereagh had written a memo-randum for the Cabinet on British policy in South America drawing lessons from the failed attack on Buenos Aires and sketching out a future line of policy which would 'relieve us of the hopeless task of con-quering this extensive country, against the temper of its population'. The British, he argued, 'in looking to any scheme for liberating South America . . . should not present ourselves in any other light than as aux-iliaries and protectors'.[7] Whereas as recently as 1806 Britain had been prepared to annex the viceroyalty of La Plata, now it was proposing to assume a role as patron and sponsor of new states breaking free from European colonial rule. In 1810 revolution broke out in the Río de la Plata and, Britain's recent attempts at conquest forgotten, the British were welcomed as allies of the new Creole governments. 1810 also saw a new commercial treaty of defence between Britain and Portugal which replaced the former agreements and confirmed Britain's privi-leged status *vis-à-vis* the Braganza monarchy.

The struggle for Lisbon

Napoleon's plan had been to partition Portugal between himself and
Spain but the retreat of the Portuguese royal family to Rio de Janeiro
meant that, in effect, the Portuguese monarchy would be partitioned
between France and Britain – France had obtained the prize of Lisbon
while Britain had rescued the Portuguese fleet and had secured a privileged position in Brazil and the Atlantic. With the departure of Dom
João to Rio, General Junot ruled as a quasi-monarch in Lisbon. The
Portuguese army was disbanded and a Portuguese Legion, reformed
under a pro-French officer corps and led by Gomes Freire de Andrade
and the Marquês de Alorna, was dispatched to join the Grande Armée
in Germany. According to Madame Junot, Napoleon considered that
Portugal's government was now 'organised in a way which has never
been known in that country since the days of Pombal'.[8] Lisbon meanwhile was plundered. While important reports, maps and archives were
sent to Paris, the churches and palaces were ransacked for their valu-
ables in a more traditional military manner.

The French were not without supporters in Lisbon and a memo-
randum was even received from a group of enthusiastic supporters of
the French asking for a constitution. Junot, however, did little to cultivate a pro-French party and Portugal was placed under martial law.
Napoleon meanwhile had secured the abdication of the Spanish royal
family and had sent his brother Joseph to become king of Spain. In May
1808 revolt broke out in Spain against the occupying French army and
quickly spread to Portugal where the centre of the uprising was Porto,
already emerging as a rival to Lisbon not only economically but also as
a centre of political activism. Junot found himself unexpectedly isolated in Lisbon, his communications with France almost completely
cut by the insurrections. For some months his position remained relatively secure until, unexpectedly, a small British expeditionary force was
landed just north of Lisbon to co-operate with the northern insurgents.
Defeated at the battle of Vimeiro outside Lisbon, Junot outwitted the
British negotiators and in the Convention of Sintra obtained terms
which allowed his army to be evacuated in British ships taking with
them a large part of their plunder.

There followed three years of constant warfare in which rival British
and French armies fought to control northern Portugal with the port of
Lisbon as the main prize. Apart from a lightning campaign conducted by
Napoleon himself in Spain in 1808, this war never greatly concerned the

emperor, who was more irritated than alarmed by the continued British presence in Portugal and who was never prepared to devote adequate resources to driving the British out. However, the war that broke out in the summer of 1808 and which continued until the last French soldier left Portugal three years later meant that northern Portugal became the battlefield that was contested for the longest continuous period during the whole of the Napoleonic Wars.

The Peninsular War

The war fought in the Iberian peninsula between 1808 and 1814 occupies a peculiar place among the remembered episodes of British history. It is an often retold story of victories won on the battlefield by the uncanny skill of the Duke of Wellington and the bravery of the British soldiers. It occupies the same kind of place in the historic consciousness as the North African campaign during the Second World War and it was of comparable importance, or unimportance. British resources, carefully husbanded and committed to a minor theatre of war, eventually triumphed over an enemy most of whose strength was committed to the real struggle in Russia where the outcome of the war would actually be decided.

The narrative of this war is very well known. British forces won an important victory over Junot's army in August 1808 outside Lisbon and in the Convention of Sintra (August 1808) agreed to its evacuation. The British then occupied Lisbon but, rather than await Napoleon's attack, advanced into Spain, being forced to retreat through the snow to be evacuated from Corunna, where another victory was won over the French in January 1809, though the British commander Sir John Moore, was killed. The French then reoccupied the north of Portugal, basing themselves in Porto. Sir Arthur Wellesley took up the command a second time, drove the French from Porto and advanced into Spain where he won the battle of Talavera (28 July 1809) before retiring into Portugal for the winter. In 1810 the French mounted their third and biggest assault on Portugal, advancing on Lisbon from the north. Wellesley confronted them at Bussaco, won another victory and then retired behind the defensive lines of Torres Vedras, which the French blockaded during the winter of 1810–11 – in vain, as Lisbon was kept supplied by sea. During 1811 the British and French armies manoeuvred on the frontier of Portugal but two more battles were won at Albuera and Fuentes d'Oñoro. Between January and April 1812 the British captured the two frontier fortresses of Ciudad Rodrigo and Badajoz and inflicted another defeat on the French at Salamanca (22 July 1812). Wellesley (now Wellington) wintered his army once again in Portugal.

During 1813 the French military control of Europe began to crumble. Joseph Bonaparte evacuated Madrid and Wellington routed his army at the battle of Vittoria on 21 June 1813. The final phase of the war lasted until 1814, during which the French retreated from Spain and Wellington mounted an invasion of southern France. More battles were fought, all of them British victories.

Ever since the publication of Napier's *History of the War in the Peninsula* (which began to appear in 1828), this outline narrative has been carefully retold to burnish the reputation of Wellington and to enshrine an image of the British army forever facing overwhelming odds and winning heroic victories. However, there are aspects of the Peninsular War that are seldom given the prominence they deserve.

First, the war showed how limited Britain's ability to influence events on the continent really was. Although after the military fiascos in Buenos Aires (1807) and Walcheren (1809), Britain's military resources were concentrated in Portugal, this was not a tale of unalloyed military success. Sir John Moore's march into Spain, courageously presented by most historians as a daring blow at Napoleon's lines of communication, turned into a major military disaster which destroyed Moore's army, left Lisbon dangerously exposed and Portugal defenceless against a French invasion. The French failure to take advantage of the rout of the British army and to reoccupy Lisbon was a major strategic mistake. Although Wellington's brilliant campaign in northern Portugal in 1809 saved the situation in the short term, his invasion of Spain later that summer came close to losing another British army as he was forced to retreat precipitately from Talavera leaving behind his wounded and his artillery. By early 1810 Britain had little to show for its intervention in the peninsula while Napoleon had once more crushed armed opposition in Central Europe and had imposed the *pax napoleonica* from the Niemen to the Straits of Messina.

Meanwhile Britain's relations with its Portuguese ally were becoming increasingly difficult. The Regency Council, described in a French history of Portugal published in 1821 as a 'vain ghost of a government, a servile instrument of the despotism of the English generals',[9] increasingly resented the occupation of Portugal by the British army and wanted Wellington to post his forces on the frontier to defend Portugal against a further French invasion. Wellington, as is well known, did not believe the frontier could be defended and wanted instead to fortify

Lisbon against a possible full-scale assault by the French. As it became clear in 1810 that a large French army was assembling for the invasion of Portugal, Wellington insisted on a scorched earth policy of removing the population from the French line of advance and destroying food supplies and livestock. This almost led to a breakdown of relations with the Regency and Wellington only got his way because the Secretary to the Regents, Miguel Pereira Forjaz, who was also Minister of War, gave Wellington his full support. While the frontier fortresses were neglected, and fell to the French in August 1810, the lines of Torres Vedras were constructed to protect the capital from attack.

The second issue concerns manpower. Throughout the eighteenth century, and during the long-drawn-out conflict with France that began in 1793, Britain had suffered from a serious shortage of manpower. This had traditionally been made up by recruiting German or Swiss mercenaries or by employing Indian sepoys for the wars in the East. Government policy towards the Irish and Scottish, notably the creation of the Highland regiments after the 1745–6 rebellion, was also specifically designed to boost the strength of the armed forces. However, shortage of manpower continued to undermine the success of any British intervention on the continent, including the campaigns in the peninsula. In the end, Britain's manpower problem was solved by the Portuguese, who took effective measures to rebuild their armed forces and place these at Wellington's disposal – though in the eyes of the French 'it was no longer the Portuguese nation who took action and fought for their independence and the honour of their country, they were mercenaries in the pay of England.'[10]

Beresford and the Portuguese army[11]

During the Napoleonic Wars Portugal built up an army which acquired a European-wide reputation and, for the first time since the fourteenth century, gave Portugal some leverage in international affairs. The army also came to play a key role in Portugal's own political development. Throughout the first half of the nineteenth century Portugal experienced occupation by the British and French armies, the removal of the government to Rio followed by an attempt to occupy the Banda Oriental of the Río de la Plata, the loss of Brazil, revolutions and counter-revolutions, two full-scale civil wars and innumerable conspiracies, *coup d'états* and *pronunciamientos*. During these years the army provided many of the political leaders, including the Dukes of Saldanha and Terceira, the

Marquês de Sá da Bandeira and, across the Atlantic, Carlos Lecor and João Bonifacio. As this army played a more and more active role in Portuguese politics, it became the principal arbiter of the political direction in which the country was moving.

The emergence of the Portuguese army as an institution of national, and even European, importance, rivalling the church and the great noble families as the school of political leadership, was a consequence of the war against the French. In the seventeenth and eighteenth centuries the Portuguese army had been kept at a distance from the political centre. This was achieved by routinely appointing foreigners as commanders of the army, men not linked to domestic factions and easily dismissed. The roll call of foreign commanders included Count Schomburg, whose victories against Spain in the 1660s assured Portugal's independence, and Count Schaumburg-Lippe, who reformed the army in the 1760s, introduced a new military code and was instrumental in promoting Freemasonry in the garrison towns of Portugal.[12]

The Portuguese army of the late eighteenth century was organized largely for defensive purposes. Regiments of the regular army were raised and stationed in the provinces, and were officered by men of *fidalgo* status who traditionally resided away from the barracks. The army was small by European standards but was supplemented by militia regiments (known as the *Segunda Linha*) recruited by lot and commanded by a largely amateur officer corps of local gentry. There was also the *Ordenança*, a village guard that could be turned out in case of invasion. This was an army that did not expect to have to fight abroad, for the colonies had their own locally recruited militias, which were supplemented from time to time by military convicts sent from Portugal. Although a group of young officers, among them Gomes Freire de Andrade and the Marquês de Alorna, had used their experience of fighting the French in 1793 to carry through reforms, the army did not perform well when it had to face the Spanish invasion of 1801.

In 1808, after the uprising against the French, the Portuguese authorities in Porto had begun to organize a new army making use of the *ordenança* and militia units. These had been placed under the command of General Bernadim Freire. An English officer, Robert Wilson, had also been engaged to raise a force which became known as the Loyal Lusitanian Legion. Early in 1809 the prince regent, safely ensconced in Rio, ordered the Regency Council to recruit and train a new regular army to replace the regiments that had been disbanded by Junot or sent to join the Grande Armée.

The prince regent wanted Britain to appoint Sir Arthur Wellesley to train the new Portuguese army but he declined the appointment and another general had to be found junior enough to be willing to serve in Portugal under Wellesley's command. The choice eventually fell on Major-General William Carr Beresford, who the previous year had acted as commandant of Lisbon.[13] Beresford owed his appointment in part to his experience of having led the force that occupied Madeira in 1807–8 and in part to the fact that he was already serving in Portugal and had knowledge of the complexity of Portuguese affairs. He was also a friend of Wellesley and, like Castlereagh and Wellesley himself, came from the narrow group of aristocratic families which formed the Anglo-Irish Protestant ascendancy.

In February 1809 Beresford received his appointment as commander of the Portuguese army and, although only a major-general in the British army, was immediately promoted to the rank of Marshal so that he would have seniority over all the Portuguese generals. In the past the Portuguese armed forces had suffered from divided command, the office of Marshal General often being held by someone other than the active commander of the army in the field. So Beresford was, from the start, determined that he alone would make decisions concerning the army. This was to become an obsession which eventually brought about confrontation with the Portuguese Regents.

On his arrival in Portugal he set immediately to work. 'The chaos and confusion in which I found everything here is not to be described,' he wrote to his half-sister Anne,

> nor could I myself . . . have believed that human ingenuity could have so perfectly confounded everything. Light is however beginning to appear and I hope we shall have shortly the pleasure of sending presents to England of at least a Marshal and Duke de l'Empire with a garnish of a few generals de plus.[14]

By May of 1809 he was able to put 19,000 men into the field to support Wellesley's campaign in the north of Portugal. Beresford himself commanded a corps of 6,000 men who were sent to turn Soult's left flank, pursuing the retreating French and beginning the encirclement of their main force.

After the recapture of Porto and the expulsion of Soult, Beresford resumed the task of training the Portuguese army and began to revise the general regulations. Rather than simply recreate the old army, his plan was to build a new army modelled on the British military system, a decision which was given some urgency by the fact that Portugal did not have the resources to arm, clothe or supply an army and depended on subsidies and shipments of clothing and arms from Britain. During the five years that followed his appointment, Beresford raised the army's manpower to 60,000, more than double its pre-war numbers. He did not, of course, work in a vacuum and was materially helped by the Secretary to the Regency, Miguel Pereira Forjaz, the man who was later to become his principal political opponent.

Beresford's plan was to recruit volunteer officers from the British army to work alongside their Portuguese counterparts, and eventually to brigade Portuguese regiments with British ones on campaign.[15] When Andrew Halliday published his account of Beresford's reforms in 1811, there were 213 British officers in Portuguese service.[16] The army was to be drilled to the British system of bugle calls and commands and provided with British arms and uniforms. At first the two armies had separate commissariat arrangements but this left the Portuguese short of everything as the Regency government did not pay as well or as promptly as the British. So, once the fighting had moved into Spain, a joint commissariat department was established.

To accompany these changes, the officer corps was made increasingly professional. According to Halliday, 'the old and unfit officers were either dismissed from the service, or put upon the reformed list, and young men of merit actively promoted'.[17] Beresford reserved the right to decide on promotions and made it clear that they would go to professionally competent officers, not to men of high social rank, as had happened so often in the past and still happened in the British army. The creation of a professional officer corps, as it turned out, was halfway to creating a new political elite.

Beresford also totally revised military discipline and made changes to the system of court martials. Although he himself acquired a reputation as a strict disciplinarian, he was, according to Halliday, determined to change the system he found in place.

> Marshal Beresford, early convinced of the horrid nature of this punishment [the *pancada* – beating administered with the flat of the sword], ordered a small cane to be used instead of the sword, which, though still keeping up the national method of punishing, deprived it of its fatal consequences. When his Excellency took the command of the army, the officers and

non-commissioned officers were in the habit of kicking and buffeting the poor soldiers on every occasion, and I believe, long custom had made striking the soldier lawful; he however set his face decidedly against this most abominable practice.[18]

A draft, said to have been of 50,000 men, had been called up in the summer of 1809 – not all of them volunteers, for John Aitchison, serving with the third regiment of Guards, recorded in a letter having seen them 'marched under an escort of regulars chained to one another like French conscripts'.[19] Halliday also makes it clear that the old methods of recruitment were still employed.

> The King ordains that the First Regiment of the Line shall consist of 2000 men. The Colonel finds upon examining his returns that 700 men are wanted to complete that number; he states this to the General of the province, who immediately issues an order to the Captain-Major of the district from which the First Regiment is recruited to send 700 young men to that corps; the Captain-Major, or his Deputy, passes a review of the district, picks out 700 young men, sends them to prison for a few days, *To tame them*, and as soon as the whole are collected, marches them off under an escort of his Ordenanza troops to the head-quarters of the First Regiment.

Peniche was used as a recruiting depot,

> but it is to be regretted that a healthier place could not be procured with the other advantages of the Island of Peniche, as certainly a great number of the unfortunate recruits have fallen a prey to the epidemic of that swampy spot, which no doubt acted with double effect upon the depressed, half starved, and ill treated peasants sent as recruits to this depot.

The Regents wanted the Portuguese army to concentrate on the defence of Portugal and Portuguese units did not accompany Wellesley in the summer of 1809 on his Talavera campaign which so nearly ended in disaster. When Masséna's army, usually estimated to have numbered about 80,000 men, invaded Portugal in the late summer of 1810 the Portuguese were ready to take the field against him. On 27 September the two armies faced each other on the ridge of Bussaco

near Coimbra. Masséna, who could easily have outflanked the position, made the mistake of trying to storm the heights and rout the
inexperienced Portuguese. He suffered a humiliating reverse as the
Portuguese regiments drove off the French attack. Bussaco was an
unnecessary battle which did nothing to prevent Masséna's march on
Lisbon and in no way affected the outcome of the campaign or the
war. However, it was an important victory for the morale of the new
Portuguese army, which now had the confidence to play a major part
in the conflict.

The numbers of the Portuguese army grew steadily, matching the
slow growth in the size of the British forces and in effect doubling the
manpower at Wellington's disposal. At the end of December 1810 Beresford was appointed by Wellington to command the forces watching the
advance of Soult south of the Tagus, to prevent any move he might
make to link up with Masséna. With the retreat of Masséna in March
1811 the war moved to the frontier and Beresford, in command of an
Anglo-Portuguese army, drove the French out of Campo Mayor on 25
March and forced them to retreat on Badajoz.

After the victory at Campo Mayor, Beresford opened the siege of
Badajoz. To prevent Soult, who was based in Seville, relieving the
fortress and possibly invading southern Portugal, Wellington, who had
strategic oversight of the operations, had decided that Beresford should
block Soult's advance at the village of Albuera. It was there on 16 May
that the bloodiest battle of the whole war was fought. Beresford had a
difficult task since his senior British officers caused him problems and
he had to dismiss the commander of his cavalry on the eve of the battle. It is also clear that during the battle Beresford issued orders to
protect the retreat of his army should it become necessary – a precau-
tion that would later be held against him in the pamphlet warfare that
refought the battle in the 1830s.[20]

The following year Beresford once again commanded the Portuguese forces during the advance on Madrid and at the battle of
Salamanca where he was badly wounded, retreating to Portugal with
the allied army to recuperate during the winter of 1812. Fully recovered
from his wounds at Salamanca, Beresford led the Portuguese forces at
Vittoria and in the invasion of France. He commanded the allied army
that occupied Bordeaux in March 1814 and with his Portuguese troops
played a decisive part in the battle of Toulouse in April. After the surrender of Napoleon, Beresford, who had been elected member of
parliament for the family seat of Waterford in 1812, returned to Britain

while Carlos Lecor, who had risen to be Beresford's second-in-command, returned with the army to Lisbon.

Whether Beresford was a general of the first rank has always been doubted. One of the Portuguese Regents, Ricardo Nogueira, was later to write in his unpublished memoirs,

> he is a brave soldier and a great officer for disciplining the army. Portugal owes him a great deal in this respect and his ability in getting the military laws observed brought our troops to a state of perfection that in a short space of time placed them on a par with the best in Europe. A lot of this was due to his inflexibility of character and to his being a foreigner . . . However, these good qualities of the Marshal were counterbalanced by great defects. He is extremely ambitious for power, obstinate and imprudent.[21]

Wellington trusted Beresford and this trust is a striking feature of their successful collaboration. They were portrayed in contemporary prints as the twin upholders of Portuguese independence and the Portuguese monarchy. One of the most remarkable testimonies to this trust occurred just before Waterloo. As Wellington was assembling the allied forces, he became concerned with what would happen should he be killed in action. It was reported to Earl Bathurst that

> the arrangement [he] . . . would like of all others is the transport here of 15,000 Portuguese infantry under Lord Beresford, whose rank of Marshal on the Continent would supersede that of General which the Prince [of Orange] holds in the Dutch service.[22]

Beresford, it seems, would outrank all the other allied generals and would take over the command.

After the surrender of Napoleon, it was expected that the Prince Regent would return to Portugal and Beresford's brother, Admiral Sir John Beresford, was even sent to Rio to escort him back, while none other than the former Foreign Secretary, George Canning, went as British ambassador to Lisbon to receive him. Meanwhile Napoleon escaped from Elba and seized power in Paris in March 1815. An allied army began to assemble in the Netherlands under Wellington and it was expected that Portugal would send a contingent. Transports were dispatched and Beresford went to Portugal to prepare an expeditionary

Beresford and Wellington support the crowns of Portugal and Spain.

force. The Regents, however, refused to authorize the army's departure without explicit orders from Rio which had not arrived by the time the battle of Waterloo was fought. Beresford was furious and mortified. He contemplated resignation but decided instead to go in person to put his case to Dom João. As he explained in a letter to Castlereagh, 'it is better at once to go to the fountain head to try if the stream will be clearer there', and to Wellington, 'the Governors do not . . . like my going to the Rio, and will not, they tell me, sanction it, still less give me any conveyance: but I can stand the business here no longer; and I wish to bring the whole question to a decision one way or other.'[23]

Beresford, the Regency and Dom João VI

By the time that the battle of Waterloo was fought it had become clear that Dom João was not going to return to Portugal, indeed in that year he issued the decrees that turned Brazil into a kingdom in its own right, with institutions that would make it effectively independent of Portugal. Explanations for Dom João's reluctance to return to Portugal have ranged from his inertia, to the horrific memories of the last-minute flight from Lisbon in November 1807 and his ill health. More significant was his realization that the wealth of the monarchy lay in Brazil rather than war-torn Portugal. He feared, with some justification, that if he left Rio Brazil would be lost to the Braganza monarchy. This last consideration, never given adequate weight by Britain, was nevertheless clear to a casual observer like the British naval officer James Prior who wrote in 1813, 'there is no question among those who best know the country, that, but for the timely arrival of the government, Brazil would have followed, if not preceded, the efforts of the Spanish colonies for independence.'[24]

Dom João also planned to take advantage of the revolt in Spain's colonies in the Río de la Plata to annex the Banda Oriental to Brazil. Portugal was now at peace but possessed a large and efficient veteran army. In May 1815 5,000 men were sent to Rio under Carlos Lecor and on their arrival the soldiers, called by the locals Talaverans even though none of them had fought at Talavera, were marched south to occupy the Banda Oriental. In these circumstances Beresford began to appear less the general of an occupying army and more an instrument for realizing the Prince Regent's ambitions.

Dom João also needed a strong man to provide a counterweight to the activities of the Regents. Indeed his continued control of Portugal now depended on the known hostility between the Marshal and the Regency Council. Beresford reached Rio shortly after Lecor and in November formally conducted a review of the army in Rio. He remained over a year in Brazil and acted as one of the pall-bearers at the funeral of Queen Maria in March 1816. He eventually returned to Portugal in September 1816 when he penned a rare appreciation of the new king to Wellington.

> He is extremely shrewd not a little bordering on cunning. He prides himself upon open dealing & sincerity, somewhat more than he practices it. He is very inquisitive upon all topics & reads every paper that comes to His ministers, indeed he always reads

the dispatches of all kinds before they get them. His judgment is far from being bad, indeed I think it excellent on all subjects, but he never abides by it, from timidity &a total want of resolution. He can not hold out in any instance against perseverance and then he is much more governed than he used to be by the interests & love of intrigues of His court & it is unfortunately too easy to get hold of him, as he is most susceptible to flattery & in particular to personal homage. He has many weaknesses but few if any personal vices. He is kind and good hearted & of a most forgiving disposition as he certainly bears little malice. He is most desirous of popularity and of being beloved by His people but I fear he loses their respect by His very kindness.[25]

While in Rio Beresford was assiduous in attending the court, which he found bizarre and frustrating.

It is the most motley & threadbare concern you can imagine as everyone goes without discrimination, all colours & all characters. In short the Sal d'audience is a mixture as extraordinary & shows as much equality as the antichamber of Robertspierre [sic] could have produced. There is the Duke and the beggar, the general & the soldiers all pressed [?] together. It is a strange kind of monarchical republicanism.[26]

His court attendance paid off and he established himself as one of Dom João's confidential advisers. He was promoted to the rank of Marshal General of all the armies in Portugal and Brazil and obtained from Dom João the necessary orders for the introduction of new army regulations and permission for a recruitment drive to fill the gaps in the ranks of the regiments. For the next four years he was to remain the dominant influence in Portuguese affairs and in 1817 was able to pose as the saviour of the monarchy when he uncovered the so-called 'Gomes Freire' conspiracy.[27] Three years later however, he became one of the first casualties of the 1820 revolution and was dismissed from his post as commander-in-chief.

Conclusion

The Napoleonic Wars officially ended in 1815 and Europe assumed its post-war shape in the Vienna settlement. Portugal had fought on the winning side and had contributed significantly to the defeat of the French. For the first time since the Hundred Years War it had an army which was respected in Europe and was strong enough to give it some sense of security. In other respects, however, the country emerged in a weak and divided state. Portugal paid the price for its non-participation in the Waterloo campaign, when the return of Olivença, which had been agreed in the peace preliminaries in 1814, was never implemented. Doubts were also raised whether Britain would in future continue to guarantee Portugal's independence should it be attacked by Spain.

The war had caused widespread destruction, and industry and agriculture had been severely damaged. The commercial treaty Britain had signed with Portugal in 1808 had effectively ended the old colonial system from which Portugal had derived so much of its wealth. In 1815 Brazil had been recognized as a kingdom and was well on the way to independence. Although Portuguese business interests continued for some decades to maintain a powerful position in the Brazilian economy, the end of the colonial trade monopoly proved a catastrophe for Portugal's public finances. As Portugal's great reforming minister, José Mousinho da Silveira, poetically phrased it:

> The old regime and the old laws died in Portugal when Brazil became free; and Brazil became free not when it was legally separated [from Portugal] but when its doors were opened to all flags, and Portuguese commerce came to an end, with memories of the 'plenty of Egypt'[28] which they still retained because the manna of [British] loans had prevented the development of the inevitable alternative, to work or to die.[29]

In 1815 Portugal was not only impoverished by the war, by the decline of trade with Brazil and by the absence of the Court, but it had not even got rid of the British occupation. A British army had been in permanent occupation of Lisbon since 1808 and the continued presence of Beresford and his officers in Portugal's army, and the fact that the Marshal was able to act independently of the Regency, convinced the Portuguese that in effect the British occupation was continuing. Beresford became the most hated figure in the history of Anglo-Portuguese relations, which remained tainted by 'his hateful memory, as the fiercest cannibal ever to cross our coastline'.[30]

Portuguese society remained deeply divided. The return of the soldiers who had fought in Napoleon's army, combined with the rise of

Freemasonry and the thwarted aspirations of the bourgeoisie, called into existence by Pombal's reforms, created a revolutionary mixture that would become increasingly explosive. Nor was the Anglo-French rivalry in Portugal and Spain brought to an end by the peace. While France was paying reparations to the allies, it played little part in Iberian affairs but when the expulsion of Beresford from Portugal in 1820 seemed to put an end to the British presence, the way was open for the French to reassert their influence. In 1823 a French army once again invaded Spain and found itself encamped on the borders of Portugal. Although this time it did not challenge Britain by mounting an invasion, it supported a strong diplomatic challenge to Britain's position. For the next ten years France and Britain struggled with each other for primacy in Lisbon while the Portuguese lost their Brazilian empire and slipped towards civil war.

For Portugal 1815 saw not the end of the revolutionary era but its beginning.

10

Portugal among the Great Powers: The Scramble for Africa

Portugal and the expanding global economy

Civil conflict in Portugal had lasted almost unbroken from 1820 to 1851 when the final *coup d'état* of the Duke of Saldanha brought the Portuguese civil wars to an exhausted halt, and the country settled down under a constitutional monarchy based on the much contested charter which Dom Pedro had originally bestowed on the country in 1827. Portugal was showing all the effects of nearly fifty years of war and social conflict. Although Lisbon, and to lesser extent Porto, remained cosmopolitan cities, the strategic and commercial position of the capital allowing it to indulge in the follies and luxuries of nineteenth century bourgeois culture, outside the cities there was little to ameliorate the poverty and backwardness of the countryside.

Portugal struggled to adjust its economy to the new industrial Europe but with the investment of British capital achieved a limited expansion in textile manufacture and basic infrastructure. However, raw materials such as wine, cork, oil, fish and salt still dominated the country's foreign trade, as they had done since the Middle Ages. As had happened so often in the past, emigration was seen as the only strategy available for the poor, and this strategy was now adopted also in Portugal's impoverished island communities of the Azores, Madeira and Cape Verde. Here relentless demographic pressure came up against the unyielding realities of the entailed estates (*morgados*) and three-life emphyteutic tenures that characterized rural land holding and, when these were abolished in a limited land reform in the 1830s, the large-scale capitalism of the commercial wine growers and farmers. Emigration also began from Portuguese Goa. With their relatively higher levels of education Goans found ready employment in British India and later in the century in British East Africa.

Portuguese emigration had causes specific to the conditions of rural Portugal and the islands but it formed part of the great flood of emigration from Europe as millions of people left in search of land and economic opportunity in the Americas, Australasia, Southern Africa and the Siberian steppes, creating a global redistribution of population far greater than that caused by the slave trade or by any earlier *völkerwanderung*. The main destination of Portuguese emigrants was Brazil, where the abolition of the slave trade in 1852 and of slavery itself in 1888 began to cause a shortage of agricultural labour. Between 1820 and 1909 703,000 people left Portugal for Brazil, averaging over 10,000 a year after 1870, when Portugal was affected by agricultural recession. In the last two decades of the nineteenth century between 85 per cent and 93 per cent of all Portuguese emigrants went to Brazil.[1] Many also went to the United States, which was particularly favoured by Cape Verdians, while emigrants from Madeira took their sugar growing expertise to Hawaii, and others went to Guiana, Venezuela, Argentina and even to the inhospitable coasts and highlands of southern Angola.

This Portuguese diaspora created emigrant Portuguese communities across the world with five distinct points of origin and five distinct communal identities. Although a particular feature of Portuguese emigration was the comparatively high number of those who returned home (in the late nineteenth century up to 50 per cent of migrants to Brazil eventually returned), remittances from Portuguese working overseas assumed a growing importance in supporting the Portuguese economy through the difficult years at the end of the nineteenth century. Between 1905 and 1915 more than half Portugal's annual trade deficit was covered by the 17,000 *contos* received from Brazil each year.[2]

The Cape Verde Islands and world communications[3]

An important motor of the expanding world economy in the nineteenth century was the growth of communications. Steam power applied to railways and ships had the effect of cutting the length of voyages and facilitating the bulk movement and distribution of goods, while the laying of submarine cables created the first system of telecommunications linking the continents. Portugal was to play an unexpectedly important part in this communications revolution. The strategic position of the Cape Verde Islands had been recognized by the early navigators, and fleets of all nations (and the pirates that preyed on them) routinely called at the islands to take on water and fresh provisions or to rendezvous with other vessels dispersed in storms. Water and safe anchorage were not available on all the islands and Praia on the island of Santiago had been the preferred port of call for sailing ships. As late as 1784 the anonymous author of the *Notícia Corográphica e Chronológica do Bispado do Cabo Verde* . . . listed the island of São Vicente among the 'Ilhas desertas', commenting that it was 'almost totally arid and produced no food at all'.[4] However, Porto Grande in the island of São Vicente had a wide, deep and sheltered anchorage and, in spite of the lack of water, this was increasingly used from the 1840s, first by the American warships on the anti-slave trade patrol and then by the coaling firms which provided bunkering services for steamships which needed to take on coal on the longer ocean routes.

The first attempts to set up a coaling depot were made by the East India Company in 1838; however, it was in 1850 that the development of Porto Grande really began. In that year the Royal Mail Steam Packet Company obtained a concession for a coaling station and made Porto Grande a regular stop on the voyage to the Cape and India. That year the British Consul, John Rendall, decided to move his consulate from Praia to the new port-city. Rendall was an enthusiastic advocate of Porto Grande and founded one of the earliest coaling companies. As described in his book *A Guide to the Cape de Verd Islands*, which he published with the official approval of the Foreign Office in 1856, the arid, desert island of São Vicente is hardly recognizable. 'The salubrity of St Vincent is very superior', he writes, water was in 'great abundance' six to ten feet from the surface; a road had been completed to Green Mountain (Monte Verde) and 'at present a good deal of cultivation is going on'. The harbour, he optimistically declares, can shelter 300 ships.[5]

For the rest of the century Porto Grande, which became the city of Mindelo in 1836, expanded ahead of its rivals, largely because of its ideal geographical location. In 1894 the year when it reached the height of its importance, 2,464 ships used the port – 1,881 being long-haul steamers and 34 being non-Portuguese warships, while 194,793 passengers passed through the port in transit. One hundred and fifty-six coaling ships delivered 657,634 metric tons of coal and often-quoted figures for January 1890 show Porto Grande importing 36,600 tons of coal from Cardiff, about the same as Gibraltar and exceeded only by Port Said, Singapore and Malta.[6] Between 1890 and the First World War Porto Grande maintained a fairly steady, if declining, level of activity. In 1910 301,400 tons of coal were imported and in 1913 1,414 steam ships cleared the port at a rate of about three to four a day.

When the Atlantic cables began to be laid in the 1860s, it is not surprising that São Vicente was chosen as a relay station. The first cables reached the island in 1874 and from there lines ran to the Azores, Portugal and England and via Ascension to the Cape and South America. By the end of the century lines also ran to Bathurst and Free Town in West Africa and in 1916 a wireless relay station was also in operation.

In 1836, when the city of Mindelo was officially created, São Vicente had almost no native population. The few inhabitants of the island, it was reported, went round in state of *'nudez absoluta'*.[7] The city was entirely the creation of transatlantic commerce. From the date of its foundation it was part of two competing colonial empires. The British provided all the economic activity of the city and the port developed entirely to meet the various needs of the British Empire. At the same time Mindelo was politically and administratively controlled by Portugal. This dual relationship was not unique. Parallels can be found in Madeira and, more obviously, in the east African port cities of Beira and Lourenço Marques which, nominally ruled by Portugal, became ports of great strategic and economic importance for Britain in the last years of the nineteenth century.

In the protectionist world of the late nineteenth century, Porto Grande was only able to survive by becoming another incarnation of the old Anglo-Portuguese alliance. Threats to its survival came not only from the Spanish Canaries where, by the end of the nineteenth century, a free port was thriving, but also nearer to home from the French decision to develop Dakar. This made Porto Grande all the more dependent on the British, who maintained the coal trade as a British monopoly, closed to international competition – a Foreign Office minute commenting on a German proposal made in 1905 reflected that the Portuguese foreign minister 'promised that he would never consent to granting a coaling station in Madeira or the Azores [or by implication Cape Verde] to a foreign power'.[8] Foreign, of course, meant anyone other than the British. As Augusto Vera Cruz, Cape Verde's representative in the Portuguese Senate, put it in an article published in *Gazeta das Côlonias* in 1925, 'these attempts [to introduce foreign competition] are frustrated because the British Government at once brings the project to the notice of our Government, which, always faithful to its ally, gives way'.[9] Porto Grande remained of great strategic importance to British imperial commerce. In 1913 870 British ships used the port, twice the number of Portuguese and four times the number of German vessels.[10]

The Cape Verde Islands remained the hub of the Atlantic communications system at least until the First World War and their strategic
importance was recognized by Britain in its duel with Germany for
naval and maritime supremacy. Porto Grande had been used by the
British as a port of assembly during the Ashanti War (1873–4) and during the First World War was regularly used for refuelling British
warships. At the Versailles peace conference the British suggested that
they should take over the port 'as a set-off to financial claims of Great
Britain on Portugal, or in exchange for territory captured from Germany' – just as they also considered annexing Delagoa Bay.[11]

After the war coal was rapidly replaced by oil in powering ships
and the importance of Mindelo declined, but the beginnings of long-
distance aviation once again gave the Cape Verde Islands a vital
international role. The airport on Sal was first developed by the Italians in the 1930s but assumed a great importance for South Africa
when, in the 1950s, over-flying African territories became difficult for
the apartheid regime. Possession of Sal and São Vicente gave the Portuguese great leverage in international diplomacy which Portugal by
itself would never have possessed.

Delagoa Bay

Portugal's position in the world had for long rested on its strategically
placed harbours. It was the possession of Malacca, Ormuz and Mozambique that had given Portugal such importance in Indian Ocean affairs
in the sixteenth and seventeenth centuries, and it was the capacious
and safe anchorage of Lisbon that had made Portugal so important to
Philip II of Spain and later to Britain. In the nineteenth century Mindelo
was seen as the key to Atlantic steam navigation and, unexpectedly,
Portugal found itself in possession of another strategic seaport, which
came to be seen as the key to the control of southern Africa and to
Britain's continued supremacy in the Indian Ocean.

Delagoa Bay on the coast of south-east Africa is a deep sea inlet in
whose warm, safe waters whales came to give birth and into which five
rivers empty themselves. Although not navigable, these rivers nevertheless provided highways to the high veldt of what later became the
Transvaal and to the low veldt areas of the future Mozambique. The
bay provides an exceptionally safe deep-water anchorage. To the south
the surf-beaten coast offers few natural harbours while to the north the
reefs, mangrove swamps and the sandy river deltas, swept by the

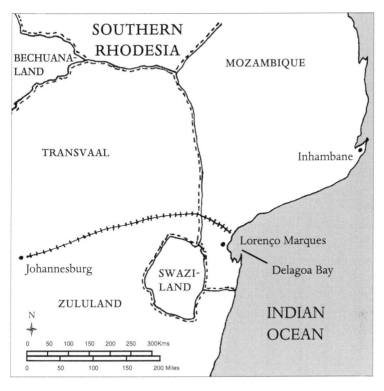

SOUTHERN RHODESIA

BECHUANA-LAND

MOZAMBIQUE

TRANSVAAL

Inhambane

Lorenço Marques

Johannesburg

SWAZI-LAND

Delagoa Bay

ZULULAND

N

INDIAN OCEAN

0   50   100   150   200   250   300Kms

0   50   100   150   200 Miles

DELAGOA BAY AND ITS HINTERLAND, LATE 19TH TO 20TH CENTURIES

Mozambique current into fantastic spits of land, offer shelter only to small sailing vessels or coastal craft.

Delagoa Bay lay too far south to be affected by the monsoons and had not been visited by Indian Ocean merchants prior to the arrival of the Portuguese. However, from 1545 the Portuguese had annually sent a ship to buy ivory there and the crews had stayed in the bay for weeks building temporary shelters on one of the islands. In the seventeenth century the bay was visited by Dutch and English vessels and in the eighteenth century first the Dutch and then a Trieste-based company had tried unsuccessfully to set up permanent trading establishments. At the end of the eighteenth century the Portuguese built a small permanent fort on the northern shores of the bay from which they traded ivory and slaves with the Ngoni kings whose states came into existence in the early part of the century. This trading station had a very precarious existence and was sacked and burnt by the Zulus in 1831. Meanwhile Commodore Owen, carrying out his survey of the East African coast

179

on behalf of the British Admiralty, had appreciated the strategic importance of the anchorage and in 1824 had signed a treaty of protection
with a local chief on the southern shore of the Bay.[12]

The first indication that Delagoa Bay was going to assume a wider
strategic importance was the arrival of Louis Trichardt, one of the leaders of the Boer *voortrekkers*, who made his way from the high veldt to
the Bay in 1839. Although the trekkers were seeking a port which
would not be controlled by the British, the existence of tsetse fly in the
low veldt regions behind the Bay meant that for the next twenty years
it would only be of limited value to the Boer republics. Although the
trade that passed through the Bay was hardly of much importance, the
British appreciated that if a viable route could be established to the high
veldt, the whole security of Britain's position in South Africa would be
threatened. The discovery of diamonds in the Orange river in 1866 and
commercially viable gold mines in 1868 made the opening of a practicable route to the Bay both urgent and, for the first time, possible. In
1869 the Portuguese authorities signed an agreement with the South
African Republic which defined the borders between the Portuguese
and Boer spheres of influence and made provision for free trade between the two.

The opening of the Kimberley mines in 1871 created an investment
boom in southern Africa and railways were planned to link the mines
to the sea, while wages paid to mine workers and the possibility of purchasing firearms began to attract migrant labour from African
communities as far north as the Zambesi. The easiest and quickest
route for labourers coming from the north was through Delagoa Bay.
As the development of the industrial mining complex was gathering
momentum, Gladstone's government became alarmed at the emergence of what looked like a Luso-Boer alliance and decided to use
Owen's dormant treaties to claim sovereignty over Delagoa Bay. Vigorously opposed by the Portuguese, Britain agreed to submit the
dispute to the arbitration of the president of France.

In 1875 the French president, Marshal MacMahon, gave his award
and judged both shores of the Bay as belonging to Portugal. This was
a decision that was to alter the whole trajectory of southern African
politics for, soon after, the award the South African Republic began to
raise funds to build a railway to the port. The prospect of an alliance
between the Boers and Portugal, which would enable the Boer
republics to pursue policies antagonistic to British interests was now
coming close to realization.

In British eyes the fact that the only really practicable port on the south-east coast of Africa was not in its control became the single most important consideration in the unfolding of the power struggle in the region. Britain's ill-fated annexation of the Transvaal between 1877 and 1881 was motivated in part by a determination that if not the port then at the very least the railway from the mines to the coast should be in British hands. Negotiations for a treaty (the Lourenço Marques Treaty), which would enable the construction of a British-controlled line, began in 1878 and the following year Britain reaped the fruits of closer co-operation when the Zulu War broke out in January 1879 and Portugal agreed to prevent arms reaching the Zulus through Delagoa Bay. However, in 1881, with the Lourenço Marques Treaty still not ratified in Lisbon, Britain was forced to restore the independence of the South African Republic and the dilemma over the future of a railway to Delagoa Bay was revived.

This time the issues were far more serious. In 1884 Germany suddenly began to flex its muscles as a power in Africa and the Boers and the Portuguese saw the possibility of a new and powerful ally. Then in 1886 major gold discoveries were made on the Rand which hugely increased the potential importance of the port and for the first time made available the funds for building the railway. Through Delagoa Bay now flowed industrial machinery, imported goods of all kinds and armaments, accompanied by thousands of migrant workers, recruited in the African kingdoms to the north to supply workers for the labour-hungry mines. The railway was eventually completed from the Bay to the Rand in 1894, swinging the balance of forces in southern Africa decisively against Britain.

Britain's fear of the development of a Boer-German axis was very real and was only marginally allayed by the comprehensive agreement over colonial boundaries reached with Germany in 1890. During the months between November 1889 and January 1890, when the Portuguese and British nearly came to blows on the Shire river in East Africa, a section of the British press strongly urged that Britain should seize control of Delagoa Bay if Portugal was unwilling to sell it. Portugal, however, refused all British offers, just as it rejected British attempts to secure control of Mindelo in Cape Verde, and it was an obsessive fear that its failure to control the Bay would enable the South African Republic to challenge Britain's supremacy in South Africa, and even its control of the Cape itself, that led Britain in 1895 to connive at the Jameson Raid, a second bungled attempt to annex the Transvaal.

After the failure of the Jameson Raid more sober policies were pursued. Lord Salisbury tried to isolate Portugal and the Boer Republics and to detach their German ally. If Germany could be persuaded to stand aside and not to interfere, British naval power would be enough to secure Britain's dominance in the region. This was the objective of the diplomacy that led to the signing of the secret treaty between Britain and Germany in 1898. This treaty defined spheres of British and German influence in the Portuguese colonies in anticipation of a virtually bankrupt Portugal having at some stage to surrender its colonial empire. The southern part of Mozambique, the most important part of which was Delagoa Bay, was declared to be in the British sphere. If Portugal sought a loan from either Britain or Germany, the surrender of Delagoa Bay would be one of the key conditions. The surrender of Delagoa Bay to Britain was now seen as inevitable and in 1899 Montague Jessett published a book which was virtually a prospectus for a prosperous future for Lourenço Marques and the Bay region under British rule. The Bay, he wrote,

> is of the highest value both from a commercial and a strategical point of view. In brief, it is the key to South Africa, and means much more to us than the mere acquisition of further territory, for it ensures to us the proud position as the paramount Power in South Africa, and is a most important factor in the maintenance of peace.[13]

By this time Portugal had begun to profit hugely from its possession of Delagoa Bay and the increasingly beleaguered ministers of the Portuguese Monarchy, even had they wished to, would have found any surrender of Portuguese territory to Britain a political impossibility. Nevertheless, deprived of the possibility of German support, Portugal had no option but to bow to the realities of British political supremacy in Southern Africa. This was not how the situation was seen in Britain. The Anglo-German agreement had allowed for the free economic development of the Bay and the city of Lourenço Marques and Britain remained deeply concerned that German business and German capital would succeed where German sabre rattling had failed. These anxieties weighed with Britain as Chamberlain and Milner argued for an aggressive policy towards the Transvaal, a policy which was to lead to war in October 1899.[14]

Once war had been declared Portugal complied with British demands to close Lourenço Marques to the Boers and to allow Britain to use the port to supply its armed forces. Carlos de Faria e Maia, who was the interim director of the Lourenço Marques railway, described vividly how the war ebbed and flowed up and down the line. From the outset the corridor from the Transvaal to Lourenço Marques was thronged with refugees of all kinds. These included President Kruger, who was smuggled across the border secretly by the Portuguese in September 1900 and departed a month later on board a Dutch warship. Large numbers of Africans also fled across the border and were followed by stragglers from the fighting,

> especially Americans, Irish and Germans . . . A Dutch Red Cross train crossed the frontier . . . full of wounded. Some of them had wounds made by bullets which had passed through them from side to side. The doctor, who had a long beard, distributed cigars to the onlookers from a cigar case bearing the picture of Kruger. The wounded greeted the Portuguese flag with hurrahs.[15]

The Boer refugees were dispatched by sea to Europe.

Portugal's compliance with British military demands proved highly advantageous and culminated in 1901, while the fighting was still in progress, when Britain and Portugal signed the *modus vivendi*, an agreement which would guarantee fifty per cent of the Rand traffic to the port of Lourenço Marques in exchange for the right to recruit labour in Mozambique. The future of southern Mozambique was in this way effectively tied to industrial South Africa but this did not put an end to the problems, real and imagined, caused by South Africa's major port being in the possession of Portugal. Soon after the establishment of the Union of South Africa in 1910, General Smuts approached Britain with a scheme to seize control of the port of Lourenço Marques and after the First World War again tried unsuccessfully to force Portugal to surrender control of the railway as a condition for a South African loan.[16]

Through possession of this strategic port the Portuguese remained key players in southern African politics and compelled a reluctant Britain and South Africa to treat Portugal in some respects as an equal.

The background to the scramble for Africa

Portugal's possession of the harbours of Mindelo and Lourenço Marques had already forced Portuguese concerns into the thinking of the great powers, but in the last third of the nineteenth century Portugal became, in addition, one of the four largest colonial powers in Africa, occupying territory which, as a famous map published during the dictatorship of Salazar demonstrated, was comparable in size to western Europe.

Portugal and Spain had partitioned South America between themselves in the sixteenth century and had gradually established their control over the native American population. The settlement of North America meanwhile had lagged far behind and until the eighteenth century was largely confined to the eastern seaboard, Newfoundland and the banks of the St Lawrence. The great scramble for North American land really began in the nineteenth century and between 1800 and 1860 the continent had been partitioned between the British, Americans and Russians – though the Russians sold their stake to the US in 1867. This expansion involved the ruthless expropriation of the native Americans and in some places their genocide, and an equally ruthless war against independent Mexico to seize a large part of its territory. This relentless imperial expansion, and the virtually uncontrolled exploitation of the continent's natural resources that accompanied it, was given momentum by mass immigration, mostly from Europe, and by vast capital investment in communications, symbolized by the construction of the Union Pacific railway between 1862 and 1869.

Where the United States led the way the major European powers were to follow. Russia, which had explored the arctic regions of Asia in the sixteenth and seventeenth centuries, now began to expand southwards towards India and China, annexing huge tracts of land, displacing native rulers and planting settlements of peasants, exiles and soldiers across the whole of central Asia. Capital investment followed, notably the building of the trans-Siberian railway which began in 1889.

Britain had participated in the partition of North America, Canada taking the lion's share of the continent's territory, and was busy expropriating land in Australia and New Zealand. Germany, Italy and France meanwhile had remained preoccupied with the internal politics of Europe and North Africa. Prior to the 1870–71 war France had shown little interest in sub-Saharan Africa, while German capital looked for outlets, and German industry for markets, in the Ottoman empire. As late as 1880 Germany apparently had no aspirations to become a colonial power in Africa, though German scientists, missionaries and explorers had done much to expand Europe's knowledge of the African interior.

'Portugal is not a small country.' A propaganda poster of the Salazar regime.

Between 1840 and 1875, thanks largely to the newly appreciated prophylactic properties of quinine, significant scientific work was undertaken to map the interior of Africa and explore the major river systems. There was also some growth of European and Indian trade with Africa – commodities like palm oil, ivory and rubber having a ready market in Europe and Asia. However, trade in the natural products of Africa, conducted through the ports of the east and west coasts, had continued for centuries without any outsider trying to expropriate African land. The first outsider to realize the potential wealth to be derived from seizing and exploiting African land and population was Mehemet Ali, the Ottoman viceroy of Egypt. Between 1840 and 1870 armed Egyptian expeditions had conquered and annexed the whole of the modern Sudan, had pushed up the Nile to modern Uganda and had expanded along the Red Sea coast and into Somalia. This Egyptian imperial expansion had been fuelled by the trade in slaves and, to a lesser extent, ivory. It resulted in a vast land empire ruled from Cairo through its outpost in Khartoum. When the Egyptian government went bankrupt in 1876, its European creditors established a joint debt commission to supervise the country's finances. This led in turn to military intervention in 1882 which forced the debt commission to take responsibility for Egypt's huge territorial empire. The policy adopted in 1884 by the Europeans, who now effectively controlled Egypt, was to abandon this empire and to withdraw Egyptian forces from the interior – the first example of a bungled decolonization and by no means the last.

The only other area where significant territorial expansion had taken place was in the extreme south, where in the 1840s Boer pastoralists had occupied the high veldt between the Orange and the Limpopo rivers. However, this had not led to any further expansion and forty years later these pastoral republics had done little more than consolidate the territory they had occupied.

Portugal's Third Empire

During the middle years of the nineteenth century the Portuguese made a number of largely unsuccessful attempts to turn their long-established commercial activities in Africa into territorial possession. The Portuguese had feared that the loss of Brazil, whose independence they finally recognized in 1825, would put an end to their long-standing economic relations with their former colony, although in the event Portuguese trade, investment and emigration meant that Brazil remained Portugal's principal economic partner for half a century more. Indeed, until the 1850s, remittances from traders based in Brazil and profits from capital invested in the slave trade continued to be a major source of external income for Portugal and provided the capital base for a number of Portugal's banks and investment houses.[17]

Nevertheless the civil wars in Portugal, which began as a struggle over the constitution between rival factions of the ruling elite, soon turned into a struggle to establish a new economic order. The victory of the supporters of Dom Pedro in 1834 had been followed by sweeping reforms. Entails and long leases, the religious orders and the restrictive royal monopolies (including the monopolies on ivory from Africa) were all swept away, foreign capital was introduced and an attack was finally mounted on the slave trade, the last bastion of the old world economy and one which was still dominated by Portuguese capital. In the African coastal colonies successive Portuguese governments tried to stimulate settlement, free trade and investment but this had little chance of success while Brazil still imported slaves. In western Africa there was some progress in growing coffee and cocoa in São Tomé and Príncipe but plans to extend formal government control over land in the interior of Angola and to introduce Portuguese settlers were less successful, the starveling settler colony planted in 1840 at Moçamedes being the sole achievement. By 1870 most of the settlement schemes and campaigns of pacification had failed – notably in the Zambesi valley, where Portuguese military failure had served to enhance the power of the Afro-Portuguese elites, who continued to profit from an extensive internal slave trade.

Meanwhile the idea was being promoted in Portugal that Africa might become the new Brazil. The reports of explorers increasingly painted a picture of an interior rich in resources where Portuguese traders from both the east and west coasts were already well established and which could provide the opportunities for Portugal to accumulate the capital needed for its own development. Africa was seen as 'the only means remaining to the country to free itself from foreign dependency'.[18] In 1875 the Lisbon Geographical Society was founded with the objective of mobilizing public opinion and organizing expeditions to turn this idea into a reality.

In spite of the concern expressed by some British missionary societies that the Portuguese in east and west-central Africa were still actively engaged in the internal slave trade and maintained a society based on slavery, there was no sign that Britain or any other European country was particularly interested in trying to thwart Portugal's aspirations. Indeed, soon after its annexation of the Transvaal in 1877, Britain began negotiations with Portugal which were limited to making sure that the river systems of central Africa, the mouths of which were wholly or partly in Portuguese control, would remain open to British trade. For his part the Portuguese Foreign Minister, João de Andrade Corvo, believed that Portugal would benefit from co-operation with Britain, which would result in an expansion of commerce and capital investment. His vision of a liberal empire was remarkably different from that which predominated among the colonial powers after the partition of Africa. As Valentim Alexandre explains:

> This expansion ought to take place not by military action but rather by 'peaceful means, through action by its nature belonging to civilization' which would attract 'the goodwill of the native populations'. For this it would be necessary to put

an end to forms of oppression which up to that time had marked the Portuguese presence – the slave trade, slavery and forced labour.[19]

To this end Corvo implemented legislation in 1875 which put an end to all forms of compulsory labour – at least on paper.

The treaty negotiations, which were carried on at ambassadorial level, showed that Britain was prepared to allow Portugal to pursue its ambitions, provided that any territory it acquired would remain open to British trade. The negotiations subsumed the issue of the building of the Lourenço Marques railway and a package began to emerge whereby, in return for Britain financing the railway from Lourenço Marques to the then British-controlled Transvaal, Portugal would lower its tariffs on the Zambesi and allow free access to traders and missionaries both there and in the estuary of the Congo. This was very much in keeping with the main objectives of British foreign policy throughout the nineteenth century. Provided free trade was guaranteed, Britain was prepared to offer protection to regimes of many different kinds and saw no particular advantage to be gained from enlarging its formal empire. In Portugal, however, opinions were bitterly divided. While the treaty was attacked by Republicans as showing a 'scandalous subservience' towards Britain and as losing 'precipitately all the advantages which had been obtained by the French arbitration', it was also strongly defended, not least by the former governor general of Mozambique, the Visconde de Arriaga, who interestingly made a comparison with Mindelo which, as a result of international commerce, had already become 'a European city' (*uma cidade europea*) and who maintained that 'maritime and land transit through Lourenço Marques will produce a result the same and indeed much greater, because Lourenço Marques, unlike São Vicente, is surrounded by land which is very fertile and of huge extent.'[20]

Meanwhile the mid-nineteenth century expansion of the global economy had begun to falter. This has been attributed to a banking crisis in Vienna in 1873 which set off a chain reaction of protectionist measures by the major European economies. Britain's trading position remained sufficiently strong for protectionism at first to make little headway, but for Portugal the threat of recession presented serious problems. Portugal's trade with Brazil had declined from 15 per cent of Portugal's overseas trade in the 1840s to 10 per cent by 1880[21] and Portugal's economy now depended increasingly on the export of its textiles and wines to Africa, on colonial re-exports to Europe and on the remittances of emigrants. All these were endangered by the world-wide economic downturn. Central Africa now ceased to be the vaguely defined aspiration for a New Brazil and became a market essential for Portugal's very survival. The completion of the treaties with Britain became a vital first step towards guaranteeing these markets.

Just as the empire began to assume huge importance to Portuguese business, it started to acquire iconic importance in the struggle between Portuguese Monarchists and the growing Republican movement. The early imperial history of Portugal, symbolized by the achievements of the great conquistadors and writers of the fifteenth and sixteenth centuries, became a political property which was vehemently fought over. In the 1880 the Republicans used the celebration of the three hundredth anniversary of the death of Luís de Camões to propagate their vision of a revived Portuguese state. Eighteen years later they would be trumped by the Monarchists, whose celebrations of the four hundredth anniversary of the first voyage of Vasco da Gama deliberately sought to outdo the Republicans and shore up the Monarchy.

In these difficult political circumstances the events unfolding in Africa could not be considered from any point of view except that of nationalist aspiration. Important as the empire was to Portuguese business, it had become of even greater importance to Portuguese politicians.[22]

The Berlin Conference

Britain and Portugal, having failed to reach an agreement over the building of the Lourenço Marques railway, were able to begin negotiations in 1882 for a Congo Treaty which was signed in February 1884. This was the last flicker of life for Andrade Corvo's policies with regard to Africa. The treaty was designed to settle all outstanding colonial questions between Britain and Portugal, recognizing Portugal's sovereignty over both banks of the lower Zaire in return for an agreement to limit Portuguese claims in East Africa on the Shire river and a set of commercial proposals that would secure freedom of navigation on the Zaire and Zambesi and a lowering of commercial customs tariffs. This treaty, which like its predecessor the Lourenço Marques Treaty would have effectively recognized Portuguese claims to be the paramount colonial power in central Africa, was opposed by missionary and commercial pressure groups in Britain and bitterly denounced in Portugal by the Progressista opposition party and the Republican press, which used terms like 'rapine' and 'robbery' to describe its terms. As the historian Valentim Alexandre tersely puts it, 'the myth of spoliation began to gain substance'.[23]

It was at this stage that Bismarck decided to intervene. It is now clear that Bismarck's decision to declare protectorates over the coastal areas of south-west Africa, Tanganyika and Cameroon was not the result of a well-thought-out colonial policy but was a move in a power game in which the Chancellor sought to maintain German supremacy in Europe and to divide Germany's rivals. If he thought about Africa in the long term, he seemed to imagine that German protectorates would not involve expensive military campaigns or colonial administrations. One of his major objectives was to limit the expansion of British influence in Africa and he refused to accept the Anglo-Portuguese treaty, which would have resolved, on a bilateral basis, the international dispute over jurisdiction in the region of the lower Zaire.

The Berlin Conference met in November 1884 and finished its deliberations in February 1885. Portugal, which had played little part in European diplomacy in the previous fifty years, could hardly be ignored in a region where it was the only European country with a real presence, but it has often been represented as a mere pawn at the Conference, with its claims brushed aside and its influence negligible. However, in his classic account of Portugal's role at the Conference, the Marquês de Lavradio claimed that Portugal's adamant refusal to recognize the claims of King Leopold's International Association was in part successful.

> The recognition by the Powers of the International Association, the pressure exerted on Portugal to recognize it and the resistance of the Portuguese government to the desires of the king of the Belgians which all of Europe supported, for some time disturbed the Berlin Conference and irritated Bismarck, but it saved a great part of the territories which the Association wanted to take from us.[24]

Eventually the Conference marked out spheres of influence in the Zaire basin which excluded Britain and severely limited Portugal's claims. Portugal's claim to the left bank of the Zaire was only recognized at its mouth, while the whole vast and largely unexplored Zaire basin was declared to be a Free State, ruled by Leopold of the Belgians and underpinned by the sanctions of the Conference powers. Of still greater importance was the attempt by the Conference powers to define what criteria would be used to recognize future territorial claims. Portugal had traditionally based its claims on the fact that it was the first European state to explore the coast of Africa, and on the agreement with Castile enshrined in the 1494 Tordesillas treaty and the subsequent Papal Bulls. These claims had for long been disputed by other Europeans, notably by the British, who maintained that only effective occupation could establish sovereign rights. The effective occupation of their own lands by Africans was not considered to amount to a title in international affairs – the British radical Henry Labouchère being one of the few European politicians of the time prepared to state publicly (in the context of British and Portuguese disputes on the Shire river) that 'the disputed territory in reality belongs neither to us nor to the Portuguese, but to the native inhabitants.'[25]

The consequences of establishing 'effective occupation' as a legal principle were largely unforeseen. Far from limiting international rivalry by establishing universally acknowledged criteria, it precipitated a veritable stampede to occupy the African interior. In this Portugal led the way, largely because it already had trading stations, and even some settlements, in the interior of Angola and Mozambique and had a long tradition of cultural and commercial influence across the whole of central Africa.

The Ultimatum

So, in the aftermath of the Berlin Conference, Portugal pushed rapidly ahead with establishing effective occupation in the regions where it had always had an informal presence. The Congo Free State had been created to peg back Britain's commercial and missionary influence and the French and Germans saw Portugal as another surrogate which would confine Britain to the southern end of the continent and which was so weak that it would be dependent on French and German support to survive. Portugal found that France and Germany were willing to negotiate and it embarked on a round of high-level diplomacy, which resulted in formal treaties with France in 1886 and Germany in 1887. These fixed borders and defined spheres of influence in upper Guinea and in the south of Angola. To these treaties Portugal appended a map, the famous *Mapa Cor de Rosa*, which showed a band of Portuguese territory stretching from Angola to Mozambique – the new Brazil of Portuguese statesmen's dreams.

The Portuguese, however, were aware that since the Berlin Conference, treaties needed to be backed up by effective occupation, and organized a series of expeditions which were to establish a string of fortified settlements across the continent. There appeared to be little opposition to these plans. Germany and France had tacitly recognized these claims and Britain had, in effect, recognized Portugal's prior claims to central Africa in the negotiations for the Lourenço Marques and Congo treaties. What changed this alignment of interests and led to the real scramble for central African land was the discovery of gold on the Rand in 1886. Once the extent of the reef was realized its potential to transform the politics of southern Africa was immense. The capital invested in the gold mines was mostly British while the fiscal benefits of industrialization went to the Transvaal government, enabling it to purchase arms and build the long-awaited railway to Delagoa Bay. The economic and political centre of gravity rapidly altered and the long-term future of the region suddenly seemed to lie with Pretoria rather than Cape Town.

The extent of the gold-bearing reef in the Transvaal soon gave rise to the conviction that another reef lay to the north, in the region of modern Zimbabwe from which gold had been traded for hundreds of years. The race to occupy the land north of the Limpopo, which lay within the area that Portugal had claimed in the *Mapa Cor de Rosa*, attracted a mass of speculators as well as political agents from the governments of the Transvaal, the Cape and Portugal, though sometimes it was not clear where political interests ended and the speculative interests of mineral flotations began. Among the mining speculators was Cecil Rhodes, who had been slow to acquire claims on the Rand and wanted to be ahead of the field when the expected new reef to the north was discovered.

So, while Rhodes's agent Rudd obtained a mining concession from Lobengula, the Ndebele king, Rhodes hastened to London to turn these mineral rights into political gold. The Charter of the British South Africa Company was granted in 1889 with its famous 'open' clauses, which defined its limits only as lying to the north of the Transvaal and to the west of Portuguese territory.

The two years between the granting of Rhodes's charter and the Anglo-Portuguese agreement that was eventually signed in May 1891 thrust Portugal brutally into the forefront of international politics and brought Britain and its ally to the brink of war. In fact, with the sole exception of the Fashoda crisis of 1898, these events were the closest that European powers came to fighting over the partition of Africa.

During 1889, while Rhodes was preparing expeditions to claim as much territory as he could, the Portuguese were sending military missions up the Zambesi and Shire and into Mashonaland ahead of Rhodes's efforts. Alarmed at the success of the Portuguese, Lord Salisbury, the British prime minister, issued an ultimatum in January 1890 threatening war if Portugal did not halt its occupation of the interior. Faced with the prospect of – at the very least – a naval blockade of Lisbon and Lourenço Marques the Portuguese gave way and stopped their expeditions. This allowed Rhodes space to send his pioneer column into the future Southern Rhodesia and to organize expeditions to cross the Zambesi to secure the copper-bearing regions to the north.

At first Portugal was reluctant to abandon its claims to central Africa and the first draft of an agreement allowed it a corridor linking its territory in the east and the west. This was rejected and it took further pressure from the unfolding events in Africa to persuade Portugal eventually to settle for the frontiers of Angola and Mozambique, which, with a few minor adjustments, were to become permanent.

In Portugal the Ultimatum of 1890 caused a 'nationalist wave [which] had a strong impact on the political and ideological life of the country, leaving deep marks in its collective memory'.[26] The Portuguese felt at the time that they had been hard done by, first at the Berlin Conference and then in the Anglo-Portuguese agreement. Viewed from one perspective this was justified. In 1884 Portugal was the only European power with any settlements in the interior of central Africa and it was the only country which had extensive commercial ties with the African states of the interior. No other Europeans had a presence that came anywhere near to that of the Portuguese. Portugal's claims to territory were, therefore, far stronger than those of other Europeans. Moreover the Portuguese moved faster and with more effect to establish effective occupation in response to the new criteria laid down in the Berlin Act. They had to be stopped in their tracks by Britain, which used its naval and military muscle to force compliance. Viewed from another perspective, however, Portugal had secured a vast territorial empire which made it a colonial power on a par with Germany and in consequence a major participant in colonial conferences and in the international negotiations that surrounded the establishment of European rule throughout Africa. As far as sub-Saharan Africa was concerned Portugal had established itself as one of the 'big four'. Moreover it soon became apparent that its importance extended far beyond the boundaries of its own colonies.

Railway politics

Railways had contributed more than any other factor to the opening up and settlement of the interior of the United States, Canada and Argentina and were to play a similar role for the Russians in Central Asia. By the 1870s similar ideas were abroad for 'opening up' Africa. The Portuguese Minister, Andrade Corvo, had believed that the building of railways could be the basis for a new co-operation between Britain and Portugal and committed himself to securing British capital for a railway across Goa to Mormugão and from the Transvaal to Lourenço Marques.

The Anglo-Portuguese agreement of 1891 had secured for Britain the largest part of the mineral-bearing regions of central Africa, and the Boer War was soon to establish British dominance over South Africa as well. However, the rich resources of these colonies were landlocked. Although Rhodes talked about a Cape to Cairo railway and actually took steps to construct a railway and telegraph linking the mines of central Africa to the Cape, the logistics of a route of such length placed a large obstacle in the way of rapid economic development. The shorter, more direct routes to the sea, however, had to cross territory controlled by the Portuguese. The importance of the rail route from the Transvaal to Lourenço Marques had already been recognized and the fact that the final stretch of the railway and the port remained in Portuguese hands enabled Portugal to negotiate very favourable financial terms first with the Transvaal and then with the Union authorities. The port of Lourenço Marques and the labour contracts with the Rand mines became one of the most successful ways in which the Portuguese economy earned foreign exchange.

Rhodes realized that the Portuguese not only controlled the Transvaal's access to the sea but sat astride any route linking the Rhodesias to the Indian Ocean. As Baron de Rezende, the representative of the Moçambique Company in Manica, put it in a letter to his superiors in October 1890:

> In the plans of the English, apart from enlarging their territory, there is above all the necessity to communicate with the Pungue and the coast and they do not have any other means of doing this except to cross this part of the country. To achieve their ends they will do as much as they have to.[27]

Twice, in 1890 and 1891, Rhodes sent armed expeditions to try to seize control of a corridor which would link Rhodesia with the sea. These expeditions led to armed clashes with the Portuguese in Manica and might have succeeded but for the determination shown by Lord Salisbury to prevent Rhodes's swashbuckling tactics from derailing the prospects for a long term settlement. In the end Rhodes had to settle for a contract to build a railway through Portuguese territory to the port of Beira, which was completed in 1898.

Meanwhile the Moçambique Company, which had been entrusted with the administration of the territory between the Zambesi and the Sabi, passed by stages into the hands of Libert Oury, a Belgian financier backed by South African capital. Oury worked closely with the Portuguese, having seen how counterproductive the confrontational style of Smuts over Delagoa Bay had been. Under Oury's guidance a second railway was built to connect Nyasaland to the sea at Beira, while the Zambesi was bridged at Sena in 1935.

Angola had also shared in the railway boom. The Katanga copper mines were hostages to the long rail haul to South Africa, the only alternative being the cumbersome river and rail transport organized by the Congo Free State. In 1902, however, Portugal signed a contract with Tanganyika Concessions to build a railway to link Katanga to Lobito Bay in Angola. The negotiations had been carried on in secret because Portugal was convinced that the British government, having recently signed the secret agreement with Germany, was anxious that the railway to the Cape would continue to have a strategic monopoly of transport to and from the copper mines. The signing of the contract for what became known as the Benguela railway was therefore a gesture of independence by a Portugal that believed its interests were being overridden by the British in South and Central Africa.[28]

Africa, a mixed blessing

Portugal's determination to compete in Africa at the level of the great powers had mixed consequences. In 1892 Portugal defaulted on its international debt and faced the prospect of losing its empire almost as soon as it had been acquired. That it did not do so was in part the result of the flow of wealth from the empire – re-exports of colonial produce, the hard currency earned by the ports and railways and the remittances of the migrant labourers who kept the Rand mines working. And there were other benefits to be derived from being an imperial power. There is little doubt, as many Portuguese themselves believed, that the African empire, and the importance it gave Portugal in the international arena, put an end to any serious possibility that the unification of the Iberian peninsula might follow the unifications of Italy and Germany. The outcome of the scramble for Africa had acted as a guarantee of Portugal's independent status in the world.

On the domestic front, however, the establishment of its African empire did little to prevent Portugal sliding once again towards political instability. The co-operation between Britain and Portugal, which Andrade Corvo believed would secure alike the survival and stability of Portugal and the peaceful development of the empire in Africa, appeared to have failed. Hostility towards Britain had been first aroused in 1880 by the Lourenço Marques Treaty and then by the Congo Treaty in 1884. This hostility had already been successfully exploited by the Republicans before the Ultimatum of 1890 played into their hands. The Ultimatum was received as a deep national humiliation, all the more serious as it was inflicted by Portugal's traditional ally, and this had been closely followed by the financial crisis of 1892. However, the successful Portuguese military campaigns in southern Mozambique in 1895–7 temporarily gave the illusion of a country rising to the challenge of great power status, a status which was reaffirmed in 1898 in the celebrations of the fourth centenary of Vasco da Gama's voyage to India, a celebration from which the monarchy hoped to derive strength and popularity.

By the early years of the twentieth century, however, the divisions between the urban Republicans and the Monarchists with roots in the countryside, the army and the church, were deepening as the costs and all the multifaceted problems of being a colonial power – pacification, labour, investment and administration – had to be solved under the sceptical gaze of Britain and Germany watching for the moment when Portugal's empire would slip from its grasp. The coup of 1910, which replaced the monarchy with a republic, was caused to a large extent by the constant financial, military and administrative strain imposed by the colonial empire.

11

Portugal and the
End of Empire

The Republic

During the nineteenth century Portugal's reputation in the rest of Europe had been one of backwardness and incompetence. This reputation had been earned during the campaign against the slave trade and was spread by hostile Protestant missionaries and those in Britain and Germany who were keen to expand their empires at Portugal's expense. Once it was clear that Portugal was not going to give up its colonies, however, a degree of co-operation was achieved. Some British, French and German capital was invested in the Portuguese colonies and gradually the British and South Africans came to acquire powerful economic interests, taking control of the Moçambique and Niassa Charter Companies in East Africa and the Moçamedes Company and the Benguela Railway in Angola. In addition the South African mines, through their recruitment organization WNLA, negotiated favourable recruitment agreements with Mozambique. Meanwhile the largely Belgian capital that controlled diamond mining in the Congo obtained an equally favourable position in the east of Angola with the formation of Diamang in 1921. This company enjoyed almost as great a degree of autonomy as the Mozambique charter companies and became responsible for health services, policing and general administration throughout the Lunda district.[1]

However, the unfavourable way that Portuguese colonial policy was generally viewed did not entirely disappear. In the first decade of the twentieth century there was a sustained campaign against the Portuguese cocoa companies in São Tomé and Príncipe and the forced labour practices that were employed on the cocoa plantation (roças). It is significant that this campaign was aimed at the only major sector of the Portuguese colonial economy that was not foreign-owned, for there was far less outcry directed against the policies pursued in the

Niassa Company territory or in the South African gold mines. At the 1919 Peace Conference there were suggestions that the Portuguese empire might be redistributed between the Allies, along with the German and Turkish colonies. Although this threat never materialized, the colonies continued to prove a diplomatic and economic liability to Portugal when the Ross Report, produced for the International Labour Office (ILO) of the League of Nations in 1926, focused unwelcome attention once again on Portuguese forced labour practices.[2]

Meanwhile Portugal itself became ever more unstable. In the early twentieth century most indicators showed the country to be among the most backward in Europe. Around 70 per cent of the population were illiterate and of the 143,000 people who were classified in 1917 as industrial workers, 48,000 were women and 22,000 minors, most of whom were employed in units of 20 or less. Although a majority of the population worked in the agricultural sector, Portugal was seldom able to feed itself and in the early years of the Republic food imports pushed the defecit in balance of trade to an unmanageable size.[3] In 1910 the monarchy had been overthrown by the republicans, who sought to build a secular state based on an educated citizenry. Although the republicans were strong in the main towns, they had no base in the rural areas, which remained Catholic and monarchist. After 1910 the country became ever more divided and few governments lasted more than a month or two. Aubrey Bell, an English writer and literary critic, whose witty prose disguised a deep sympathy for Portugal, commented in 1915 that

> the splendid Avenida de Liberdade [in Lisbon] has never become popular and is apt to be deserted . . . It seems to be too far from the centres of gossip: before you had walked from the Praça dos Restauradores to the Praça do Marquêz de Pombal and back a ministry might have fallen.[4]

The republican leaders thought they saw an opportunity to create national unity and safeguard Portugal's empire by entering the First World War on the side of the Allies. Aware that the republican ideal, in particular its anti-clericalism, was not shared by the majority of the population, they hoped that 'if the process of political mobilization around the new regime could be joined to the process of generating patriotic enthusiasm, as is characteristic of a national emergency, the danger of Monarchism might be definitively removed.'[5] However, their attempts to enter the war against Germany initially failed when Britain rejected the offer to join the alliance, and then came to grief with the costly military failures in France and Africa. Portugal emerged from the war humiliated and deeply in debt.

After the war the republicans were able to implement their policy of devolving power in the colonies to High Commissioners, who were granted a wide degree of autonomy. Such a policy, on paper, addressed many of the problems which the over-centralized regime of the monarchy had brought to the fore, but in Angola it led to a rapid growth of debt and a depreciation of the colonial currency, which threatened to drag the domestic economy of Portugal down with it. The Portuguese republic appeared to represent 'the tendency of parliamentary government to breed systematic corruption and favouritism',[6] especially, one might add, in countries with underdeveloped economies where political office is the main route to wealth and where the political process is distinguished less by ideological or policy issues than by the patronage systems of rival politicians. In this respect republican Portugal was close to the experience of much of post-colonial Africa.

In 1926 a military coup placed a *junta* of generals in power – on the face of it little different from the coups which had regularly punctuated the period of the Republic and offering meagre prospects of success. 'The march on Lisbon – an imitation of the Fascist march on Rome – was the beginning of the Portuguese military dictatorship', wrote Vicente de Bragança Cunha, and he went on to describe how attempts were made to 'clear the ground for a military Dictatorship, by a propaganda of the so-called Lusitanianism . . . [but] even Theophilo Braga's patriotic enthusiasm . . . failed to convince anybody that the Lusitanians aspired to being anything beyond a collection of rival tribes devoted to the pursuit of booty.'[7] General Carmona, having promoted his rival, General Gomes da Costa, to the rank of field marshal and sent him into exile in the Azores, presided over a succession of governments which initiated important policies, particularly with regard to Africa, and which began to address the economic chaos, benefiting from the signs of economic recovery which had appeared in the last years of the Republic. However, they were not able to deal with the continued social unrest nor the weakness of Portugal's overall economic position and gradually surrendered power into the hands of the finance minister, António de Oliveira Salazar, who in 1932 became prime minister – a position he held without a break until he was incapacitated by a

António de Oliveira
Salazar.

stroke in 1968 – an example of political longevity which was quite
exceptional for any European political leader of the twentieth century.

Salazarism

Salazar did not achieve supreme power in Portugal using the methods
of other fascist leaders of the time. As Ralph Fox, a British Communist
who died in 1936 fighting Franco, described him in 1933,

> he never appears in public, nor speaks on the radio, nor
> reviews the army, nor wears a uniform, nor murders his ene-
> mies with his own hands, nor has his photo hung up in every
> shop window. He himself explains his hermit life by the need
> for thought . . . There are others who suggest that Salazar's
> retiring nature is due partly to a religious training and partly
> to a wholesome fear of assassination.[8]

There was no mass party, no street demonstrations and no dema-
goguery, nor did Salazar seek to establish a spurious national unity by
persecuting ethnic minorities. There was, however, a systematic elabo-
ration of a personality cult, though one which was very different from
that of a Hitler or a Mussolini. Salazar was presented to the public as
'an unique blend of the professor, the high church dignitary and the
ascetic'.[9] Marcello Caetano, from the start one of his closest associates
and the man who eventually succeeded him, was also a university professor (though of law not economics) as was Adriano Moreira, the
best-known of Salazar's ministers of the overseas provinces (*Ultramar*).
In all 40 per cent of all ministerial appointments during the Estado
Novo were held by university professors[10] and Portugal between 1930
and 1974 presents the only example in the history of Europe of a
regime controlled throughout by academics.

Salazar is 'a man who has had neither the taste nor the desire for
power', wrote Albert T'Serstevens in 1940, 'who was made for silent
reflection on abstract problems and who has not the least morsel of
ambition for political glory and who finds no pleasure of any kind in
the domination of his fellow man.'[11] It is difficult to recognize in these
naïve phrases the man who between 1926 and 1932 demonstrated a skil-
ful, relentless and ultimately successful pursuit of power. It took six
years for him and his supporters to control the major levers of power
and to elaborate a conservative ideology which would bring as many
interest groups as possible inside what became in the end a very capacious tent. Salazar was probably aided by the experience of the Great
Depression, which gave some justification to the brand of economic
nationalism that was to mark his rule. Although he and his propaganda
machine continually denounced the shortcomings of the republic, he
liked to maintain his republican credentials and to emphasize continu-
ity rather than the establishment of a new '*Reich*'. However, it took
some skill and intellectual sleight of hand to reconcile monarchists and
Catholics with conservative republicans, the army and big business, the
groups which formed his coalition of supporters.

Salazar was deeply conscious of the low esteem in which Portugal
was held in Europe, and of the economic weakness which meant that
its interests were ignored and the country was at the mercy of international capitalism. His avowed aim was to make Portugal less dependent
on outside forces diplomatically and economically, and the means
adopted was to concentrate power in the hands of one man to an
extent without parallel in any modern state. In 1939, as well as being

President of the Council of Ministers, he held the portfolios of Foreign Affairs, Finance and the Army. He had 'an almost obsessive concern for the minutiae of all areas of government' and achieved 'a concentration of decision-making power in the person of the dictator and a reduction of the independence of both the ministers and of the president of the republic'.[12]

He sought to strengthen the ties between Portugal and its empire and to create an autarkic economy which would make Portugal, as far as possible, self-sufficient. Portugal and its colonies would together become less dependent on imports and would generate earnings of hard currency which would provide the funds for economic development. To achieve this objective Salazar placed controls on the use of foreign exchange and brought the economies of the colonies under the direct control of Lisbon, where all budgets had to be agreed and all borrowing authorized. In the short term this threatened Portugal with severe economic recession, but compensatory measures were taken to boost trade with the colonies and to organize the production of key raw materials (sugar, tea, coffee, cotton, rice and maize), which would be given a captive market in Portugal at prices guaranteed by the state.

Restrictions were put on new foreign capital investment, though the interests of the major colonial partners of Portugal were safeguarded. Sena Sugar, the Benguela Railway, Diamang and the WNLA maintained their privileged positions in the colonies but the charters of the Moçambique and Niassa Companies were not renewed and the privileges of the largely foreign-owned *prazo* companies in Zambesia were severely curtailed. For all his nationalist rhetoric, Salazar was largely successful in winning the acquiescence and grudging support of South Africa and Britain, whose investment in building the lower Zambesi rail bridge, at the time the second longest bridge in the world, was an indication of a successful new partnership in Africa. His emphasis on stability and economic conservatism was reassuring and enabled conservative British politicians and the political media to ignore the political repression and the existence of the concentration camp in the Cape Verde Islands to which political dissidents were consigned and where most of them died.

During the 1930s and '40s Salazar steered a clever course in very dangerous international waters. Official neutrality was maintained in the Spanish Civil War and the Second World War, but it was a neutrality carefully managed to make sure that Portugal supported the winning side and could benefit from the gratitude and approval of the victors. Towards the end of the World War Portugal allowed the Americans and British to use the Azores as a base against German U-boats and in 1949, by adopting a face-saving veneer of democracy, Portugal was allowed to join NATO and benefit from its security umbrella in the post-war world, even though membership had been refused to Franco's Spain. While the Communist Party (PCP) and the liberal opposition (MUD) were unable to find common ground, plots within the regime found a rallying point first round President Oscar Carmona and then around his successor Francisco Craveiro Lopes,[13] but, secure within the Western alliance, Salazar was able to face down his critics and thwart attempts to organize a coup (*golpe*) to remove him from power.

After the war Salazar's economic austerity began to thaw. The succession of five-year development plans, limited as they were, announced a commitment to economic growth, while regulations governing foreign investment in the colonies were relaxed. Industrialization began in Mozambique and Angola and foreign companies were allowed to prospect for oil and to mine iron ore. Meanwhile Salazar's facade of democracy delivered comforting electoral victories for the official candidate in the presidential elections of 1949 and 1953.

Salazar had deliberately sought to keep Portugal out of the limelight and the policies pursued by his dictatorship were of little concern to European or world politicians. All this began to change in 1958 and by the early 1960s events in Portugal and its empire had not only become headline news but threatened to tip decisively the delicate balance achieved by Cold War diplomacy.

The crisis of the regime, 1958–62

The storm clouds began to gather for Salazar early in the 1950s, at first 'no bigger than a man's hand'. Ever since its independence in 1947 India had been putting pressure on France and Portugal to relinquish the territories they held on the Indian subcontinent. The French agreed to retire from their two enclaves in 1953 but Portugal refused even to discuss the matter. In 1954 Indian 'volunteers' invaded the Portuguese territories of Dadra and Nagar Haveli but, while the International Court was asked to rule on the legitimacy of this action, Nehru did not press the case against the much larger territories of Goa, Daman and Diu. Meanwhile Britain was faced with the Mau Mau rebellion in Kenya and France with the outbreak of an independence war in Algeria. Portugal watched and waited and began to build airstrips in its African colonies. At home opposition remained cowed and little concern was expressed when a senior colonial official and deputy in the Cortes, Henrique Galvão, broke ranks and began a virulent denunciation of the colonial regime. A report on the African colonies presented to the Cortes was followed between 1952 and 1953 by a four-volume work on the Portuguese Empire co-authored with Carlos Selvagem.[14] Dismissed from the army, Galvão was arrested in 1952 but escaped abroad.

In 1958 presidential elections were due once more and the official Salazarist candidate, Admiral Américo Tomás, was duly groomed to stand for election. It had been customary for opposition candidates to withdraw in protest before polling day but in 1958 a charismatic figure appeared to contest the election. General Humberto Delgado was an air force general and came from the highest echelons of the military establishment. His disillusionment with Salazar was personal as much as political but, having broken ranks, he began to breathe the heady fumes of his own radical rhetoric and released among his audiences a massive wave of hostility to the regime. In politics people are almost always far clearer about what they oppose than what they support and it mattered little that Delgado's plans for Portugal and the colonies were vague. Sufficient was the reply that he is alleged to have given to a journalist who asked what he would do about Salazar were he elected president. 'I will dismiss him' was the laconic reply that summed up the common political platform of all those who backed his campaign.

Delgado did not win the election, which was duly rigged, and fled into exile, returning to Portugal from time to time in disguise in circumstances that became more and more bizarre. He was eventually assassinated in 1965 by agents of PIDE, the Portuguese secret police.[15] Delgado had failed to win but had shown the depths of the discontent beneath the surface in Portugal and had drawn the attention of the world to the unresolved issue of the future of the African colonies.

In 1960 the United Nations, which Portugal only joined in 1955 six years after it joined NATO, established a Special Committee on Decolonization to speed up the implementation of the decolonization process. The same year Salazar mounted a major propaganda exercise, which deliberately placed Portugal and its colonies in the spotlight. The occasion was the five hundredth anniversary of the death of Henry the Navigator. Celebrations, international conferences and prestige publications, the most remarkable being the *Portugaliae Monumenta Cartographica*,[16] sought to steal the initiative from the growing number of Portugal's critics. One consequence of this was that renewed scholarly attention began to be focused on the history of the Portuguese colonies. If Portuguese history had been neglected in the past outside Portugal, it was now to become the subject of an increasing number of detailed studies. Among these were a series of lectures given by Charles Boxer on race relations in the Portuguese empire. When these were published in 1963 they caused a huge furor in Portugal, and in Britain and America helped to align the academic establishment with the radical politics of African nationalism.[17] Salazar's bid to enlist academia on Portugal's side had backfired.

Already by this time the empire was in crisis. Britain had begun to grant independence to its African colonies in 1957 and in 1960, following rioting in the Congo, the Belgians decided precipitately to withdraw from theirs. The capital of the Congo lay close to the Portuguese colony of Angola, and large numbers of Angolans lived in Leopoldville and had formed political organizations which were banned in their homeland. Events in the Congo, and the apparent ease with which the Belgians had been persuaded to leave, influenced events across the border. Early in 1961 an insurrection broke out in Luanda when armed men tried to free prisoners from the jail. This was easily put down by the local security forces and few people attached much credibility to the claims of the exiled nationalists who had formed the MPLA that they were responsible. What attracted far more attention was Galvão's dramatic hijacking of a Portuguese cruise liner, the *Santa Maria*. Before seeking asylum in Brazil, he and his men sailed around the South Atlantic for ten days proclaiming that they had liberated a piece of Portuguese territory.

Following the suppression of the insurrection in Luanda, there were a series of rural outbreaks in northern Angola directly inspired by events across the frontier. These revolts were poorly organized and extremely violent. White plantation-owners and black migrant workers were massacred by armed men set in motion by the FNLA in the Congo. African independence movements, which since the suppression of Mau Mau had been largely non-violent, had suddenly erupted into savagery. The Portuguese responded in kind. Salazar was determined that there would be no Belgian-style retreat. The army was reinforced and settler militias were mobilized. The rebellious rural areas were rapidly reoccupied and this was followed by extensive killings of those thought to be involved and the flight of even larger numbers of refugees across the border into the Congo.

These events attracted the full glare of world publicity as the Protestant missions in the Congo published horrific accounts of the security operations and directly accused the Portuguese of targeting the Protestant churches.[18] Portugal's civilizing mission that had been trumpeted so widely the year before was now shown up in all its brutal reality.[19]

Salazar's suppression of the Angolan uprisings was complete by the end of the year (it had taken the British four years to defeat Mau Mau in Kenya), but by then he had received another humiliating exposure to the realities of international politics. In December 1961, faced with an imminent political challenge from radical nationalists led by Krishna Menon, Nehru decided to seize the Portuguese enclaves in India. On 19 December Indian forces invaded Goa, Daman and Diu, which surrendered without a struggle. Salazar had appealed to Britain and the Anglo-Portuguese alliance but it had always been Britain's interpretation of the terms of the alliance that it only guaranteed the integrity of mainland Portugal, not the overseas colonies or provinces. In the event Britain remonstrated with India but took no action.

Salazar's hard line in Angola, and his intransigence in refusing to accept India's intervention in Goa, stemmed at least in part from his having successfully survived an attempt from inside the regime to replace him. Little was heard at the time about the plot against Salazar but it was the most serious challenge that he faced in his long political career. It was led by General Júlio Carlos Botelho Moniz and a group of senior generals, among whom was the commander of the Lisbon garrison. It also seems that the plotters had the support of Craveiro Lopes, a former president, and General Francisco da Costa Gomes, who was later to emerge as the radical president of Portugal after the successful coup of 1974. The plot was betrayed to Salazar, who acted swiftly against the conspirators. The conspiracy was at least in part a response to the critical events in Angola and Salazar's crushing of the opposition was tantamount to a clear declaration that there was to be no retreat in Africa and that the pure doctrine of Salazarism, which asserted the unity of Portugal and its colonies in one indivisible nation, was not to be tampered with. Although there was a half-hearted and wholly unsuccessful attempt at military revolt the following year, the events of 1961 had in the end left the prime minister stronger than ever. There were to be no further serious challenges to him before he was incapacitated by a stroke in 1968.

If the events in India and Angola had achieved nothing else, they had thrust Portugal and its affairs into the forefront of international concerns.

The colonial war, 1961–74

The fighting that broke out in Angola in 1961 was the beginning of more than a decade of guerrilla warfare which spread to Guiné in 1963 and Mozambique in 1964.

Seen in retrospect these wars were not so much a military confrontation as an ideological struggle on a world stage, and a conflict between rival groups of African nationalists who sought to inherit power in the post-colonial era. The wars were also, of course, the instruments which ultimately broke the Portuguese regime and brought about a fundamental change of direction for Portugal itself.

In Angola and Mozambique the Portuguese army had little difficulty in containing the weak and disorganized efforts of the African guerrillas to infiltrate the country. In Angola the war was confined to remote border regions and the rival nationalist forces spent as much time fighting each other as they did fighting the Portuguese. In Mozambique the bitter conflicts within Frelimo and the frequent defections from its leadership were not finally resolved till 1970, when the armed forces of the movement were hammered by a major Portuguese offensive in the north – the famous Operation Gordian Knot. It was not until 1972 that any significant military offensive could be mounted against the Portuguese and by that time political events were on the move. In Guiné the nationalist forces operating out of neighbouring Senegal and Guinea were able to pin the Portuguese down to fortified camps throughout much of the rural interior but the Portuguese retained control of the towns and the regions where the majority of the population lived.

It was on the world stage that the really important phase of the war took place. The Portuguese sought allies among conservative political groups in Europe and the United States and courted the regime in Brazil, taking advantage of the 150th anniversary of Brazil's independence in 1972 to return the body of Dom Pedro, the first Emperor of Brazil, a gesture which the Portuguese Foreign Minister, Rui Patrício, claimed 'deeply touched the heart of the Brazilian people'.[20] The Portuguese also tried, eventually with some success, to obtain NATO help by representing the wars as a security risk for the western alliance. The Portuguese also established close cooperation with the South Africans and Rhodesians to present a common front against black nationalism. The struggle, Salazar maintained, was one of multiracial Christian civilization against racist, Communist, black nationalism. The Portuguese claimed that their record of economic progress was far superior to that of most independent African countries and that 'anti-Portuguese terrorism would have ended a long time ago if it were not for the outside support it gets.'[21] The support of the Vatican was important to both sides. In 1967 Salazar secured a great propaganda coup when the pope visited Portugal to celebrate the fiftieth anniversary of the Fatima visions. Only four years later, however, the Vatican had shifted its position and the leaders of the nationalist movements were received in audience in Rome.

The nationalist movements operated more effectively on the international stage than on the battlefield. Nationalist politics was late to develop in the Portuguese African colonies and for the most part grew up among exiles living abroad. Nationalist activity was particularly strong among the BaKongo exiles in Kinshasa who were able to build on a tradition of radical Christian religious movements. Their vision of an Africanist alternative to Portuguese rule was, however, opposed by Creole and mestizo exiles who formed the MPLA sometime around 1958. In Mozambique a nationalist movement was even later to emerge, Frelimo only being formed in 1962 on the fragile base of small exile groups in Tanzania, Zambia and Malawi. A divergence in outlook soon became apparent between 'Africanists' among the ethnic Makonde and the educated radicals and Creoles from the urban areas of the south. This culminated in the assassination of Frelimo's first leader Eduardo Mondlane in 1969. In Guiné the PAIGC was dominated from the start by Cape Verdean Creoles, who established total control of the movement in 1964 with the purge and execution of 'Africanist' opposition elements.

The MPLA, Frelimo and PAIGC, all controlled by an educated Creole elite, cooperated closely together and elaborated a socialist discourse which proved highly effective in securing the support of radical intellectuals in the West and the non-aligned movement in general. Already by the late 1960s there was some disillusionment among the supporters of African independence with what had occurred in the former British, French and Belgian colonies. There were allegations of neo-colonialism and of a failure to secure change beyond a hauling down of the flag of the colonial powers. The Portuguese African nationalists, especially Amílcar Cabral, talked of more radical change, of a liberation from the forms of capitalism and tribalism which had persisted in other African countries. These ideas were eagerly adopted by Western intellectuals hungry for a new vision which would offer a radical alternative to both Western capitalism and Eastern Bloc Communism.

In retrospect the naivety of those who found in Cabral, Neto and Machel messiahs of a new world order is little short of staggering and was brutally revealed in the aftermath of independence as Angola and Mozambique collapsed into bloody civil war and the leaders of Guiné massacred those associated with the Portuguese, expelled the Creoles and quickly reverted to a traditional rural society which knew nothing of Cabral's socialist utopia. While the war continued, however, the cause of African nationalism in the Portuguese colonies was a dominant theme of academic African studies and helped to form opinion about post-colonial Africa throughout much of western Europe and the United States. The Portuguese African colonies assumed an importance in their demise which they had never had during their heyday.

The Portuguese Revolution

Salazar suffered a stroke in 1968 and died the following year. He was replaced by a longtime stalwart of the regime, Marcello Caetano, an academic lawyer and historian who had held many ministerial and administrative posts. Caetano never wielded the authority within the regime that Salazar had done and for five years maintained an uneasy balancing act between those who sought to modernize the New State and those opposed to any significant change of direction. As a result Caetano's government often seemed rudderless, not least in its policy towards Africa. By 1973 it had become clear that support for the regime was haemorrhaging fast and a secret organization among junior army officers, the Movimento das Forças Armadas (MFA), began preparing the way for a coup. Aware of dissidence in the army, Caetano tried to flush out his enemies by demanding a public oath of loyalty from the leading generals. António de Spínola and Francisco da Costa Gomes refused and resigned. At the same time Spínola's book *Portugal e o Futuro,* which appeared early in 1974 and was rapidly translated into French and English, was seen as a direct challenge to Caetano and as a bid for power.

After at least one false start the coup was launched on 25 April 1974, the signal for the various elements to move famously being given by the Portuguese folk song *Grândola, Vila Morena* being played on the radio. The military took control of Lisbon with no casualties and Caetano and president Tomás resigned power into the hands of Spínola, who was installed as interim head of government.

The coup, although so clearly signalled over the previous months, took the world by surprise. The American ambassador, for example, was absent in the Azores and, when he found he could not get back to Lisbon, flew to Boston 'to attend a class reunion at Harvard Law School'. The Deputy Chief of Mission left in charge received a phone call in the middle of the night but 'hung up and went back to sleep'.[22] Only one press photographer captured the key scenes and his pictures were syndicated to every newspaper throughout Europe.

The revolution left Portugal in the hands of a very diverse and uneasy coalition of forces. As so often in politics, people were united by what they opposed, not by what they planned for the future. The men who overthrew Caetano ranged from traditionalists on the right, through the middle ground of social democracy to Communists and anarchists on the left, while the military played the key active role in the events of April and were to continue to play a key role for the next two years. These factions did not agree on a future shape for Portugal nor on what to do about Africa. The manifesto of the MFA had merely stated that there must be a political solution to the wars in Africa, but what this meant in practice no one was clear.

The African colonies did, indeed, present the most urgent problem. In the latter stages of the war the Portuguese high command had increasingly recruited African soldiers to fight the guerrillas. Indeed, there were more Africans fighting for the Portuguese than for nationalists. More of the cost of the war had also been transferred to the colonies, which had benefited considerably from the increased expenditure on infrastructure and services since the outbreak in 1961. Caetano had also made the first tentative steps towards devolving some power onto the local Portuguese community in Africa and elections had actually been held in 1973. However, three features of the colonial situation in April 1974 stood out.

First, the tight control that Lisbon had maintained since 1930 meant that the Portuguese community in the colonies had no control over the administration and security forces and no political institutions which could be used to implement a settler takeover. There was no local settler leadership and no settler hands on the levers of power. So the possibility of a settler regime such as that which established itself in Rhodesia was never an option. The second key factor was that no one had seriously considered the possibility of decolonization and no plans had been drawn up for a handover of power. As early as 1969 a Portuguese official spokesman had pointed out the contradictions involved in the United Nations calling for the implementation of 'the freely expressed will of the peoples' while at the same time demanding an immediate transfer of power to the nationalist guerrilla movements,[23] no one had given any thought to what exactly would be involved in transferring power to the local population,

The third factor, which in the end decided the course of events, was that the MFA effectively took control of the security situation in the colonies and made the unilateral decision to cease military operations. The soldiers retreated into their armed camps and barracks and let it be known that their priority was to be repatriated as soon as possible.

So Portugal had to resolve two problems at the same time: how to devise a stable new order for itself and how to put an end to its rule in Africa. As António José Telo wrote twenty-five years later, 'no one was in any doubt that the evolution of the internal situation was going to depend above all else on finding a solution to the wars in Africa.'[24] The two issues became intertwined in a complex manner in the months that followed the revolution. The man who had the clearest sense of direction was General Spínola. As acting president he was able to take initiatives both at home and abroad and it was soon suspected that he was aiming to establish a Gaullist, presidential constitution in Portugal. At the same time he set out a programme for the colonies which would have provided for an interim period of two years during which democratic institutions could be built, and which would be followed by referenda on their constitutional future. This was the only attempt made by any Portuguese leader to think through the process of decolonization but, as Norrie Macqueen was to write, 'the circumstances in which he attempted to implement it were hopelessly difficult . . . Neither the timescale nor the necessary stability of environment were available'.[25]

Spínola was deeply distrusted by the left-wing politicians and by the African nationalist leaders. They believed that he was trying to limit progress towards democracy and socialism and was seeking to deny the African colonies their independence. Throughout the summer of 1974 the radical officers in the MFA, in conjunction with the socialist politicians, conducted a parallel diplomacy which undermined all Spínola's initiatives. They made it clear to the African nationalists not only that the Portuguese army would no longer fight but that Spínola's 'roadmap' was not supported in Portugal itself. This reinforced the intransigence of the African nationalist leaders who refused an official ceasefire and demanded nothing short of immediate independence.

Spínola's policies brought together the forces of the left in a new coalition, which forced his resignation in September 1974. He was succeeded by General Francisco da Costa Gomes, the veteran of the

Botelho Moniz coup of 1961, with Vasco Gonçalves as prime minister. The government and the MFA were now controlled by forces of the left and there were Communist sympathizers in the government. However, the window of opportunity for action was small. Elections for a constituent assembly were to be held in April and there were fears that before that a right-wing coup might be attempted. There was a clear sense of urgency to resolve the outstanding issues in Africa while political conditions were favourable.

Negotiations proceeded rapidly and by January 1975 agreements had been reached for the independence of all the colonies. Guiné was handed over to the PAIGC with no interim period of joint administration. In São Tomé and Cape Verde elections were to be held but with no opposition candidates allowed and with a firm date for independence agreed. In Mozambique there were to be no elections and an interim administration was installed in September 1974 to rule the country for nine months until independence in July 1975. Only in Angola was a gesture made towards holding elections prior to independence and at Alvor in January 1975 it was agreed to set up an interim administration, with all three African nationalist groups represented, to organize elections prior to independence, which was set for November 1975. In the event fighting between the nationalist factions made the Alvor accord a dead letter.

The independence agreements for Africa, once signed, sealed and out of the way, allowed Portugal to turn its attention to its own internal problems. In April the elections brought a clear majority to the centre parties with the Communists and the Christian Democrats left stranded on the political margins – Mário Soares's Socialists (PS) winning 38 per cent of the vote and the Communists (PCP) only 13 per cent.

During the summer of 1975, while the details of the constitution were worked out, radical agitation in the capital created the impression that a Communist takeover was imminent. This stimulated a right-wing backlash that effectively expelled the Communist party organization from the northern part of the country. Portugal stared for the first time at the prospect of armed conflict between the radicals of Lisbon and the increasingly hostile rural areas. The confusion of the times comes out clearly from an unofficial British Labour Party account of the events of the summer of 1975. The author, Audrey Wise, was unable to decide if the anti-Communist movement was orchestrated by the Socialists or secretly by the extreme right. The violence erupted in Aveiro after a rally held by Mário Soares and began with stones smashing the windows of PCP offices, but the pattern of attacks changed. 'They now use groups coming in cars and throwing incendiaries, and people on the streets are reluctant to take part in this kind of attack.' Forest fires in the northern mountains are very common in the summer months and there is a rooted Portuguese belief that these are either caused by arsonists or by corrupt politicians with some arcane purpose to be gained. The fires could be seen as in some way fuelling the hostility to the Communists. 'The very latest kind of attack is different again – an aeroplane is now being used to drop incendiaries on forests . . . At one and the same time this is a dangerous escalation of violence and can do enormous damage, and it is also an expression of the weakness of the fascists.'[26]

The army once again proved decisive in deciding Portugal's future. The MFA chose Colonel Ramalho Eanes as its leader and he established a close working relationship with Mário Soares, the socialist leader. Eanes was able to use the army to recapture control of the streets and in the first parliamentary elections held in April 1976 the triumph of the centre left was confirmed. Significantly the army was given a formal role in the constitution as the guarantor of democracy.

The Portuguese Revolution in the history of Europe and Africa

Diogo Freitas do Amaral, who founded the right-wing Christian Democrat (CDS) party in 1974, said of the Revolution in Portugal that it was 'a political miracle, a Portuguese miracle, to have succeeded in avoiding a dictatorship of the Left without allowing the country to descend into civil war or slide back into a dictatorship of the right.'[27] The triumph of moderate social democracy in Portugal soon acquired huge significance for Europe's future. At first it had seemed that the revolution might usher in a democratically elected Communist regime, which would install Communism at the heart of NATO itself. The Revolution also rapidly led to decolonization in Africa. This resulted in the short term in an extension of the Cold War to that continent but at the same time heralded the endgame of white supremacy in the southern part of the continent. The Portuguese Revolution was also the first of the revolutions that put an end to western Europe's right-wing dictatorships. The fall of Caetano was followed a few months later by the fall of the military regime in Greece and the following year by the demise of fascist Spain with the death of General Franco.

The revolution also occurred at a crucial moment in the evolution of the European community. In 1973 Britain (and Denmark) had eventually joined the Common Market, leaving the rival EFTA, of which Portugal was a member. Portugal had also been drawn into the orbit of the Common Market. Emigration from Portugal to France and Germany had risen sharply in the 1960s and towards the end of the decade Portuguese banks had increasingly directed their investment towards Europe and away from the empire. Some of the younger figures in Caetano's government had advocated a closer association with Europe and this was also being considered by the opposition politicians. It was the socialist leader Mário Soares who most clearly perceived that Portugal's future lay in Europe and that disencumbering itself from Africa was an urgent first step to take.

The Portuguese revolution was also a defining moment for European Communism. The Communist Party in Portugal had been by far the best-organized opposition movement, even though it had had to operate underground. When the Revolution occurred the Communists were able to play a key role in taking over land and businesses, in dominating the trades unions and media and in placing their members in key positions in the MFA and the government. Moreover, the Communists had an experienced and able leader in Álvaro Cunhal. No other Communist party in Western Europe had come so close to real power in the state. However, the Communist influence peaked with the decolonization of the African provinces. On the streets it was challenged by extreme socialist or anarchist elements, while it lost ground to the PS in capturing middle opinion. The elections of April 1975 revealed how small its electoral support really was. The failure in Portugal, in circumstances that were uniquely favourable for the Communists, became in the longer term a failure for Communism in general.

The process of decolonization in Africa was little short of disastrous. For Portuguese politicians and the MFA the sole objective was to leave Africa as soon as possible with the minimum amount of disturbance. This was achieved, even in Guiné, and Portugal withdrew its administrative and military personnel without violence. However, in none of the other colonies was any serious attempt made to negotiate the terms of the handover. Portugal never insisted on genuine elections being held which would test opinion and validate the successor regimes. No post-independence constitutions were agreed and no provisions were made for the legal, economic or institutional future of the new states. Questions of debt and private property were unresolved and no legal or economic framework was left behind. In São Tomé and Cape Verde independence was granted, although it was by no means clear that the successor regimes had majority support within the island communities and the proposition that Cape Verde might remain part of Portugal, like the other island groups of the Azores and Madeira, was never tested.

The consequence of the precipitate withdrawal of the Portuguese was that Angola descended at once into civil war. Mozambique enjoyed a few years of uneasy government by a radical guerrilla movement before also sliding into a civil war even more violent than that of Angola. Guiné experienced an immediate blood-letting as supporters of the colonial regime were rounded up and killed, before experiencing a collapse of civil government and reversion to a pre-colonial rural economy. São Tomé remained relatively peaceful but its economy rapidly deteriorated until it became one of the poorest countries in Africa. Moreover the precipitate nature of Portugal's retreat plunged southern Africa into a decade of warfare as the rivalries of western and eastern blocs were fought out on the battlefields of Angola and in the guerrilla bush campaigns in Rhodesia and Mozambique.

The Portuguese have always claimed that, in quitting Africa in the way they did, there was no other course open to them. Getting out as soon as possible was the only option. Given the unwillingness of the army to continue to carry out military operations in the colonies, Portugal indeed had few means of maintaining the colonial government for an interim period. However, by far the most important consideration was the lack of any will among the political elite in Portugal to try to negotiate a properly managed transfer of power and this lack of will arose from the deep divisions and lack of trust among the politicians in Portugal itself. Any staged handover of power would have appeared to the left as an attempt to delay or even thwart decolonization and there were even fears that a delaying action in the colonies might somehow be translated into a delay in introducing full democracy in Portugal, while any protection extended to settler businesses and property could be represented as interfering with the transition to socialism in the domestic setting.

Although, after the initial shock of the revolution, there was intense international interest in the unfolding of events in Portugal, there was no attempt by the international community to help Portugal carry out a phased decolonization. The rivalries of the Cold War meant that anything short of an immediate handover could be exploited to their advantage by the eastern or the non-aligned bloc. The struggle for the future of Africa was going to be fought out by Africans themselves and there was little to be gained by interfering with the departure of the Portuguese from the scene.

Epilogue

After the excitement of the 1974 April Revolution and the retreat from Africa Portugal assumed the stance of a small state with small ambitions, but history seldom allows a country to escape its past so easily. By 1986 the Portuguese were prepared to begin to come to terms with their imperial past and a Commission was established to celebrate the early history of Portuguese expansion with something of the same dedication to the theme that had previously been shown by Salazar. In 1996 Portugal worked with Brazil to create an international organization of Portuguese-speaking countries – in some people's eyes a linguistic and cultural shadow empire – and in 1998 it organized Expo'98, a highly successful international fair to celebrate Vasco da Gama's epic voyage to India five hundred years earlier. Portugal's profile in the world was becoming increasingly pronounced. In 1998 José Saramago was awarded the Nobel Prize for Literature and in 2004 the Portuguese prime minister, José Manuel (Durão) Barroso, became the twelfth president of the European Commission. Thirty years after the April Revolution had apparently ended Portugal's role as an imperial power, Portugal was once again a player of significance on the European (and world) stage.

The constitution of 1976 that finally produced a democratically elected government had brought stability to Portugal under the unlikely leadership of the distinctly uncharismatic army colonel António Ramalho Eanes, who served two terms as president from 1976–85. In choosing him it was as though the country was visibly exhausted from the excitements brought about by dictators, generals and anarchists. In 1980 the constitution was amended to remove the constitutional role of the army council as guarantors of democracy and in 1989 a second amendment ended the 'irreversibility' of the nationalizations that had taken place in 1975. By that time democracy had come to mean a return to a sort of *rotativismo* which saw Socialists (PS) and Social Democrats (PSD) alternate in power.

The dominant political figure during these years was Mário Soares, who was twice prime minister from 1976–8 and 1983–5 and then president of Portugal from 1986–96. This veteran leader of the Socialists possessed political capital, built up in the years of opposition to Salazar and Caetano, which seemed to be well-nigh inexhaustible. Soares, a more or less enthusiastic convert to the European idea, had the satisfaction of bringing Portugal into full membership of the European Community in 1986. Portugal's recognition of its European destiny had had a long gestation. While Salazar had remained determined to retain the empire and with it the economic independence of Portugal and a strong currency, he and his successor Marcello Caetano had nevertheless pursued policies of economic convergence with the rest of Europe. During the 1960s Portugal's regulated industries had developed a strong export orientation, principally in textiles, and this, together with tourism, built up substantial currency reserves. Portugal joined EFTA and in 1961 GATT, the IMF and the World Bank. In 1972, after the UK had decided to join the European Community, Portugal signed a free trade agreement with the EEC while pursuing a policy of disinvestment in Africa. Portugal was becoming a 'European' country and it was a European destiny for which the Portuguese people themselves voted – if not in the ballot box then with their feet, for in the late 1960s emigration to France and Germany reached huge and unsustainable proportions. With the 1974 Revolution, as Jorge Braga de Macedo wrote, 'the domestic objective constraining European integration changed'[1] and in 1977, one year into its first democratic government, formal application was made to join the European Community.

By joining Europe Soares had provided Portugal with an answer to what would otherwise have been a real dilemma. Without its empire and the leverage which this gave Portugal in international affairs, the country would have been weak and vulnerable. However, it has been one of the triumphs of the European Union that within its community small ethnicities can survive without being swallowed by larger empires or predatory nation states, as had happened so often in the preceding centuries. The suggestion, first floated in 2002, that the Cape Verde Islands might one day seek membership of the EU offered a further fascinating prospect of the scattered bones of the old Portuguese empire one day reassembling under the protection of an overarching Europe.

Having joined the European community Portugal immediately began to benefit from European funding. EU money financed major infrastructure projects which promoted employment and economic growth. The large numbers of *retornados* – former settlers and Africans who had served the colonial regime – whose arrival in Portugal in 1975 had increased the national population by 10 per cent were quickly absorbed. With the stimulus of EU funding Portugal developed a taste for modernity which could be seen in its architecture and in the readiness with which it adopted modern styles of living after long years of conservative repression. Like the Republic of Ireland, another country whose long tradition of emigration had substantially influenced its culture and sense of identity, Portugal soon found that it was attracting immigrants, not only from Portuguese-speaking countries but from eastern Europe. The centuries-old haemorrhage of population to Brazil was remarkably reversed.

In some ways Portugal was unprepared for the consequences of joining Europe. Rapid economic growth produced an unregulated building boom which covered the hills round Lisbon with concrete, clogged the roads with traffic and led to an urban sprawl that crept northwards along the highways towards Coimbra and along the southern Algarve coast to provide timeshares and golf courses for expatriate British and Germans. Some of the major infrastructure projects, like the Vasco da Gama bridge designed to provide Lisbon with a second Tagus crossing, were embarked upon with little or no concern for their environmental impact.[2] Environmental degradation marched abreast with prosperity and much of the old Portugal was swept away with an almost unseemly haste. Nowhere was this more apparent than in the island of Madeira. Long one of the poorest parts of Portugal, generating waves of emigrants in the nineteenth and twentieth centuries, Madeira acquired autonomous status in 1976 and embarked upon a heady economic expansion which turned Funchal into a sprawling metropolis swallowing up the surrounding mountainsides.

Although decolonization (with the single exception of Macao) had been completed in 1975 the imperial legacy remained and gradually dragged Portugal back into a world of wider commitments. Although the makers of the Revolution had tried to sever links with Africa, Portugal found itself forced to play a role in the bloody Angolan civil war – if only because of the knowledge it possessed of Angolan conditions. Portugal hosted the discussions which led to the Bicesse Accords which were signed in May 1991 and made provision for elections which it was hoped would end the Angolan civil war. Portugal also began to provide modest aid to its former colonies which served to knit up the economic and social networks that had been so rudely torn apart in 1975. Portuguese

experts returned to São Tomé to try to revive the flagging cocoa production and Portuguese banks played a leading role in the rapidly expanding
Cape Verdian economy. Portuguese diplomacy was also active in help-
ing to resolve the Indonesian occupation of East Timor in 1999,
Portugal's prime minister, António Guterres, admitting to a *Financial
Times* reporter in a disarming manner, 'I think that to be honest we have
a debt to the East Timorese. We were the colonial power, and we did not
do much for them.'[3] To the scarcely concealed delight of Portuguese
politicians East Timor opted to use Portuguese as one of its official languages when its independence was officially recognized in 2002.

The most important sign that Portugal would try to build a new role
for itself on the ruins of its empire was the creation in 1996 of CPLP
(Comunidades dos Países de Língua Portuguesa). During the wars of liberation the Portuguese African colonies had worked closely with each
other and had provided a common front during the negotiations leading
to decolonization. These links had continued after independence and
had at times assumed considerable importance, for example when São
Tomé experienced a military coup and sought aid from its Portuguese-
speaking allies. Portugal had been largely excluded from these African
discussions and had reacted in a negative way to Guiné joining the CFA
franc zone in 1994 and Mozambique seeking (and obtaining) entry into
the Commonwealth in 1995. So Portugal welcomed the initiative of
Brazil to build on the experience of linguistic cooperation that had begun
in 1989 with the IILP (Instituto Internacional da Língua Portuguesa) and
to create an organization at government level to coordinate cooperation
between Portuguese-speaking countries in 1996. This brought together
Portugal, Brazil, East Timor and the five African states which, the CPLP
proudly announced, together constituted 7.2 per cent of the world's land
surface. Language and a shared colonial past proved the unifying basis,
indeed the only basis, for this institution and its creation was a recognition that the Portuguese language was not only an official language of
international bodies in Europe, South America and Africa but was the
seventh most widely spoken language in the world, and hence a significant vehicle for educational and cultural exchange. Portuguese language
and the culture associated with it, it was hoped, would also bridge the
ethnic and linguistic differences that threatened to tear Timor apart and
would help to build cooperation between Brazil and Africa. If the world-
wide importance of the Portuguese language owed more to Brazil than
Portugal it nevertheless conferred on European Portugal a status in the
world it might not otherwise have achieved.

In 1986, ten years after securing its liberal democracy, the Portuguese government established the Comissão Nacional para as Comemorações dos Descobrimentos Portugueses. Towards the end of every century Portugal has traditionally celebrated twenty years of centenaries, extending from the death of Camões in 1580 to the turn of the next century when Cabral's discovery of Brazil requires recognition. On the way the Portuguese have to come to terms with Vasco da Gama, whose status as national icon has always been somewhat controversial. The Comissão proved enormously energetic and productive, producing an impressive range of historical publications and scholarly editions. Significantly this revival was focused, as it had been under Salazar, on the early days of imperial expansion, when Portugal could realistically claim to be a world power and there were centenaries to prove it. With few exceptions, however, it was left to non-Portuguese to look at the post-1800 imperial history, which in Portugal was still deemed too sensitive an issue for most historians to touch. In striking contrast to Spain, which did not seem to have found a way of celebrating its the imperial past, the work of the Comissão helped to create a national historiography which offered the Portuguese an appreciation of their role in initiating globalization and made their imperial story central to an understanding of the modern world.

References

Introduction

1 Maria Isabel Barreno, 'The Loss of Memory' in Fátima Monteiro, José Tavares, Miguel Glatzer and Ângelo Cardoso, *Portugal: Strategic Options in a European Context* (Lanham, MD, 2003), p. 10; Maria Isabel Barreno, Maria Teresa Horta and Maria Velho da Costa, *Novas Cartas Portuguesas* (Lisbon, 1972).
2 This theme has already been extensively explored. See Ana Maria Homem de Mello, *Oito Séculos de Portugal na Cultura Europeia* (Lisbon, 1992).
3 Nuno Severiano Teixeira, 'Between Africa and Europe: Portuguese Foreign Policy, 1890–1986', in *Modern Portugal*, ed. António Costa Pinto (Palo Alto, CA, 2003), p. 60.
4 *Internationale Spectator* [Netherlands], 18 May 1949, quoted in S. J. Bosgra and C. van Krimpen, *Portugal and NATO* (Amsterdam, 1969) p. 4.
5 Baillie W. Diffie, *Prelude to Empire: Portugal Overseas before Henry the Navigator* (Lincoln, NE, 1960), p. 41.
6 José Moraes Sarmento, *The Anglo-Portuguese Alliance and Coast Defence* (London, 1908), quoted in V. de Bragança Cunha, *Revolutionary Portugal (1910–1936)* (London, 1936), pp. 185–6.
7 Ibid.
8 Reported in *The Guardian*, 17 July 2007.
9 Manuel Rafael Amaro da Costa, *Economic Humanism in the Overseas Provinces* (Lisbon, 1962), p. 11.

1 The Second Crusade and the Capture of Lisbon

1 R. A. Fletcher, 'Reconquest and Crusade in Spain, *c.* 1050–1150', in *The Crusades*, ed. Thomas F. Madden (Oxford, 2002), pp. 51–68.
2 Jean Flori, 'Ideology and Motivations in the First Crusade', in *Palgrave Advances in the Crusades*, ed. Helen J. Nicholson (Basingstoke, 2005), pp. 15–36. Quotation from p. 29.
3 Matthew Bennet, 'Military Aspects of the Conquest of Lisbon', in *The Second Crusade: Scope and Consequences*, ed. Jonathan Phillips and Martin Hoch (Manchester, 2001), pp. 71–89. Quotation from p. 75.
4 Jonathan Riley-Smith, 'Early Crusaders to the East and the Costs of Crusading, 1095–1130', in *The Crusades*, ed. Madden, pp. 155–71. Quotation from p. 163.

5   Susan Edgington, 'Albert of Aachen, St Bernard and the Second Crusade',
    in *The Second Crusade*, ed. Phillips and Hoch (Manchester, 2001), p. 61.

6   José Mattoso, *História de Portugal*, vol. II (Lisbon, 1993), p. 64.

7   The MS usually known as *De Expugnatione Lyxbonensi* is now thought to have
    been written by a priest called Raoul in the form of a letter to another priest,
    Osbert of Bawdsey in England. It survives in a single copy in the library of Cor-
    pus Christi College, Cambridge. There have been a number of editions of this
    manuscript. The edition, with translation, used here is that of Charles Wendell
    David, *De Expugnatione Lyxbonensi* (New York, 1936), reprinted with a new intro-
    duction by Jonathan Phillips with the title *The Conquest of Lisbon* (New York,
    2001). The other account survives in three copies and is usually known as *The
    Lisbon Letter*. It was also written by a priest, called Winand, and was addressed
    to the archbishop of Cologne. A discussion of this text and its origin, with an
    English translation, is contained in Susan Edgington, 'Albert of Aachen, St
    Bernard and the Second Crusade', in *The Second Crusade*, ed. Phillips and Hoch,
    pp. 54–70. The text of both manuscripts with Portuguese translation were pub-
    lished in 1935 by José Augusto de Oliveira. See J. A. de Oliveira, *Conquista de Lis-
    boa aos Mouros (1147)* (Lisbon, 1935, 2nd edn 1936). Neither Edgington nor
    Phillips refer to Oliveira's edition and translation. The most recent Portuguese
    edition is Aires A. Nascimento, ed., *A Conquista de Lisboa aos Mouros: Relato de
    um Cruzado* (Lisbon, 2001), with an introduction by Maria João Branco.

8   José Hermano Saraiva, *História Concisa de Portugal*, 19th edn (Lisbon, 1998) p. 47.

9   It has been argued that twelfth-century Christian armies in the Iberian penin-
    sula did not have the technical capacity to take fortified cities. Matthew Ben-
    nett, 'Military Aspects of the Conquest of Lisbon', in *The Second Crusade*, ed.
    Phillips and Hoch, pp. 71–89.

10 David, *The Conquest of Lisbon*, p. 85.

11 Ibid., p. 103.

12 Ibid., p. 111.

13 Ibid., p. 113.

14 Edgington, 'Albert of Aachen, St Bernard and the Second Crusade', p. 64.

15 Ibid., p. 64.

16 Ibid., p. 65.

17 David, *The Conquest of Lisbon*, p. 177.

18 Maria João Branco, 'Introdução', in *A Conquista de Lisboa aos Mouros*, ed. Nasci-
    mento, p. 11.

19 Ibid., p. 35.

20 Ibid., p. 11.

21 Maria João Branco, 'A Conquista de Lisboa Revisitada', *Arqueologia Medieval*, vii
    (2001), p. 224.

22 Branco, 'Introdução', *A Conquista de Lisboa aos Mouros*, ed. Nascimento, p. 12.

23 David, *The Conquest of Lisbon*, pp. 92–3.

24 Ibid., p. 181.

25 Álvaro da Veiga Coimbra, 'Ordens Militares de Cavalaria de Portugal', *Revista
    Histórica de São Paulo*, xxvi (1963), p. 24.

26 David, *The Conquest of Lisbon*, p. 91.

2 The Hundred Years War and the Crisis of Portugese Independence

1 Bailey W. Diffie, *Prelude to Empire: Portugal Overseas before Henry the Navigator* (Lincoln, NE, 1960), p. 41.
2 José Mattoso, *História de Portugal*, vol. II (Lisbon, 1993), p. 168.
3 For these events see the classic account by P. E. Russell, *The English Intervention in Spain and Portugal in the Time of Edward III and Richard II* (Oxford, 1955).
4 Ibid., p. 169.
5 A. H. de Oliveira Marques, *Daily Life in Portugal in the Late Middle Ages* (Madison, WI, 1971), p. 189.
6 Derek Lomax and R. J. Oakley, *The English in Portugal 1367–87* (Warminster, 1988), p. 73. This book consists of extracts from Fernão Lopes's *Chronicles of Dom Fernando and Dom João.*
7 Ibid., pp. 119–27.
8 Russell, *The English Intervention in Spain and Portugal in the Time of Edward II and Richard II*, p. 334.
9 P. E. Russell, chapter 8 of *Portugal, Spain and the African Atlantic, 1343–1490* (Aldershot, 1995).
10 John Bourchier, Lord Berners, trans., *The Chronicles of Froissart*, ed. G. C. Macaulay (London, 1913), vol. II, chap. 34, p. 347.
11 Peter Reid, *A Brief History of Medieval Warfare: The Rise and Fall of English Supremacy at Arms 1314–1485* (London, 2008), p. 241.
12 Russell, *The English Intervention in Spain and Portugal in the Time of Edward III and Richard II*, p. 397.
13 João Gouveia Monteiro, *A Guerra em Portugal* (Lisbon, 1998), pp. 291–2, and *Aljubarrota 1385: A Batalha Real* (Lisbon, 2003).

3 Portugal and the Discoveries

1 By far the most reliable general English account of fifteenth-century Portuguese expansion is Bailey W. Diffie and George D. Winius, *Foundations of the Portuguese Empire, 1415–1580* (Oxford, 1977); the most recent general account in Portuguese is A. H. de Oliveira Marques, *A Expansão Quatrocentista*, Nova História da Expansão Portuguesa, vol II (Lisbon, 1998).
2 P. E. Russell, *Prince Henry 'the Navigator'* (New Haven, CT, and London, 2000), p. 76.
3 The economic forces behind fifteenth-century Portuguese expansion in Morocco and in the Atlantic were explained in Vitorino de Magalhães Godinho, *A Economia dos Descobrimentos Henriquinos* (Lisbon, 1962).
4 Russell, *Prince Henry 'the Navigator'*, pp. 30–31.
5 David Lopes, *A Expansão em Marrocos* (Lisbon, 1989), p. 47.
6 Maria Leonor García da Cruz, 'As controvérsias ao tempo de D. João III sobre a política portuguesa no Norte de África', *Mare Liberum*, xiv (1997), pp. 117–98.
7 J.R.C. Martyn, *The Siege of Mazagan* (New York, 1994).
8 For an English account of the wars in Morocco seen from a Moroccan viewpoint see Weston F. Cook, *The Hundred Years War for Morocco* (Boulder, CO, 1994).

9   For a detailed account of European enterprise in the Canary Islands see David
    Abulafia, *The Discovery of Mankind* (New Haven, CT, 2008).

10 T. Bentley Duncan, *Atlantic Islands* (Chicago, IL, 1972); a near contemporary
    description of the discovery and settlement of Madeira is given by Alvise da
    Cadamosto, see G. R. Crone, ed., *The Voyages of Cadamosto* (London, 1937).

11 Jacinto Monteiro, *Alguns aspectos da história açoriana nos séculos xv–xvi* (Angra,
    1982).

12 C. R. Beazley and Edgar Prestage, *The Chronicle of the Discovery and Conquest of
    Guinea*, 2 vols (London, 1896–9), p. 258, and Léon Bourdon, trans., *Chronique de
    Guinée (1453)* (Paris, 1994), p. 244.

13 Beazley and Prestage, *The Chronicle of the Discovery and Conquest of Guinea*,
    p. 261, and Bourdon, trans., *Chronique de Guinée (1453)*, p. 247.

14 Crone, ed., *The Voyages of Cadamosto*.

15 João Paulo Oliveira e Costa, 'D. Afonso v e o Atlântico a base do projecto
    expansionista de D. João II', *Mare Liberum*, xvii (1999) pp. 39–71.

16 For this maritime struggle between Portugal and Castile see P. E. Russell,
    'Castilian Documentary Sources for the History of Portuguese Expansion in
    Guinea in the Last Years of the Reign of Dom Afonso v', in P. E. Russell, *Portu-
    gal, Spain and the African Atlantic 1343–1490* (Aldershot, 1995).

17 The best study of Elmina is J. Bato'ora Ballong-Wen-Mewuda, *São Jorge da
    Mina 1482–1637* (Lisbon and Paris, 1993).

18 The most detailed English account of these voyages is provided by Eric Axel-
    son, *Congo to Cape: Early Portuguese Explorers* (London, 1973).

19 Elizabeth Mancke, 'Empire and State', in *The British Atlantic World, 1500–1800*,
    ed. David Armitage and Michael Braddick (Basingstoke, 2002), p. 176.

20 Elizabeth Mancke, 'Power, Space, and the Making of Early Modern Empires',
    paper presented to the Ohio Seminar in Early American History and Culture,
    at Ohio State University, 2003.

21 Quoted in João Rocha Pinto, 'Le Vent, le Fer et la Muraille', in *Lisbonne hors les
    Murs*, ed. Michel Chandeigne (Paris, 1990), p. 234.

22 See Sanjay Subrahmanyam, *The Career and Legend of Vasco da Gama* (Cam-
    bridge, 1997).

4 The First European Maritime Empire

1   The most important work in English on the Portuguese empire is undoubtedly
    C. R. Boxer, *The Portuguese Seaborne Empire* (London, 1969). Other general ac-
    counts are Sanjay Subrahmanyam, *The Portuguese Empire in Asia, 1500–1700*
    (London, 1993) and Malyn Newitt, *A History of Portuguese Overseas Expansion,
    1400–1668* (London, 2005). See also Francisco Bethencourt and Diogo Ramada
    Curto, eds, *Portuguese Oceanic Expansion, 1400–1800* (Cambridge, 2007).

2   M. N. Pearson, *The New Cambridge History of India: 1: The Portuguese in India*
    (Cambridge, 1987), pp. 57–8.

3   Quoted in Joan-Pau Rubiés, *Travel and Ethnology in the Renaissance: South India
    through European Eyes, 1250–1625* (Cambridge, 2000), p. 223.

4   For a discussion of these works see C. R. Boxer, *Two Pioneers of Tropical Medi-
    cine: Garcia d'Orta and Nicolás Monardes,* in Diamante, 14, 1963) and *South China*

in the Sixteenth Century (London, 1953)

5 Rubiés, *Travel and Ethnology in the Renaissance*, p. 253.

6 Rebecca Catz, *The Travels of Mendes Pinto* (Chicago, IL, 1989), pp. 149, 152.

7 Francisco Carletti, *My Voyage Round the World*, ed. Herbert Weinstock (London, 1964).

8 Leonard Blussé, *Strange Company: Chinese Settlers, Mestizo Women and the Dutch in VOC Batavia* (Dordrecht, 1986), p. 165.

9 A.J.R. Russell-Wood, *A World on the Move: The Portuguese in Africa, Asia, and America, 1415–1808* (Manchester, 1992), p. 175. This book provides a detailed discussion of the dissemination of plants and animals by the Portuguese.

5 The Union with Spain and the Armada, 1578–89

1 Letter dated Lisbon, 3 Feb 1580, in Viktor von Klarwill, ed., *The Fugger News-letters*, Second Series (London, 1926), pp. 35–6.

2 Augusto Salgado, *Os Navios de Portugal na Grande Armada* (Lisbon, 2004), p. 33.

3 John Guilmartin, *Galleons and Galleys* (London, 2002), p. 155.

4 For the preparations made in Lisbon, see Salgado, *Os Navios de Portugal na Grande Armada*, pp. 32–63.

5 Letter of the Duke of Medina Sidonia to Philip II, 14 June 1588, in *The Great Enterprise. The History of the Spanish Armada*, ed. Stephen Usherwood (London, 1988), pp. 89–90.

6 Letter of Edmund Palmer, 15 July 1589, quoted in R. B.Wernham, *After the Armada* (Oxford, 1984), p. 130.

6 The Portugese Restoration and the General Crisis of the Seventeenth Century

1 T. Bentley Duncan, 'Navigation between Portugal and Asia in the Sixteenth and Seventeenth Centuries', in *Asia and the West: Encounters and Exchanges from the Age of Exploration*, ed. C. K. Pullapilly and E. J. van Kley (Notre Dame, IN, 1986), p. 22.

2 J. H. Elliott, *The Count-Duke of Olivares* (New Haven, CT, and London, 1986), p. 530.

3 J. H. Elliott, *Richelieu and Olivares* (Cambridge, 1984), p. 64.

4 Elliott, *The Count-Duke of Olivares*, p. 26.

5 Christian Hermann and Jacques Marcadé, *Les royaumes ibériques au XVIIe siècle* (Liège, 2000), p. 142.

6 António de Oliveira, 'Levantamentos Populares do Algarve em 1637–1638', *Revista Portuguesa de História*, XX (1983), p. 33.

7 Anon, *O Sebastianismo: breve panorama dum mito português* (Lisbon, 1978), p. 10.

8 Abbé Vertot, *The History of the Revolutions of Portugal*, 5th edn (London, 1754), p. 26.

9 Vertot, *The History of the Revolutions of Portugal*, p. 16.

10 Letter of François Lanier, Lisbon, 27 July 1643, printed in Edgar Prestage, *Informes de Francisco Lanier sobre Francisco de Lucena e a côrte de D. Joâo IV* (Coimbra, 1931), p. 13.

11 Quoted in I. S. Révah, *Le Cardinal de Richelieu et la Restauration du Portugal* (Lisbon, 1950), p. 8.
12 See letters from the Crown to the Duke, printed in ibid., pp. 55–97.
13 Vertot, *The History of the Revolutions of Portugal*, p. 46.
14 Fernando Dores Costa, *A Guerra da Restauração 1641–1668* (Lisbon, 2004), p. 15.
15 For the trial of Lucena see Prestage, *Informes de Francisco Lanier sôbre Francisco de Lucena e a côrte de D. Joâo IV.*
16 Costa, *A Guerra da Restauração 1641–1668*, p. 14.

7 Portugal, the Inquisition and the Triumph of English Merchant Capitalism

1 Francisco Bethencourt, 'Portugal: a Scrupulous Inquisition', in Bengt Ankerloo and Gustav Henningsen, *Early Modern European Witchcraft* (Oxford, 1990), p. 407.
2 António José Saraiva, *Inquisição e Cristãos-Novos* (Porto, 1969), pp. 38–40.
3 Letter patent of Dom Manuel to the Jews of Safi, 1509 in *Les Sources Inédites de l'Histoire du Maroc: Archives et Bibliothèques de Portugal, Tome I (1486-1516)*, ed. Pierre Cenival (Paris, 1934), pp. 174–6.
4 For details of these tortuous negotiations see Saraiva, *Inquisição e Cristãos-Novos*, pp. 60–73.
5 Charles Amiel, 'Inquisitions Modernes: Le Modèle Portugais', *Histoire de Portugal. Histoire Europeenne* (Paris, 1987), p. 53.
6 Ibid., p. 54.
7 Francisco Bethencourt and Philip Havik, 'A África e a Inquisição Portuguesa', *Inquisição em África*. Revista Lusófona de Ciência das Religiões, V–VI (2004), p. 22.
8 Jean Pierre DeDieu, 'The Inquisition and Popular Culture in New Castile', *Inquisition and Society in Early Modern Europe* (London, 1987), p. 130.
9 Amiel, 'Inquisitions Modernes: Le Modèle Portugais', p. 56.
10 Charles Dellon, *Account of the Inquisition at Goa* (London, 1815), p. 114.
11 Abbé Vertot, *The History of the Revolutions of Portugal*, 5th edn (London, 1754), p. 82.
12 This is discussed at length in Carl A. Hanson, *Economy and Society in Baroque Portugal* (Minneapolis, MN, 1980)
13 António José Saraiva, *A Inquisição Portuguesa*, 3rd edn (Lisbon, 1964), p. 81.
14 Michèle Tailland, *Inquisition et Société au Portugal. Le cas du tribunal d'Évora, 1660–1821* (Paris, 2001), p. 46.
15 DeDieu, 'The Inquisition and Popular Culture in New Castile', pp. 134–5.
16 Fernanda Olival, 'A Visita da Inquisição à Madeira em 1591–92', *Actas. III Colóquio Internacional de História da Madeira* (Funchal, 1993), p. 496.
17 Quoted in I.-S. Révah, 'Les Marranes', *Revue des Etudes Juives*, CXVIII (1959–60), p. 47.
18 Saraiva, *Inquisição e Cristãos-Novos*, p. 9.
19 Hanson, *Economy and Society in Baroque Portugal*, p. 77.
20 Saraiva, *A Inquisição Portuguesa*, p. 109.
21 This was written by Francisco Peña in the introduction to the 1578 edition of

Manuel de los Inquisidores. Quoted in DeDieu, 'The Inquisition and Popular Culture in New Castile', p. 143.

22 Dellon, *Account of the Inquisition at Goa*, p. 107.

23 Olival, 'A Visita da Inquisição à Madeira em 1591–92', p. 499.

24 Tailland, *Inquisition et Société au Portugal: Le cas du tribunal d' Évora, 1660–1821*, p. 130.

25 Boyd Alexander, ed., *The Journal of William Beckford in Portugal and Spain 1787–1788* (London, 1954), p. 61.

26 Timothy Walker, *Doctors, Folk Medicine and the Inquisition* (Leiden, 2005), pp. 27, 385.

27 For this treaty and its aftermath see L.M.E. Shaw, *The Anglo-Portuguese Alliance and the English Merchants in Portugal, 1654–1810* (Aldershot, 1998).

28 Bethencourt, 'Portugal: A Scrupulous Inquisition', in Bengt Ankerloo and Gustav Henningsen, *Early Modern European Witchcraft*, pp. 404, 406.

29 Bernard Shaw, *Saint Joan* (London, 1924), Scene VI, p. 77.

8 The Lisbon Earthquake, the Enlightenment and Crisis Politics

1 Milton Friedman, quoted in Naomi Klein, *The Shock Doctrine* (New York, 2007), pp. 6–7.

2 The figures for wine imports are in H.E.S. Fisher, *The Portugal Trade* (London, 1971), p. 28.

3 Text in L.M.E. Shaw, *The Anglo-Portuguese Alliance and the English Merchants in Portugal, 1654–1810* (Aldershot, 1998), p. 212.

4 David Erskine, ed., *Augustus Hervey's Journal* (Rochester, 2002), pp. 76, 126, 143.

5 Thomas Chase, 'Mr Chase's Narrative of Earthquake at Lisbon', *The Gentleman's Magazine*, vol. LXXXIII (1813), pp. 105–10, 201–6, 314–17. Printed in *The Lisbon Earthquake of 1755: Some British Eye-witness Accounts*, ed. Judite Nozes (Lisbon, 1987), p. 57.

6 Maria Guiffré, *The Baroque Architecture of Sicily* (New York, 2008).

7 'An Account of the late Dreadful Earthquake and Fire, which destroyed the City of Lisbon. The Metropolis of Portugal. In a Letter from a Merchant Resident there, to his Friend in England', J. Payne (London 1755) reprinted in *The Lisbon Earthquake of 1755*, pp. 26–7.

8 Quoted in T. D. Kendrick, *The Lisbon Earthquake* (London, 1955), p. 89.

9 Quotation from Jean-Paul Poirier, *Le Tremblement de Terre de Lisbonne* (Paris, 2005), p. 118. See also Kendrick, *The Lisbon Earthquake*, pp. 53–4.

10 João Pedro Ferro, 'Deutsche Einflüsse in Portugal', *Aufsätze zur Portugiesischen Kulturgeschichte*, xx (1988–92), pp. 156–76.

11 Jorge Borges de Macedo, *A Situação Económica no Tempo de Pombal*, 2nd edn (Lisbon, 1982), p. 70.

12 Quoted in Klein, *The Shock Doctrine*, pp. 6–7.

13 Guilherme de Oliveira Santos, *O Processo dos Távoras* (Lisbon, 1979), p. 24.

14 The pamphlet published in Cork, Dublin and London in 1759 was entitled *The Genuine legal Sentence pronounced by the High Court of Judicature of Portugal upon the conspirators against the life of His Most Faithful Majesty; with the just motives for the same* and was published by Order and Authority of the said Tribunal.

15 Oliveira Santos, *O Processo dos Távoras*, p. 25.

16 For an account of this imprisonment by a Jesuit who survived twenty years in the dungeons of the fortress of São Julião see Mauriz Thoman, *M.Thomans ehemaligen Jesuitens und Missionars in Asien und Afrika. Reise und Lebensbeschreibung. Von ihm selbst verfasset* (Augsburg, 1788). See also Malyn Newitt, 'Mauriz Thoman's Account of the Imprisonment of the Jesuits of the Province of Goa', *Metahistória: História questionando História* (Lisbon, 2007), pp. 459–70 and the works cited there.

17 Kenneth Maxwell, *Pombal, Paradox of the Enlightenment* (Cambridge, 1995), p. 103.

18 Ibid., p. 160.

9 Portugal's Moment of Truth: The French and British Struggle for the Control of Lisbon

1   Boyd Alexander, ed., *The Journal of William Beckford in Portugal and Spain, 1787–1788* (London, 1954), pp. 194–5.

2   Kirsten Schultz, *Tropical Versailles* (New York and London, 2001), pp. 49–50.

3   Richard Beale Davis, *The Abbé Corrêa in America, 1812–1820* (Providence, RI, 1993). This was originally published in *Transactions of the American Philosophical Society*, XLV (1955).

4   José Joaquim da Cunha de Azeredo Coutinho's *Ensaio Económico sobre o Commercio de Portugal e suas Colônias* (Lisbon, 1794).

5   John Barrow, *Voyage a la Cochinchine, par les Iles de Madère, de Teneriffe et du Cap Verd, Le Brésil et l'ile de Java, traduits de l'anglais, avec des notes et additions par Malte Brun* (Paris, 1807), pp. 59, 252.

6   Laure Junot, *Memoirs of the Duchess D'Abrantes*, 8 vols (London, 1833–5), vol. VI, p. 227.

7   Quoted in H. S. Ferns, *Britain and Argentina in the Nineteenth Century* (Oxford, 1960), pp. 47–8.

8   Junot, *Memoirs of the Duchess D'Abrantes*, vol. VI, p. 61.

9   Jean-René Durdent, *Beautés de l'Histoire du Portugal* (Paris, 1821), p. 350.

10 Ibid., p. 350.

11 This section of the chapter is based on a paper entitled 'Lord Beresford' written for the city of Porto's celebration of the two hundredth anniversary of the expulsion of the French army from northern Portugal.

12 A. H. de Oliveira Marques, 'Graf zu Schaumburg-Lippe und sein Einfluss auf die Portugiesische Freimauerei', *Aufsätze zur Portugiesischen Kulturgeschichte*, XX (1988–92), pp. 177–9.

13 See also Malyn Newitt and Martin Robson, eds, *Lord Beresford and British Intervention in Portugal, 1807–1820* (Lisbon, 2004).

14 Public Record Office of Northern Ireland (PRONI), t3285\1\1, W. C. Beresford to Lady Anne Beresford, 23 April 1809.

15 There are numerous accounts of Beresford's reorganization of the Portuguese army. See in particular C.W.C. Oman, *Wellington's Army* (London, 1912, reprinted 1968) and H. V. Livermore, 'Beresford and the Reform of the Portuguese Army', *A History of the Peninsular War*, ed. Paddy Griffiths, vol. IX

(London, 1999), pp. 121–44.

16　Andrew Halliday, *Observations on the Present State of the Portuguese Army as organised by Lieutenant-General Sir William Carr Beresford* KB. *Field Marshal and Commander in Chief of that army with an account of the different military establishments and laws of Portugal* (London, 1811), pp. 145–9.

17　Ibid., p. 15.

18　Ibid., pp. 69–70.

19　W.F.K. Thompson, ed., *An Ensign in the Peninsular War: The Letters of John A itchison* (London, 1981), p. 48.

20　Mark Thompson, *The Fatal Hill* (Sunderland, 2002).

21　Biblioteca Nacional de Lisboa, Codice 6848-6853, Ricardo Raymundo Nogueira, 'Memória das cousas mais notáveis que se tratarem nas conferencias do governo d'estes reinos desde o dia 9 de agosto de 1810, em que entrei a servir o logar de um dos governadores até a 5 de fevereiro de 1820', quoted in *Lord Beresford and British Intervention in Portugal, 1807–1820*, ed. Newitt and Robson.

22　Arthur Richard Wellesley, 2nd Duke of Wellington, ed., *Supplementary Despatches and Memoranda of Field Marshal Arthur Duke of Wellington*, 15 vols (London, 1858–72), vol. X, Torrens to Earl Bathurst, Ghent, 8 April 1815, pp. 41–3.

23　Ibid., vol. XI, Beresford to Wellington, Lisbon, 8 July 1815, pp. 18–19.

24　James Prior, *Voyage along the Eastern Coast of Africa . . . in the Nisus Frigate* (London, 1819), p. 99.

25　University of Southampton, Wellington Papers, WP 1/519, Beresford to Wellington, 22 September 1816.

26　University of Southampton, WP 1/519 Beresford to Wellington, 22 September 1816.

27　The Gomes Freire conspiracy was investigated in depth by Raul Brandão who published three editions of his work between 1914 and 1922. A fourth edition incorporating final corrections was issued in 1990 with the title *Vida e Morte de Gomes Freire*, 4th edn (Lisbon, 1990). Beresford's own lengthy account of the conspiracy can be found among the correspondence between himself and Sir John Beresford in the North Yorkshire Record Office in Northallerton ZBA 21/10/75 and ZBA 21/10/76. These documents were published in Newitt and Robson, eds, *Lord Beresford and British Intervention in Portugal 1807–1820*.

28　Literally 'onions of Egypt' (*cebolas de Egipto*) – a reference to Numbers 11:4.

29　Quoted in Magda Pinheiro, 'Reflexões sobre a História das Finanças Públicas Portuguesas no Século XIX', *Ler História*, I (1983), p. 49.

30　From Simões de Almeida, 'Política. O Governo Britânico e a Democracia P ortuguesa', *Imparcialidade*, IX (August 1882), p. 1, quoted in Gabriela Gândara Terenas, 'Media Coverage of Nineteenth Century Anglo-Portuguese Protests: Quillinan *versus* Bright', *Revista de Estudos Anglo-Portugueses*, XVI (2007), p. 95. Beresford was demonized to such an extent that the real role he played in Portuguese affairs has been obscured. He still remains the unsympathetic bully described so brilliantly in Rose Macaulay, 'King Beresford: *Este Britânico Odioso*', *They Went to Portugal Too* (Manchester, 1990) and in Luís de Sttau Monteiro's play *Felizmente há Luar* (Lisbon, 1962).

10 Portugal among the Great Powers: The Scramble for Africa

1 Figures from S. Engerman and João César das Neves, 'The Bricks of an Empire, 1415–1999: 585 years of Portuguese Emigration', *European Journal of Economics*, XXVI (1997), pp. 494, 499.

2 W. G. Clarence-Smith, *The Third Portuguese Empire, 1825–1975* (Manchester, 1985), p. 87.

3 This section is based on M. Newitt, 'Mindelo: A Side Light on Anglo-Portuguese Relations', unpublished paper presented at the conference 'The Portuguese Atlantic: Africa, Cape Verde and Brazil' in Mindelo in July 2005.

4 António Carreira, ed., *Notícia Corográphica e Chronológica do Bispado do Cabo Verde . . .* (Lisbon, 1985), p. 36.

5 John Rendall, *A Guide to the Cape de Verd Islands* (London, 1856), pp. 2–3, 27.

6 Ernesto J. de Carvalho e Vasconcellos, *As Colonias Portuguezas* (Lisbon, 1903), table facing page 26; João de Sousa Machado, *Estudo sobre o Commercio do Carvão no Porto Grande da Ilha de S. Vicente e no Porto da Luz em Gran Canaria* (Lisbon, 1891), pp. 34–5. According to the figures given by Villaça, 1896 was the peak year with 3,056 ships, but he was giving figures for Cape Verde as a whole. António Eduardo Villaça, *Relatório Propostas de Lei e Documentos* (Lisbon, 1890), p. 232.

7 *Linhas Gerais da História do Desenvolvimento Urbano de Mindelo*, Républica de Cabo Verde (Lisbon, 1984), p. 13.

8 National Archives (London) (NA) FO 63/1427, Minute attached to Vice-consul Rice to FO St Vincent, 1 June 1905.

9 NA FO 371/11094, British Vice-consul to Lancelot Carnegie, St Vincent, 26 September 1925, enclosing article from *Gazeta das Colonias*, no. 21, 25 April 1925.

10 Alexandre D'Almeida, *A Colónia de Cabo Verde* (Lisbon, 1929), p. 35.

11 NA FO 608/119/23, Admiralty to Foreign Office, 18 January 1919.

12 Caetano Montez, *Descobrimento e Fundação de Lourenço Marques* (Lourenço Marques, 1948); Gerhard Liesegang, 'Dingane's Attack on Lourenço Marques', *Journal of African History*, X (1969), pp. 565–79.

13 Montague George Jessett, *The Key to South Africa: Delagoa Bay* (London, 1899), p. xii.

14 Peter Henshaw, 'The "Key to South Africa": Delagoa Bay and the Origins of the South African War', *Journal of Southern African Studies*, XXIV (1998), pp. 527–43.

15 Carlos Roma Machado de Faria e Maia, *Guerra anglo-boer de 1899-1902 na fronteira de Lourenço Marques e de Gaza,* separata from *O Instituto*, vol. 102 (Coimbra, 1943), p. 33.

16 Simon Katzenellenbogen, *South Africa and Southern Mozambique* (Manchester, 1982).

17 For the continuation of Portugal's economic ties with Brazil see Clarence-Smith, 'Illegitimate and Legitimate Commerce, 1820s to 1850', in *The Third Portuguese Empire*, pp. 22–60.

18 Angela Guimarães, 'A Ideologia colonialista em Portugal no último quartel do século xix', *Ler História*, i (1983) p. 77. This article discusses the idea of colonialism espoused by the Lisbon Geographical Society.

19 Valentim Alexandre, *Velho Brasil Novas Áfricas* (Lisbon, 2000), p. 150.

20 Quotations from Visconde da Arriaga, *Exame sobre o Tratado relativo a Bahia e Territorio de Lourenço Marques concluido entre Portugal e a Inglaterra em 30 de Maio de 1879* (Lisbon, 1882), pp. 6, 49.

21 Figures from Clarence-Smith, *The Third Portuguese Empire*, p. 64.

22 This was strongly argued by Richard Hammond in 'Uneconomic Imperialism: Portugal in Africa before 1910', in *Colonialism in Africa 1870–1960*, ed. L. H. Gann and Peter Duignan, 2 vols (Cambridge, 1969), vol. i, pp. 352–82.

23 Valentim Alexandre, 'A Questão Colonial no Portugal Oitocentista', in Valentim Alexandre and Jill Dias, *O Império Africano, 1825–1890* (Lisbon, 1998), p. 112; see also Gabriela Gândara Terenas, 'Media Coverage of Nineteenth Century Anglo-Portuguese Protests: Quillinan *versus* Bright', *Revista de Estudos Anglo-Portugueses*, xvi (2007), pp. 85–100.

24 Marquês de Lavradio, *Portugal em África depois de 1851* (Lisbon, 1936), p. 93.

25 Quoted in Robert Howes, 'The British Press and Opposition to Lord Salisbury's Ultimatum of January 1890', *Portuguese Studies*, xxiii/2 (2007), p. 162.

26 Alexandre, *Velho Brasil Novas Áfricas*, p. 149.

27 João de Rezende to Administrador Delegado da Companhia de Moçambique, 8 October 1890, in *Documentos Relativos aos Acontecimentos de Manica (setembro a dezembro de 1890)* (Lisbon, 1891), pp. 18–19.

28 S. E. Katzenellenbogen, *Railways and the Copper Mines of Katanga* (Oxford, 1973).

11 Portugal and the End of Empire

1 Jorge Varanda, '"A bem de nação": Medical Science in a Diamond Company in Twentieth-century Colonial Angola', unpublished PhD thesis, University College, London (2007).

2 E. A. Ross, *Report on the Employment of Native Labour in Portuguese Africa* (New York, 1925).

3 Filipe Ribeiro de Meneses, *União Sagrada e Sidonismo: Portugal em Guerra (1916–18)* (Lisbon, 2000), pp. 45–7.

4 Aubrey Bell, *Portugal of the Portuguese* (London, 1915), pp. 41–2.

5 Ribeiro de Meneses, *União Sagrada e Sidonismo: Portugal em Guerra (1916–18)*, p. 23.

6 David D. Roberts, 'Comment: Fascism, Single-Party Dictatorships, and the Search for a Comparative Framework', *Contemporary European History*, xi (2002), p. 456.

7 V. de Bragança Cunha, *Revolutionary Portugal (1910–1936)* (London, 1937), p. 219.

8 Ralph Fox, *Portugal Now* (London, 1933), p. 61.

9 Freppel Cotta, *Economic Planning in Corporative Portugal* (London, 1937), p. 3.

10 António Costa Pinto, 'Elites, Single Parties and Political Decision-making in Fascist-era Dictatorships', *Contemporary European History*, ii (2002), p. 434.

11 Albert T'Serstevens, *L'Itinéraire Portugais* (Paris, 1940), p. 114.

12 Costa Pinto, 'Elites, Single Parties and Political Decision-making in Fascist-era Dictatorships', p. 432.

13 Jean-François Labourdette, *Histoire du Portugal* (Paris, 2000), pp. 590–95.

14 Henrique Galvão and Carlos Selvagem, *Império Ultramarino Português*, 4 vols (Lisbon, 1952–3).

15 A detailed account of PIDE's pursuit of Delgado was published by Peter Deeley and Judith Bull, 'Who Killed Delgado?', *Observer*, 26 April 1970.

16 Armando Cortesão and Avelino Teixeira da Mota, *Portugaliae Monumenta Cartographica*, 6 vols (Lisbon, 1960).

17 C. R. Boxer, *Race Relations in the Portuguese Colonial Empire, 1415–1825* (Oxford, 1963); J. S. Cummins and Luís de Sousa Rebello, 'The Controversy over Charles Boxer's *Race Relations in the Portuguese Colonial Empire 1415–1825*', *Portuguese Studies*, XVII (2001), pp. 233–46.

18 Len Addicott, *Cry Angola* (London, 1962).

19 For these events see John Marcum, *The Angolan Revolution*, 2 vols (Cambridge, MA, 1969); René Pélissier, *Les Guerres Grises* (Orgéval, 1977); Fernando Andresen Guimarães, *The Origins of the Angolan Civil War* (London, 1998).

20 *Press conference by the minister of Foreign Affairs, Dr Rui Patrício*. Given at the P alácio das Necessidades on 9 February 1972 (Lisbon, 1972), p. 22.

21 *Press conference by the minister of Foreign Affairs, Dr Rui Patrício*, p. 9.

22 Kenneth Maxwell, *The Making of Portuguese Democracy* (Cambridge, 1995), pp. 66–7.

23 For an intelligent exploration of this contradiction see *Statement made by the representative of Portugal, Dr Bonifácio de Miranda, in the plenary of the XXIV General Assembly of the United Nations, on 20 November 1969, commenting on the Manifesto of Lusaka*, Ministry of Foreign Affairs (Lisbon, 1970).

24 António José Telo, 'A Revolução e a Posição de Portugal no Mundo', in *Portugal e a Transição a Democracia (1974–1976)*, ed. Fernando Rosas (Lisbon, 1999), p. 285.

25 Norrie Macqueen, *The Decolonization of Portuguese Africa* (Harlow, 1997), p. 92.

26 Audrey Wise, *Eyewitness in Revolutionary Portugal* (Nottingham, 1975), p. 58.

27 Diogo Freitas do Amaral, 'O Papel da Assembleia Constituinte em 1975–76', *Portugal e a Transição a Democracia (1974–1976)*, ed. Rosas, p. 211.

Epilogue

1 Jorge Braga de Macedo, 'Portugal's European Integration: The Limits of External Pressure', in Fátima Monteiro, José Tavares, Miguel Glatzer and Ângelo Cardoso, *Portugal: Strategic Options in a European Context* (Lanham, MD, 2003), p. 68.

2 See discussion in Carlos Pereira da Silva, 'Environmental Issues in Portugal', in *Contemporary Portugal: Dimensions of Economic and Political Change*, ed. Stephen Syrett (Aldershot, 2002), p. 171.

3 Quoted in David White, 'Taking an Intensive Refresher in EU affairs', *Financial Times*, 30 November 1999.

Bibliography

This bibliography consists only of works cited in this book

Abulafia, David, *The Discovery of Mankind* (New Haven, CT, 2008)

Addicott, Len, *Cry Angola* (London, 1962)

Alexander, Boyd, ed., *The Journal of William Beckford in Portugal and Spain, 1787–1788* (London, 1954)

Alexandre, Valentim, and Jill Dias, *O Império Africano, 1825–1890*, Nova História da Expansão Portuguesa, x (Lisbon, 1998)

Alexandre, Valentim, *Velho Brasil Novas Áfricas* (Lisbon, 2000)

Almeida, Alexandre D', *A Colónia de Cabo Verde* (Lisbon, 1929)

Amaro da Costa, Manuel Rafael, *Economic Humanism in the Overseas Provinces* (Lisbon, 1962)

Amiel, Charles, 'Inquisitions Modernes: Le Modèle Portugais', *Histoire de Portugal. Histoire Européenne* (Paris, 1987)

Anon., *O Sebastianismo: breve panorama dum mito português* (Lisbon, 1978)

Arriaga, Visconde da, *Exame sobre o Tratado relativo a Bahia e Território de Lourenço Marques concluido entre Portugal e a Inglaterra em 30 de Maio de 1879* (Lisbon, 1882)

Azeredo Coutinho, José Joaquim da Cunha de, *Ensaio Económico sobre o Commercio de Portugal e suas Colónias* (Lisbon, 1794)

Ballong-Wen-Mewuda, J. Bato'ora, *São Jorge da Mina, 1482–1637* (Lisbon and Paris, 1993)

Barreno, Maria Isabel, Maria Teresa Horta and Maria Velho da Costa, *Novas Cartas Portuguesas* (Lisbon, 1972)

Barreno, Maria Isabel, 'The Loss of Memory', in Fátima Monteiro, José Tavares, Miguel Glatzer and Ângelo Cardoso, *Portugal: Strategic Options in a European Context* (Lanham, MD, 2003), pp. 25–31

Barrow, John, *Voyage à la Cochinchine, par les Iles de Madère, de Teneriffe et du Cap Verd, Le Brésil et l'ile de Java, traduits de l'anglais, avec des notes et additions par Malte Brun* (Paris, 1807)

Beazley, C. R., and Edgar Prestage, *The Chronicle of the Discovery and Conquest of Guinea*, 2 vols (London, 1896–9)

Bell, Aubrey, *Portugal of the Portuguese* (London, 1915)

Bennet, Matthew, 'Military Aspects of the Conquest of Lisbon', in *The Second Crusade: Scope and Consequences*, ed. Jonathan Phillips and Martin Hoch

(Manchester, 2001), pp. 71–89

Bentley Duncan, T., 'Navigation between Portugal and Asia in the Sixteenth and Seventeenth Centuries', in *Asia and the West: Encounters and Exchanges from the Age of Exploration*, ed. C. K. Pullapilly and E. J. van Kley (Notre Dame, IN, 1986)

Bethencourt, Francisco, 'Portugal: A Scrupulous Inquisition', in Bengt Ankerloo and Gustav Henningsen, *Early Modern European Witchcraft* (Oxford, 1990), pp. 403–22

—, and Philip Havik, 'A África e a Inquisição Portuguesa', *Inquisição em África*. Revista Lusófona de Ciência das Religiões, V–VI (2004), pp. 21–7

—, and Diogo Ramada Curto, eds, *Portuguese Oceanic Expansion, 1400–1800* (Cambridge, 2007)

Blussé, Leonard, *Strange Company: Chinese Settlers, Mestizo Women and the Dutch in VOC Batavia* (Dordrecht, 1986)

Borges de Macedo, Jorge, *A Situação Económica no Tempo de Pombal*, 2nd edn (Lisbon, 1982)

Bosgra, S. J., and C. van Krimpen, *Portugal and NATO* (Amsterdam, 1969)

Bourchier, John, Lord Berners, trans., *The Chronicles of Froissart*, ed. G. C. Macaulay (London, 1913)

Bourdon, Léon, trans., *Chronique de Guinée (1453)* (Paris, 1994)

Boxer, C. R., ed., *South China in the Sixteenth Century* (London, 1953)

—, *Race Relations in the Portuguese Colonial Empire 1415–1825* (Oxford, 1963)

—, *Two Pioneers of Tropical Medicine: Garcia d'Orta and Nicolás Monardes*, in Diamante, 14 (London, 1963)

—, *The Portuguese Seaborne Empire* (London, 1969)

Bragança Cunha, V. de, *Revolutionary Portugal (1910–1936)* (London, 1937)

Branco, Maria João, 'A Conquista de Lisboa Revisitada', *Arqueologia Medieval*, VII (2001), pp. 217–34

—, 'Introdução', *A Conquista de Lisboa aos Mouros, Relato de um Cruzado*, ed. Aires A. Nascimento (Lisbon, 2001)

Brandâo, Raul, *Vida e Morte de Gomes Freire*, 4th edn (Lisbon, 1990)

Brooks, Mary, *A King for Portugal* (Madison, WI, 1964)

Carletti, Francisco, *My Voyage Round the World*, ed. Herbert Weinstock (London, 1964)

Carreira, António, ed., *Notícia Corográphica e Chronológica do Bispado do Cabo Verde* (Lisbon, 1985)

Carvalho e Vasconcellos, Ernesto J. de, *As Colônias Portuguezas* (Lisbon, 1903)

Catz, Rebecca, ed., *The Travels of Mendes Pinto* (Chicago, IL, 1989)

Cenival, Pierre, ed., *Les Sources Inédites de l'Histoire du Maroc: Archives et Bibliothèques de Portugal*, Tome I (1486–1516) (Paris, 1934)

Chandeigne, Michel, ed., *Lisbonne hors les Murs* (Paris, 1990)

Clarence-Smith, W. G., *The Third Portuguese Empire, 1825–1975* (Manchester, 1985)

Coimbra, Álvaro da Veiga, 'Ordens Militares de Cavalaria de Portugal', *Revista Histórica de São Paulo*, XXVI (1963), pp. 21–34

Cook, Weston F., *The Hundred Years War for Morocco* (Boulder, CO, 1994)

Cortesão, Armando, and Avelino Teixeira da Mota, *Portugaliae Monumenta Cartographica*, 6 vols (Lisbon, 1960)

Costa, Fernando Dores, *A Guerra da Restauração 1641–1668* (Lisbon, 2004)

Costa Pinto, António, 'Elites, Single Parties and Political Decision-making in Fascist-era Dictatorships', *Contemporary European History*, II (2002), pp. 429–54

—, ed., *Modern Portugal* (Palo Alto, CA, 2003)

Cotta, Freppel, *Economic Planning in Corporative Portugal* (London, 1937)

Crone, G. R., ed., *The Voyages of Cadamosto* (London, 1937)

Cruz, Maria Leonor García da, 'As controvérsias ao tempo de D. João III sobre a política portuguesa no Norte de África', *Mare Liberum*, XIV (1997), pp. 117–98

Cummins, J. S., and Luís de Sousa Rebello, 'The Controversy over Charles Boxer's *Race Relations in the Portuguese Colonial Empire 1415–1825*', *Portuguese Studies*, XVII (2001), pp. 233–46

David, Charles Wendell, *De Expugnatione Lyxbonensi* (New York, 1936), reprinted with a new introduction by Jonathan Phillips as *The Conquest of Lisbon* (New York, 2001)

Davis, Richard Beale, *The Abbé Corrêa in America 1812–1820* (Providence, RI, 1993); originally published in *Transactions of the American Philosophical Society*, XLV (1955)

DeDieu, Jean Pierre, 'The Inquisition and Popular Culture in New Castile', in *Inquisition and Society in Early Modern Europe*, ed. Stephen Haliczer (London, 1987), pp. 129–46

Deeley, Peter, and Judith Bull, 'Who Killed Delgado?', *The Observer*, 26 April 1970

Dellon, Charles, *Account of the Inquisition at Goa* (London, 1815)

Diffie, Bailey W., *Prelude to Empire: Portugal Overseas before Henry the Navigator* (Lincoln, NE, 1960)

—, and George D. Winius, *Foundations of the Portuguese Empire, 1415–1580* (Oxford, 1977)

Documentos Relativos aos Acontecimentos de Manica (setembro a dezembro de 1890) (Lisbon, 1891)

Durdent, Jean-René, *Beautés de l'Histoire du Portugal* (Paris, 1821)

Edgington, Susan, 'Albert of Aachen, St Bernard and the Second Crusade', in *The Second Crusade: Scope and Consequences*, ed. Jonathan Phillips and Martin Hoch (Manchester, 2001), pp. 54–70

Elliott, J. H., *Richelieu and Olivares* (Cambridge, 1984)

—, *The Count-Duke of Olivares* (New Haven, CT, and London, 1986)

Engerman, S., and João César das Neves, 'The Bricks of an Empire, 1415–1999: 585 Years of Portuguese Emigration', *European Journal of Economics*, XXVI (1997), pp. 471–510

Erskine, David, ed., *Augustus Hervey's Journal* (Rochester, 2002)

Faria e Maia, Carlos Roma Machado de, *Guerra anglo-boer de 1899–1902 na fronteira de Lourenço Marques e de Gaza*. Separata from *O Instituto*, vol. 102 (Coimbra, 1943)

Ferns, H. S., *Britain and Argentina in the Nineteenth Century* (Oxford, 1960)

Ferro, João Pedro, 'Deutsche Einflüsse in Portugal', *Aufsätze zur Portugiesischen Kulturgeschichte*, XX (1988–92), pp. 156–76

Fisher, H.E.S., *The Portugal Trade* (London, 1971)

Fletcher, R. A., 'Reconquest and Crusade in Spain, c. 1050–1150', in *The Crusades*, ed. Thomas F. Madden (Oxford, 2002)

Flori, Jean, 'Ideology and Motivations in the First Crusade', in *Palgrave Advances in the Crusades*, ed. Helen J. Nicholson (Basingstoke, 2005), pp. 15–36

Fox, Ralph, *Portugal Now* (London, 1933)

Galvão, Henrique, and Carlos Selvagem, *Império Ultramarino Português*, 4 vols (Lisbon, 1952–3)

The Genuine legal Sentence pronounced by the High Court of Judicature of Portugal upon the conspirators against the life of His Most Faithful Majesty; with the just motives for the same. Published by Order and Authority of the said Tribunal (Cork, Dublin and London, 1759)

Guiffré, Maria, *The Baroque Architecture of Sicily* (New York, 2008)

Guilmartin, John, *Galleons and Galleys* (London, 2002)

Guimarães, Angela, 'A Ideologia colonialista em Portugal no último quartel do século xix', *Ler História*, I (1983), pp. 69–79

Guimarães, Fernando Andresen, *The Origins of the Angolan Civil War* (London, 1998)

Haliczer, Stephen, 'The First Holocaust: The Inquisition and the Converted Jews of Spain and Portugal', in *Inquisition and Society in Early Modern Europe*, ed. Stephen Haliczer (London, 1987), pp. 7–18

Halliday, Andrew, *Observations on the Present State of the Portuguese Army as organised by Lieutenant-General Sir William Carr Beresford KB. Field Marshal and Commander in Chief of that army with an account of the different military establishments and laws of Portugal* (London, 1811)

Hammond, Richard, 'Uneconomic Imperialism: Portugal in Africa before 1910', in *Colonialism in Africa 1870-1960*, ed. L. H. Gann and Peter Duignan, 2 vols (Cambridge, 1969), vol. I, pp. 352–82

Hanson, Carl A., *Economy and Society in Baroque Portugal* (Minneapolis, MN, 1980)

Henshaw, Peter, 'The "Key to South Africa": Delagoa Bay and the Origins of the South African War', *Journal of Southern African Studies*, xxiv (1998), pp. 527–43

Hermann, Christian, and Jacques Marcadé, *Les Royaumes ibériques au xviie siècle* (Liège, 2000)

Homem de Mello, Ana Maria, *Oito Séculos de Portugal na Cultura Europeia* (Lisbon, 1992)

Howes, Robert, 'The British Press and Opposition to Lord Salisbury's Ultimatum of January 1890', *Portuguese Studies*, xxiii (2007), pp. 153–66

Jessett, Montague George, *The Key to South Africa: Delagoa Bay* (London, 1899)

Junot, Laure, *Memoirs of the Duchess D'Abrantes*, 8 vols (London, 1833–5)

Kamen, Henry, *The Duke of Alba* (New Haven, CT, 2004)

Katzenellenbogen, Simon, *Railways and the Copper Mines of Katanga* (Oxford, 1973)

—, *South Africa and Southern Mozambique* (Manchester, 1982)

Kendrick, T. D., *The Lisbon Earthquake* (London, 1955)

Klarwill, Viktor von, ed., *The Fugger Newsletters*, Second Series (London, 1926)

Klein, Naomi, *The Shock Doctrine* (New York, 2007)

Labourdette, Jean-François, *Histoire du Portugal* (Paris, 2000)

Lavradio, Marquês de, *Portugal em África depois de 1851* (Lisbon, 1936)

Liesegang, Gerhard, 'Dingane's Attack on Lourenço Marques', *Journal of African History*, x (1969), pp. 565–79

Linhas Gerais da História do Desenvolvimento Urbano de Mindelo, República de Cabo Verde (Lisbon, 1984)

Livermore, H. V., 'Beresford and the Reform of the Portuguese Army', *A History of the Peninsular War*, ed. Paddy Griffiths (London, 1999), vol. ix, pp. 121–44

Lomax, Derek, and R. J. Oakley, *The English in Portugal 1367–87* (Warminster, 1988)

Lopes, David, *A Expansão em Marrocos* (Lisbon, 1989)

Macaulay, Rose, 'King Beresford: *Este Britânico Odioso*', *They Went to Portugal Too* (Manchester, 1990)

Macedo, Jorge Braga de, 'Portugal's European Integration: The Limits of External Pressure', in Fátima Monteiro, José Tavares, Miguel Glatzer and Ângelo Cardoso, *Portugal: Strategic Options in a European Context* (Oxford, 2003), p. 68

Macqueen, Norrie, *The Decolonization of Portuguese Africa* (Harlow, 1997)

Magalhães Godinho, Vitorino de, *A Economia dos Descobrimentos Henriquinos* (Lisbon, 1962)

Mancke, Elizabeth, 'Empire and State', in *The British Atlantic World, 1500–1800*, ed. David Armitage and Michael Braddick (Basingstoke, 2002)

—, 'Power, Space, and the Making of Early Modern Empires', paper presented to the Ohio Seminar in Early American History and Culture, at Ohio Stte University, 2003

Marcum, John, *The Angolan Revolution*, 2 vols (Cambridge, MA, 1969)

Martyn, J.R.C., *The Siege of Mazagan* (New York, 1994)

Mattoso, José, *História de Portugal*, vol. II (Lisbon, 1993)

Maxwell, Kenneth, *Pombal, Paradox of the Enlightenment* (Cambridge, 1995)

—, *The Making of Portuguese Democracy* (Cambridge, 1995)

Miranda, Bonifácio de, *Statement made by the representative of Portugal, Dr Bonifácio de Miranda, in the plenary of the XXIV General Assembly of the United Nations, on 20 November 1969, commenting on the Manifesto of Lusaka* (Lisbon, 1970)

Monteiro, Jacinto, *Alguns aspectos da história açoriana nos séculos XV–XVI* (Angra, 1982)

Monteiro, João Gouveia, *A Guerra em Portugal* (Lisbon, 1998)

—, *Aljubarrota 1385. A Batalha Real* (Lisbon, 2003)

Monteiro, Luís de Sttau, *Felizmente há Luar* (Lisbon, 1962)

Montez, Caetano, *Descobrimento e Fundação de Lourenço Marques* (Lourenço Marques, 1948)

Nascimento, Aires A., ed., with an introduction by Maria João Branco, *A Conquista de Lisboa aos Mouros. Relato de um Cruzado* (Lisbon, 2001)

Newitt, Malyn, and Martin Robson, eds, *Lord Beresford and British Intervention in Portugal, 1807–1820* (Lisbon, 2004)

Newitt, Malyn, 'Mindelo: A Side Light on Anglo-Portuguese Relations', unpublished paper presented at the conference 'The Portuguese Atlantic: Africa, Cape Verde and Brazil' in Mindelo, July 2005

—, *A History of Portuguese Overseas Expansion 1400–1668* (London, 2005)

—, 'Mauriz Thoman's Account of the Imprisonment of the Jesuits of the Province of Goa', *Metahistória. História questionando História* (Lisbon, 2007), pp. 459–70

Nozes, Judite, ed., *The Lisbon Earthquake of 1755: Some British Eye-witness Accounts* (Lisbon, 1987)

Olival, Fernanda, 'A Visita da Inquisição à Madeira em 1591-92', *Actas. III Colóquio Internacional de História da Madeira* (Funchal, 1993), pp. 493–519

Oliveira, António de, 'Levantamentos Populares do Algarve em 1637–1638', *Revista Portuguesa de História*, XX (1983), pp. 1–98

Oliveira, J. A. de, *Conquista de Lisboa aos Mouros (1147)* (Lisbon, 1935, 2nd edn 1936)

Oliveira e Costa, João Paulo, 'D. Afonso v e o Atlântico a base do projecto expansionista de D. João ii', *Mare Liberum*, xvii (1999), pp. 39–71

Oliveira Marques, A. H. de, *Daily Life in Portugal in the Late Middle Ages* (Madison, wi, 1971)

—, 'Graf zu Schaumburg-Lippe und sein Einfluss auf die Portugiesische Freimauerei', *Aufsätze zur Portugiesischen Kulturgeschichte*, xx (1988–92), pp. 175–9

—, *A Expansão Quatrocentista*, Nova História da Expansão Portuguesa, vol. ii (Lisbon, 1998)

Oliveira Santos, Guilherme de, *O Processo dos Távoras* (Lisbon, 1979)

Oman, C.W.C., *Wellington's Army* (London, 1912, reprinted 1968)

Padfield, Peter, *Tide of Empires, vol. i: 1481–1654* (London, 1979)

Parker, Geoffrey, *Europe in Crisis 1598–1648* (Brighton, 1980)

Patrício, Rui, *Press Conference by the Minister of Foreign Affairs Dr Rui Patrício. Given at the Palácio das Necessidades on 9 February 1972* (Lisbon, 1972)

Pearson, M. N., *The New Cambridge History of India: vol. i: The Portuguese in India* (Cambridge, 1987)

Pélissier, René, *Les Guerres Grises* (Orgéval, 1977)

Pinheiro, Magda, 'Reflexões sobre a História das Finanças Públicas Portuguesas no Século xix', *Ler História*, i (1983), pp. 47–67

Pinto, João Rocha, 'Le Vent, le Fer et la Muraille', *Lisbonne hors les Murs*, ed. Michel Chandeigne (Paris, 1990), pp. 229–36

Poirier, Jean-Paul, *Le Tremblement de Terre de Lisbonne* (Paris, 2005)

Prestage, Edgar, *Informes de Francisco Lanier sobre Francisco de Lucena e a côrte de D. Joâo iv* (Coimbra, 1931)

Prior, James, *Voyage along the Eastern Coast of Africa... in the Nisus Frigate* (London, 1819)

Reid, Peter, *A Brief History of Medieval Warfare: The Rise and Fall of English Supremacy at Arms, 1314–1485* (London, 2008)

Rendall, John, *A Guide to the Cape de Verd Islands* (London, 1856)

Révah, I. S., *Le Cardinal de Richelieu et la Restauration du Portugal* (Lisbon, 1950)

—, 'Les Marranes', *Revue des Etudes Juives*, cxviii (1959–60), pp. 29–77

Ribeiro de Meneses, Filipe, *União Sagrada e Sidonismo. Portugal em Guerra (1916–18)* (Lisbon, 2000)

Riley-Smith, Jonathan, 'Early Crusaders to the East and the Costs of Crusading, 1095–1130', in *The Crusades*, ed. Thomas F. Madden (Oxford, 2002), pp. 155–71

Rodrigues-Salgado, M. J., *Armada 1588–1988: The Official Catalogue* (London, 1988)

Rosas, Fernando, ed., *Portugal e a Transição a Democracia (1974–1976)* (Lisbon, 1999)

Rubiés, Joan-Pau, *Travel and Ethnology in the Renaissance: South India through European Eyes, 1250–1625* (Cambridge, 2000)

Russell, P. E., *The English Intervention in Spain and Portugal in the Time of Edward iii and Richard ii* (Oxford, 1955)

—, *Portugal, Spain and the African Atlantic 1343–1490* (Aldershot, 1995)

—, *Prince Henry 'the Navigator'* (New Haven, ct, and London, 2000)

Russell-Wood, A.J.R., *A World on the Move: The Portuguese in Africa, Asia, and America 1415–1808* (Manchester, 1992)

Salgado, Augusto, *Os Navios de Portugal na Grande Armada* (Lisbon, 2004)

Saraiva, António José, *A Inquisição Portuguesa*, 3rd edn (Lisbon, 1964)

——, *Inquisição e Cristãos-Novos* (Porto, 1969)

Saraiva, José Hermano, *História Concisa de Portugal*, 19th edn (Lisbon, 1998)

Sarmento, José Moraes, *The Anglo-Portuguese Alliance and Coast Defence* (London, 1908)

Shaw, George Bernard, *Saint Joan* (London, 1924)

Shaw, L.M.E., *The Anglo-Portuguese Alliance and the English Merchants in Portugal, 1654–1810* (Aldershot, 1998)

Schultz, Kirsten, *Tropical Versailles* (New York and London, 2001)

Sousa Machado, João de, *Estudo sobre o Commercio do Carvão no Porto Grande da Ilha de S. Vicente e no Porto da Luz em Gran Canaria* (Lisbon, 1891)

Subrahmanyam, Sanjay, *The Portuguese Empire in Asia, 1500–1700* (London, 1993)

——, *The Career and Legend of Vasco da Gama* (Cambridge, 1997)

Tailland, Michèle, *Inquisition et Société au Portugal: Le cas du tribunal d' Évora, 1660–1821* (Paris, 2001)

Teixeira, Nuno Severiano, 'Between Africa and Europe: Portuguese Foreign Policy, 1890–1986', in *Modern Portugal*, ed. António Costa Pinto (Palo Alto, CA, 2003), pp. 60–87

Terenas, Gabriela Gândara, 'Media Coverage of Nineteenth Century Anglo-Portuguese Protests: Quillinan *versus* Bright', *Revista de Estudos Anglo-Portugueses*, XVI (2007), pp. 85–100

Thoman, Mauriz, *M.Thomans ehemaligen Jesuitens und Missionars in Asien und Afrika. Reise und Lebensbeschreibung. Von ihm selbst verfasset* (Augsburg, 1788)

Thompson, F. K., ed., *An Ensign in the Peninsular War: The Letters of John Aitchison* (London, 1981)

Thompson, Mark, *The Fatal Hill* (Sunderland, 2002)

T'Serstevens, Albert, *L'Itinéraire Portugais* (Paris, 1940)

Usherwood, Stephen, ed., *The Great Enterprise: The History of the Spanish Armada* (London, 1988)

Varanda, Jorge, '"A bem da nação": Medical Science in a Diamond Company in Twentieth-century Angola', unpublished PhD thesis (University College, London, 2007)

Villaça, António Eduardo, *Relatório Propostas de Lei e Documentos* (Lisbon, 1890)

Vertot, Abbé, *The History of the Revolutions of Portugal*, 5th edn (London, 1754)

Walker, Timothy, *Doctors, Folk Medicine and the Inquisition* (Leiden, 2005)

Wellesley, Arthur Richard, 2nd Duke of Wellington, ed., *Supplementary Despatches and Memoranda of Field Marshal Arthur Duke of Wellington*, 15 vols (London, 1858–72)

Wernham, R. B., *After the Armada* (Oxford, 1984)

White, David, 'Taking an Intensive Refresher in EU Affairs', *Financial Times*, 30 November 1999.

Wise, Audrey, *Eyewitness in Revolutionary Portugal* (Nottingham, 1975)

Acknowledgements

I would like to thank all the students at King's College London who took my courses on the history of Portugal and who indirectly stimulated me to write this book. I am grateful to Joan Newitt for drawing the maps.

Index

Maranhão e Para,
Company 144, 145
Marchioni bank 60, 64
Mardel, Karl 140
Mardijkers 79
Mare clausum 80
Mare liberum 81
Margaret of Savoy 106–7,
108
Maria I, queen of
Portugal 158, 170
Maria Anna, queen of
Portugal 144
Marie de Savoie, queen of
Portugal 133
Mary, queen of Scots 89
Mascarene islands 49
Mashonaland 193; *see also*
Southern Rhodesia
Masséna, Marshal 45,
166–7
Master of Avis *see* João I,
Dom
Mattoso, José 22, 33
Mau Mau 203, 205, 206
Maxwell, Kenneth 148
Mazagan 53, 84
Médici, Catherine de,
queen of France 89
medicine 76, 128
Medina Sidonia, Duke of
93, 94, 95
Mediterranean 19, 31, 55,
69, 75, 78, 88, 136, 155
Mehemet Ali, 185
Melo, Francisco de 109,
110
Menon, Krishna 206
messianism 104, 105; *see
also* Sebastianism
mestizos see creoles
Methuen treaties 129, 135,
151
Mexico 78, 79, 120, 184
MFA 209, 210–11, 213, 214
Middle East 19, 20, 21, 31
migrant labour 181, 183, 196
Miguel, Infante 98

Milan 107
Military Orders; *see*
Orders of Knights
Milner, Alfred 182
Mina Coast 49, 66; *see also*
Elmina, Gold Coast
Mindelo 176–9, 181, 183,
188
mines in South Africa
180–2, 183, 192, 194, 196,
197, 198
Minho river 22
missions 72, 73, 76, 126,
146, 184, 187, 197, 207;
see also Dominicans,
Jesuits
Moçambique Company
194–5,197, 202
Moçamedes 187;
Company 197
modernization 132, 144, 151
Modus vivendi 183
Moluccas 72, 73, 79, 82
Monarchism 198
Mondlane, Eduardo 208
Mongols; empire 74; inva-
sions 19
Monomotapa 85
monopolies 70, 72, 79, 102,
186; companies 74
monsoon 179
Montesquieu 77
Montevideo 156, 157
Montiel 38
Montjuic, battle of 110
Moore, Sir John 160, 161
Moors 54; in Portugal and
Spain 19, 20, 22, 23, 27,
28, 29, 30, 32, 33, 50
morgados 174, 186
Moreira, Adriano 210
Mormugão railway 194
Morocco 30, 47, 55–6, 58,
60, 61, 64, 85, 89, 93, 99,
108, 117, 131; Portuguese
wars in 50–3, 58, 83, 85,
86 88
Mosul 21

Mousinho da Silveira, José
172
Mozarabes 27; bishop of 26
Mozambique 14, 69, 74, 99,
178, 182, 183, 188, 191–2,
193, 203, 207, 208; cam-
paigns in the south 196;
independence of 212;
migrant labour from
182, 183; war in 209, 215;
see also East Africa
MPLA 205, 208
MUD 203
Mussolini, Benito 201

Naga Haveli 203
Nagasaki 72, 73
Najéra, battle of 37, 41, 45,
47
Namibia 62
Napier, William 161
Naples 107, 111, 155
Napoleon 88, 154, 155, 157,
158, 159, 161, 168, 172
Napoleonic empire 154;
continental system
155–6
Napoleonic Wars 11, 13, 15,
120, 160, 162 171–2
Natal 49
nationalism 114, 121, 129,
130, 189, 193, 201
Nationalist movements
207–9, 210–11
Nato 12, 15, 203, 204, 207,
213
naus 69
Navarre 36, 37, 41
Ndebele 192
Negapatnam 72
Nehru, Jawaharlal 203, 206
Netherlands 22, 25, 35, 55,
75, 79, 83, 87, 88, 93, 94,
99, 101, 102, 105, 128,
129, 153, 154, 168; *see also*
Antwerp, Dutch,
Flemish
Neto, Agostinho 209